An Introduction
to
Japanese Tea Ritual

An Introduction

to

Japanese Tea Ritual

Jennifer L. Anderson

State University of New York Press

Cover photo by Steve Dietz

Published by
State University of New York Press, Albany

For information, address State University of New York
Press, State University Plaza, Albany, N.Y. 12246

Production by Christine M. Lynch
Marketing by Dana E. Yanulavich

Library of Congress Cataloging-in-Publication Data

Anderson, Jennifer Lea.
    An introduction to the Japanese way of tea / Jennifer L. Anderson
        p.   cm.
    Includes bibliographical references and index.
    ISBN 0–7914–0749–7 (acid free) . — ISBN 0–7914–0750–0 (pbk. : acid
free)
    1. Japanese tea ceremony. 2. Japanese tea ceremony—Urasenke
school.   I. Title.
GT2910.A48   1991
394.1'5—dc20
                                                                                    90–49070
                                                                                    CIP

10 9 8 7 6 5 4 3 2 1

To Hōunsai, Sen Sōshitsu,

the Fifteenth Generation Grand Master of Urasenke:

For the intellectual inspiration his work provides
and for his commitment to sharing
"Peacefulness Through a Bowl of Tea" with all of us.

Contents

Part II: Organization in the Tea World

Part III: A Model Shōgo Chaji

Acknowledgments

*F*or the opportunity to study the Japanese tea ritual, I am deeply grateful to Sen Sōshitsu, the fifteenth generation grand master of Urasenke, the tea school with which I study. I hope this book contributes in a small way to his effort to share a friendly bowl of tea with the world.

I also greatly appreciate the aid given to me by the staff of the Foreign Affairs Division of the Urasenke Foundation directed by Akiko Mori. The *Urasenke Newsletter* and the *Chanoyu Quarterly*, produced by that office, are invaluable sources of scholarly information. I would particularly like to thank Gretchen Mittwer, editor of the *Chanoyu Quarterly* and Gary Cadwallader, editorial advisor to the *Urasenke Newsletter*. Their scholarship has been an inspiration to me.

Fellow practitioners have also contributed much to this work. My tea teacher, Aiko Tauchi, is thoughtful, articulate, and well-educated. She is very careful to explain the symbolism and history of *chadō* during the course of lessons or Tea events. The members of the tea club with whom I study also generously share their broad experience with Japanese culture. In addition, I have benefited and learned a considerable amount from my association with the San Francisco Urasenke *shibu*, a large group of tea practitioners that holds many gatherings during the year, and the Urasenke Foundation's San Francisco branch.

I would also like to acknowledge the advice and tea expertise of Allan Palmer, Ron Nado, Larry Tiscornia, Kimika Takechi, Christy Bartlett, and Grace Shinohara. To Joseph Justice, I owe thanks for his generosity in sharing his knowledge of both *kaiseki* cooking and the city of Kyōto.

For my anthropological training, I would like to thank Dr. Harumi Befu. Without the advice based on his extensive and insightful knowledge of Japanese culture, I could not have completed this research. I would also like to thank Dr. Bernard J. Siegel and Dr. Charles O. Frake for their comments and encouragement. I owe a special debt of gratitude to Dr. Norman Girardot for both his theoretical inspiration and his faith in this project.

Finally, I would like to thank my husband Dr. Thomas Jackson for drafting the figures in this book, Rita Naughton for the cover art, Steve Dietz, Tankōsha, and the Itsuo Museum for the photographs, my editor William Eastman, production editor Christine Lynch, and copy editor Lani Blackman. The support of my teachers, fellow tea practitioners, friends, and family have made writing this book a pleasure.

Preface

Like tea ritual itself, this book draws on a number of diverse sources for its form and character: I am a tea practitioner by avocation, an anthropologist by training, and find theology an abundant fount of theoretical inspiration.

When I first became interested in *chadō*, the "Way of Tea," I was astonished to discover that this wonderfully rich and intricate complex of rituals was virtually neglected in the anthropological literature. In fact, locating Tea in its cultural and historical matrices on the basis of the information available in this country was almost impossible.

After ten years of practice and intensive research (both here and in Japan), I am more convinced than ever of the need for a behavior-oriented, English language introduction to tea ritual—one that helps the reader understand the development of *chadō*'s value system and explains precisely how practitioners express their beliefs in the tearoom.

Of course, there are many people, Japanese and non-Japanese, who know more about *chanoyu* than I. Unfortunately, those who lack the opportunity or desire to study Tea with these individuals have few opportunities to avail themselves of their expertise. As a novice, I felt a strong need for a book that would help me understand why people follow "The Way of Tea." This book was born of that desire.

Unless specifically noted, the contents of this work are based entirely on Tea as it is practiced through Urasenke. Urasenke is the largest tea school in Japan and the most accessible to non-Japanese. My informants are almost exclusively members of that structure. We share its values, symbolic language, and practical lore.

By custom, an individual commits to one school (and one school only) for a lifetime. Thus, while my observations indicate my experience is representative of that of tea practitioners at large, neither I nor anyone else can claim omniscience regarding the total phenomenon of tea ritual. (Urasenke also discourages members from commenting on the internal affairs of other schools in the interests of maintaining good relationships within the tea community.)

In further contrast to standard ethnographic practice, I have described a "model" tea ritual rather than a series of actual events. There are several reasons for this. First, size constraints limit the scope of this book to the fundamentals. Trying to describe the subtle nuances of a real gathering to an audience unfamiliar with the basic standards of Tea would be like trying to comment on the strategy of a game of chess without first explaining its rules.

Second, I feel a strong obligation to protect the privacy of my fellow tea practitioners. My situation is not analogous to that of the anthropologist who goes into the field for several years, returns to the academic setting, and candidly reveals a great deal of personal information about the people with whom he or she has worked.

I interact with my sources of information on an almost daily basis and will do so for the rest of my life. Many of my cohort will read and discuss this book. If I were to describe a typical, less than perfect, tea gathering, I might inadvertently embarrass some sensitive soul who is doing the best they can with the materials at hand: At real gatherings, minor compromises of orthodoxy inevitably occur. This does nothing to diminish the importance of the ideal. It only confuses the uninitiated.

Most of the factual information included in this book is common knowledge for tea practitioners. I have collected it by witnessing and participating in hundreds of tea gatherings and practice sessions—some within my own tea group, others in San Francisco, and many during extensive field work in Kyōto. I have also verified each assertion of fact with several tea teachers and with the Japanese literature. Any errors, however, are my personal responsibility and undoubtedly result from my status as a relative novice.

I would also like to make it very clear from the outset that I am not (and have never been) employed by Urasenke. I do not represent the tea school, and I am not a "tea master." The closest Japanese equivalent of "tea master" is "sōshō," a term usually reserved for the heads of the tea schools and their heirs. The Japanese employ a whole range of special titles for other kinds of expert tea practitioners. I am only an advanced student. Expertise takes a lifetime to acquire—not a decade.

The term "grand master" also needs clarification. Grand master is generally used to refer to the head or (o)*iemoto* of a school of the traditional Japanese arts (*iemoto*). (The *iemoto* system will be more fully discussed in chapter 7.)

Since it is confusing to refer to both the school and its leader as *iemoto*, I shall preface references to the individual who directs the school with the honorific "(o)" as is common among tea practitioners. The honorifics "(o)" and "(go)" otherwise appear only in situations where they are consistently used by tea practitioners of both sexes.

To avoid further perplexing the reader, I have established a few additional conventions for this text: The word "Tea" (capitalized in English) is meant to stand either for *chanoyu* or *chadō* (the latter more properly defined as "the Way of Tea" implying the spiritual content of *chanoyu*).

Neither *chadō* nor *chanoyu* will be referred to as "tea ceremony." Sen Sōshitsu objects to the indiscriminate use of this common English translation and I concur. "Ceremony" evokes a false impression of liturgical rigidity. Furthermore, the term's analytical utility is limited by the failure of anthropologists to agree on its theoretical definition. In this book, "ceremony" will be used only to refer to the most overtly religious tea rituals (services where tea is offered to spiritual entities).

The reader should also be aware that the terms applied to tearoom roles (like host and guest) are genderless in Japanese. Unfortunately, the English language virtually mandates the use of gender-specific nouns and pronouns. I have therefore decided to use masculine pronouns: Primarily because Japanese men have historically dominated tea ritual. But, also because I want to counter the western image of *chadō* as an exclusively female pastime.

Tea master's personal names create yet another problem of nomenclature. Typically, they have a number of names appropriate to different stages in their lives. An Urasenke (o)*iemoto* has a proper name used in his youth, a generation name used in his capacity as (o)*iemoto*, a Buddhist name bestowed on him by his Zen mentor, and a posthumous name. He may also acquire additional artistic pseudonyms. To prevent confusion, I allude to Urasenke (o)*iemoto* by the names most commonly used by tea people.

Finally, Japanese born prior to the Meiji era will be referred to surname first in the traditional Japanese fashion. Japanese-surnamed authors discussed or cited in this work will be listed surname first if they are primarily active in Japan and surname last if they publish in English.

Having established these preliminary understandings, let us begin to examine that multi-faceted, cultural gem—*chadō*.

Chapter I

The Nature of Tea Ritual

INTRODUCTION

*F*ollowing the Way of Tea (*chadō*) has three main components: *dō*, the philosophy; *gaku*, the academic content;
and *jitsu*, practice. As an anthropologist, I was initially
intrigued by the relationship between the philosophical content
of Tea (*dō*) and the way in which these beliefs develop and are
expressed, that is, the scholarly aspects (*gaku*) of tea ritual
(*chanoyu*). However, in the course of ten years of actual practice
(*jitsu*), I became convinced that analysts without extensive tearoom experience are unlikely to produce meaningful research
on this fascinating subject.

Tea must be interpreted in context. The purpose of this
book is to better prepare the reader to appreciate *chanoyu* by
anticipating his or her need to locate the event among its historical, social, and symbolic coordinates. By sharing my understanding of the relationship between Tea and universal concepts such as those of religion and ritual, I hope to stimulate
others to think analytically about the "Way of Tea."

Despite the fact that *chadō* is one of the richest, most sophisticated, and vital products of the human mind, westerners know
very little about it. There are good reasons for this. Tea is not easily accessible to the casual observer. Anyone in Japan or near a
large Japanese community may have a chance to observe the ritual preparation of tea, but, without disciplined and conscientious
study, the symbol system, which conveys its meaning, cannot be
interpreted. *Chadō* is a "way" of life and it assumes a lifetime
commitment. Brief exposures to Tea produce little insight.

Happily, the doors of the Tea world are beginning to open to non-Japanese. In the last thirty years, it has become possible for people outside Japan to study *chanoyu* seriously and to take part in Tea's yearly cycle of events. The grand masters of Urasenke have been particularly active in stimulating this trend. They have encouraged people from many nations to practice at their headquarters in Kyōto and have made it possible for many more to study in their own countries. Some, like myself, have been privileged to do both.

PUTTING THIS RESEARCH IN CONTEXT

My perspective as ethnographer and tea student seems to perplex both fellow-practitioners and professional colleagues, so I would like to be very clear about my biases. Let me begin by emphasizing my belief that an anthropologist's first obligation is to his or her informants. We have historically been guests in other cultures and we have a real obligation to respect our hosts. This is particularly true in a world where the fragile tissues of traditional culture need to be cherished and protected more than ever.

As an initiate of the advanced level (*okuden*) of the Urasenke tea school (those of the 'secret' or orally transmitted tea procedures) and an assistant tea instructor, I have accepted an obligation to adhere to orthodox exegeses of Tea philosophy. This includes respecting the interpretations of meaning espoused by my superiors in the school hierarchy as well as their right to dictate goals and procedures. By custom, the ultimate arbiter of meaning in all Japanese schools of the traditional arts (*iemoto*) is the grand master or (*o*)*iemoto*. I and all my fellow students enter into a social contract with our (*o*)*iemoto* and those senior to us historically and in terms of practical experience. They dedicate their lives to developing and sharing *chadō*, and we agree to respect the tradition and pass it on intact.

Accepting this responsibility raises questions about my objectivity among fellow professionals. Some seem to confuse the mental posture necessary for producing a critical analysis with that of being strictly critical. But, there need be no conflict between commitment to the subject matter and its faithful presentation. I will discuss some of the less desirable aspects of the tearoom behavior as they contribute to our understanding of Tea's value system. But, experience has taught me that it is counterproductive, both intellectually and in terms of interpersonal relationships, to discuss deviation in situations where a clear conception of the norm is lacking.

It should be obvious that I am not presenting my work as that of an impartial observer—I doubt if any ethnographer honestly could. Anthropologists select their area of specialty because some aspect of it is attractive to them. The quality of analyses produced by individuals who do not like or respect the people with whom they work should be suspect.

My perspective is exclusively that of an anthropologist who is learning ritual in a uniquely circumscribed and highly structured environment (that of the tearoom). Because I have been functioning under these particular circumstances for many years and have cross-checked my information with numerous other practitioners and the written literature, I feel confident that my training differs little from that of native participants and that it is comprehensive (for my level of expertise). I do not, however, claim my experience is typical or exemplary in any way.

As regards my academic outlook, I prefer not to identify with either the posture of the super-objective "ivory tower" scholar (the etic position) or hypersensitive insider (the emic position). My approach to ethnography is best described by Robert Feleppa's (1986) linguistically based research model.

Feleppa views ethnography as a work of translation, pointing out that: "Translation does not *reflect* pre-existing structure, it *creates* a structure" (1986, 250; the emphasis is Feleppa's). He goes on to explain that while linked to the cognitive framework of both the observer and the subject, the translation itself must be viewed as an independent framework for description rather than a distortion of another reality.

Like a responsible translator, I have tried to create a model that is scrupulously faithful to the vocabulary and grammar of Tea as it is experienced by my teachers and fellow students. My work can be labeled that of an insider only to the extent that Tea practitioners recognize it as descriptively accurate. I reject a predominantly outside or "objective" approach because I have found explanations of meaning presented symbolically in the tearoom and in the Tea literature fully adequate and reconcilable with anthropological theory. Let us consider some of these ideas.

SOME FUNDAMENTAL IDEAS ABOUT TEA RITUAL

An introduction to the religious aspects of Chadō

Much evidence suggests the relationship between tea ritual and the larger cultural milieu should be evaluated by the criteria applied to the cognitive systems we call "religions." To begin with, the words selected by Japanese to describe Tea in English clearly propose a direct correlation between *chadō* and religion. Okakura Kakuzō (1863–1913), the scholar whose work effectively brought Tea to the attention of the western popular consciousness, labeled Tea "the religion of aestheticism" and "a cult founded on the adoration of the beautiful among the sordid facts of everyday existence." He also said Tea is "a religion of the art of life" and "a sacred function at which the host and guest join to produce for that occasion the utmost beatitude of the mundane." Finally, he observed that "Teaism was Taoism in disguise" (Okakura 1956, 34). The present grand master of Urasenke, Sen Sōshitsu, also says "Tea is the practice or realization of religious faith, no matter what you believe in" (*Urasenke Newsletter* [Winter 1978], no. 15).

If Sen Sōshitsu and Okakura Kakuzō are correct, the task of analyzing the "Way of Tea" can best be accomplished by: (1) exploring definitions of religion and ritual appropriate to systems of thought such as Tea philosophy in the light of their potential contribution to our understanding of *chadō*. And, (2) investigating the manner in which the actual practice of tea ritual manifests its underlying rational.

Exploring definitions of religion

One of the most thought provoking definitions of religion is that of Clifford Geertz. He maintains that religion is:

> (1) a system of symbols which acts to (2) establish powerful, pervasive, and long-lasting moods and motivations in men by (3) formulating conceptions of a general order of existence and (4) clothing these conceptions with such an aura of factuality that (5) the moods and motivations seem uniquely realistic (Geertz 1973, 90).

Geertz emphasizes the manner in which a particular set of symbols functions to create a psychic environment conducive to the creation of a perception of reality that relieves the anxiety normally associated with the suspicion "that life is absurd and the attempt to make moral, intellectual, or emotional sense out of experience is bootless" (Geertz 1973, 108).

Religion, Geertz suggests, achieves its ends through ritual "by inducing a set of moods and motivations—an ethos—and defining an image of cosmic order—a world view—by means of a single set of symbols " (Geertz 1973, 118). In other words, in the course of acting out an ideal or postulated cosmic order, ritual practitioners make alternatives seem plausible, not only in an explanatory sense but also as a paradigm for interaction with the ambient physical (and social) environment.

Geertz's definition emphasizes the fact that the communication of meaning in religion takes place through symbols. It also highlights the two central functions of religion: (1) postulating an ideal order to existence, and (2) providing a way for humans to alter or adapt to their perception of that system. Finally, it accentuates ritual's role in reconciling the real and the ideal.

The problem with Geertz's definition is that it provides no criteria that allows us to distinguish between behaviors pertaining to worldly concerns from those centering on cosmic anxieties and strategies for dealing with them. There is no doubt that one can make something *like* a religion out of a political ideology, for instance, but the meaning that religion has for the individual requires a condition of desired personal satisfaction not spelled out in this particular case.

For comprehensiveness and analytical utility, I prefer to work with Norman J. Girardot's definition. He defines religion as "a system of symbolic thought and action that is 'focused on salvation' and interpretively grounded in mythical or cosmological 'formulations of a general order of existence'" (Girardot 1983, 6). Girardot also maintains that "religion as a cultural system of symbols is concerned with a means of transforming, temporally or permanently, some 'significant ill' that is seen to be part of the cosmological or existential order of human life" (Girardot 1983, 6).

(Note that Girardot does not refer to "salvation" as being saved from damnation or oblivion, a prominent characteristic of the Judeo-Christian tradition. Salvation can also mean being rescued from Chaos, a central concern of Eastern religions.)

The strong point of Girardot's definition is its emphasis on salvation, an idea that I interpret as providing a personal link between the concept of cosmological order and individual behavior. Finding salvation is finding the means to transform that "significant ill" to which Girardot refers. What this definition lacks is Geertz's notion of clothing cosmological imagery with an aura of veracity—an idea that has significant implications for the role of rituals, like those associated with Tea, in religion.

What is a "ritual"?

The functionalist approach to interpreting ritual   To most English speakers, the word "ritual" connotes a particular class of formal, solemn, and repetitive events. However, as we have just learned, Geertz's and Girardot's more careful analysis suggests that rituals can also be viewed as physical behaviors that integrate a culture's higher-order cognitive models with the daily lives of its members.

Most inquiries into the character of ritual have focused on answering two central questions: (1) Why do people engage in the behavior? And, (2) How do they achieve their goals? Those concerned primarily with discovering what ritual "does" take the functionalist approach, while those interested in the way ritual works concentrate on structure.

Norman J. Girardot contends that the aim of all religious behavior is "periodically recovering in this lifetime a condition of original wholeness, health or holiness" (1983, 7); while the grand master of Urasenke, Sen Sōshitsu XV, says the purpose of practicing *chadō* is: "to realize tranquillity of mind in communion with one's fellow men within our world" (Sen 1979b, 9). Girardot is speaking in theoretical terms and the grand master is referring specifically to Tea, but they are saying the same thing—people engage in religious ritual because they feel it can help reconcile them with the incomprehensible.

Evan M. Zuesse's concepts of "confirmatory" and "transformatory" ritual provide additional insight into this phenomenon. Zuesse believes events intended to reconcile the transcendental and the mundane while preserving the essential integrity of each domain may be identified as confirmatory ritual. In contrast, transformatory ritual serves to regenerate or reintegrate parts of the cognitive structure when its integrity is threatened by internal or external change. Zuesse sees the main function of both kinds of ritual as anchoring the perceived order in higher realms (Zuesse 1987).

The idea that an individual or group practices ritual to confirm or transform their perception of universal order has important implications for understanding tea ritual. Tea history and observations of tearoom behavior strongly suggest that disparate personal interpretations of external conditions may compel some of the religiously inclined to focus on preserving the "mythical or cosmological formulata of a general order of existence," while others concentrate on rectifying whatever they perceive to be a "significant ill." In practice this means that some ritual practitioners seek merely to confirm the "fitness" of their relationship with the "Ultimate," while others actively attempt to symbolically transform themselves, the transcendent order, or both.

While Zuesse's bipartite approach to ritual function has the potential to illuminate some of the continuities and juxtapositions that synthesize tea history, tea practice, and the Japanese perception of *chanoyu*, the utility of his terminology is severely constrained by restricting its application to categories of behavior perceived as strictly dichotomous. For example, Zuesse labels taboos, blessings, rituals of meditation, and some kinds of prayers "confirmatory"; while, he considers rituals of initiation, healing, and divination "transformatory."

My research suggests that some very inclusive and complex rituals, like *chadō*, may be alternately or concurrently "confirmatory" or "transformatory," depending on the immediate spiritual requirements of their ritual constituencies. In fact, practitioners' ability to reconcile a ritual's symbolic content with the ambient cultural milieu by selectively emphasizing either "confirmatory" or "transformatory" aspects of the behavior may determine the evolutionary viability of the activity.

I believe every tea event mirrors the ambiguity created by the dual confirmatory and transformatory constituents in its development. The strain is minimal in the more advanced tea procedures (*temae*) and offertory ritual (*kucha* and *kencha*) because these rites are solidly rooted in the confirmatory tradition of temple Tea. They serve mainly to define humans not only in relation to higher powers but also to explicate the cosmic model. The conflict is most intense at the more secular *chaji* because these private gatherings incorporate the imagery of practitioners who aspired to manipulate perceptions of the transcendent through tea ritual as well as those determined to maintain the system unchanged.

Over the centuries, a distinct bias in favor of the confirmatory element in tea ritual appears to have developed. Even though the dress, manners, and surroundings of tea ritual are radically different from those of their daily lives, modern Japanese practitioners seem to leave the tearoom with a strong conviction that the "correct" order has been confirmed.

In the tearoom, the diverse Chinese and native elements in Japanese culture are synthesized and made coherent. The social order is reinforced through subtle etiquette. The rhythms of temporal existence are celebrated and the bounty of nature is glorified. Even the products of Japanese material culture are enshrined.

By behaving properly in the tearoom, the host and guest participate fully in a cooperative act of ritual world maintenance. Indeed, tea practitioners appear to perform these functions so effectively that other Japanese have come to perceive such ritual specialists as their proxies in this complex cognitive process.

This is not to say transformatory elements are completely missing from modern tea practice or that it is in any way a "failed ritual." No statistics will ever reveal the relative percentages of people who practice tea with confirmatory *vs* transformatory intentions. After all, even Sen Rikyū (1522–1591), the greatest tea master who ever lived, admitted to having experienced *chanoyu* true to his ideal (which was fundamentally transformatory) once or twice in his lifetime. The important issue here is that, though the intent of practitioners varies, *chadō* always fulfills a function beyond the simple preparation of tea. How it does so is an equally important area of inquiry.

The structuralist approach to analyzing ritual   Victor Turner was one of the first investigators to suggest approaching the problem of examining ritual from a structuralist perspective. He suggested making a careful inquiry into the interrelations between the components of ritual. His work, *The Forest of Symbols: Aspects of Ndembu Ritual,* had a catalytic effect on the debate. It presented the symbol as "the smallest unit of ritual which still retains the specific properties of ritual behaviors" (Turner 1967, 19).

Turner believed that "each kind of ritual might be regarded as a configuration of symbols, a sort of 'score' in which the symbols are notes" (Turner 1967, 48). He also suggested that rituals were integrated into a larger cultural context by multivocal symbols and observed that ritual was a mechanism which "adapts and periodically readapts the biopsychical individual to the basic conditions and axiomatic values of human social life" (Turner 1967, 43).

Raymond Firth refined this symbolic approach to ritual structure by substituting a linguistic conceptual model for Turner's musical metaphor. He defined "ritual" as ". . . a symbolic mode of communication, of 'saying something' in a formal way, not to be said in ordinary language or informal behavior." He also suggested "This idea of 'not to be said' in an ordinary way means that a special character of ritual is its reserve, its apartness, its 'sacred' quality. Its "grammar' is different from that of ordinary language." (Firth 1973, 176)

Furthering the trend toward looking at ritual "from the symbolic 'inside out' (rather than the functionalist 'outside in')," Nancy Munn elaborated upon this linguistic imagery. She concluded that ritual should be interpreted as "a symbolic intercom between the level of cultural thought and complex cultural meanings on the one hand, and that of social action and immediate event on the other" (Munn 1973, 579).

Munn also observed that particular symbols appear and reappear in different contexts within a culture's ritual matrices. She deemed it essential to investigate these units both in terms of what informants say they mean and with respect to the various social arenas in which they appear. It was her contention that, because symbols convey messages in a variety of ritual situations, they are endowed with the power to condense meaning and, ultimately, to mediate the relationship of the individual to the community at multiple levels of consciousness and utility (Munn 1973).

Munn's concept of ritual as "ritual message system" has important implications for the analysis of tea ritual. She defined "the ritual message system" as "all the forms and rules governing these forms that pertain to the ritual process as a mode of expressive communication (e.g. the symbols, the action sequences, and the rules governing these; the categories of participants and their modes of participation, etc.)" (Munn 1973, 580). In other words, Munn was not concerned merely with the meaning of individual symbols but with the way in which they relate to each other in a wider cultural milieu. As we shall see, this concept is critical in attempting to understand *chadō*.

ABOUT THIS BOOK

It should be becoming increasingly obvious that there is much more to a tea gathering than ladies in pretty *kimono* fluttering over exquisite ceramics. As the work of the forgoing theorists suggests, phenomena like Tea can be fruitfully investigated from both functionalist and structuralist perspectives. My purpose in writing this book is to propose some avenues of inquiry and establish a factual basis for further discussion.

The chapters on tea history that follow are intended to help the reader understand the way tea ritual developed. The section on the modern tea school explains how tea practitioners learn to perform tea ritual, and a detailed description of a tea gathering ensues. The book concludes with some thoughts concerning *chadō*'s relationship to Japanese culture at large.

Throughout, we will be seeking the answers to three main questions derived from Geertz's and Girardot's definitions of religion: (1) How does tea ritual aid in formulating a general order of existence? (2) How does it focus on salvation? (i.e. How does it transform some "'significant ill' thought to be part of the cosmological or existential order of human life?") And, (3) How does it clothe the resulting concept of order with an aura of factuality that influences and alters the practitioner's approach to everyday life? I hope that in seeking the answers to these questions, the reader will become inspired to travel a little further along "The Way of Tea."

Part I

The History of Chanoyu

Chapter 2

The Beginning of the Road

THE RELIGIOUS COMPONENTS OF CHINESE TEA RITUAL

An introduction to the historical dimension of tea ritual

*I*n contrast to many of the rituals studied by anthropologists, the evolution of *chadō* has been carefully chronicled by an unusually sophisticated body of observers for hundreds of years. These circumstances provide modern researchers with a unique opportunity to test the historic adaptability of specific definitions of religion. They also allow us to assess the characters of individual practitioners and evaluate their personal contributions to the development of *chanoyu* in context. Finally, the richness and detail of tea history permits the effect of particular innovations to be examined relative to their historic milieu. In sum, an awareness of the interweaving of personalities, artifacts, and ideas in *chadō* enhances every tea ritual performed today. The same should be true for the analysis of such events.

A medicinal herb becomes the stuff of legends

Overwhelmed by the complexity and sophistication of modern tea ritual, it is easy to ignore the modest relative of the camellia central to the entire behavioral system. Tea is probably native to Assam in India or southwestern China. Botanists refer to this leafy evergreen as *Thea sinensis* or *Thea assamica*. The chemical characteristics of the plant itself have contributed much to its popularity: In addition to the stimulant theine, tea contains tannin, calcium, phosphorus, potassium, a significant amount of Vitamin C, B vitamins, and some trace minerals such as fluoride.

13

Consumed in its less highly processed states and in concentrated form, tea was and is one of the most effective medicines in the ancient pharmacopoeia.

Li Shih-chen's (1518–1593) herbal (the *Pen-ts'ao kang-mu*, originally published in A.D. 1578 but considered heir to a much older tradition) attributes tea with the ability to promote digestion, dissolve fats, neutralize poisons in the digestive system, cure dysentery, fight lung diseases, lower fevers, and treat epilepsy. Tea was also thought to be an effective astringent for cleaning sores and recommended for washing the eyes and mouth (Li 1973). Obviously, tea has been designated a wonder drug for centuries.

Early references to tea in Chinese literature highlight the interaction between tea and a variety of religious systems. The first written allusion to tea may be one that chronicles an incident purported to have taken place around the sixth century B.C. Supposedly, the famous Taoist Lao-tzu was offered a bowl of tea by another adept Yin Hsi (the Keeper of the Pass). This occurred during the former's journey by ox cart from the declining Chou kingdom into the Land of Ta Chin (the eastern provinces of the Roman Empire). After enjoying the mountain hermit's hospitality, Lao-tzu agreed to leave him a copy of his famous *Tao te-ching*. Since both sages were respected as masters of esoteric "long-life" techniques, this intriguing vignette foreshadows tea's future identification with the "elixir of immortality" (Legge 1959, 50–51, Cohen 1976, 22).

In the *Book of Songs*, purported to have been composed about two hundred years after Lao-tzu's encounter with the Keeper of the Pass, an herb called *t'u* is identified with an ideograph similar to that of the modern character for tea. Whether the plant under consideration was the one we now call tea or a similar bitter herb (sow thistle) is a matter for debate (Cohen 1976). At any rate, the Chinese seem to have been drinking something resembling tea from an early date.

Real tea (*Camellia sinensis* or *assamica*) can be more reliably associated with the early history of Buddhism in China. Legend has it that tea was introduced as an aid to meditation by Bodhidharma (d. 532), the Indian monk who established Ch'an Buddhism among the Chinese around A.D. 526 (Ch'an will be discussed in more detail later.) It is said that in a fit of frustration with his inability to meditate properly, the sleepy patriarch ripped off his eyelids and threw them to the ground where they became tea plants (Cohen 1976, 23). Tea's capacity to stimulate and its eyelid-like leaf shape probably inspired the tale.

In point of fact, however, tea was most certainly known in China previous to Bodhidharma's arrival: It began appearing in Chinese dictionaries around the third century A.D.[1] Nevertheless, the story of the patriarch's eyelids probably recalls a genuine association between the Indian Buddhist missionaries and tea's impressive efficacy as medicine. Medical miracles and religious proselytism have always made a potent combination.

The Taoists attribute special powers to tea

By the T'ang Dynasty (A.D. 618–907), tea had assumed a special status in the relatively undifferentiated class of Chinese foods and medicines. It joined items like ginseng and various kinds of mushrooms at the top of the list of almost magically powerful substances that had accumulated bodies of laudatory folklore on account of their strength and efficacy.

There is nothing particularly unique about this development. The ancient Chinese perceived a mutable cosmos where spiritual and physical energy were virtually indistinguishable. Central to this ideology was a highly integrated vision of reality. Its motive force was called the "*Tao*." The *Tao* was thought to be more of a process than an entity. It was "the Way" the universe worked.

Within the *Tao*, two complementary forces were believed to interact. These were *yang* (the active, hot, male principle) and *yin* (the passive, cool, female principle). Humans were thought to have the power to manipulate the cosmic principles and so affect their fate. Through such media as properly propitiating spiritual forces (usually gods or ancestors), correctly balancing the *yang* and *yin* aspects of digestible materials, and, orienting buildings and graves to harmonize with the flow of power in the universe, the Chinese hoped to achieve salvation by integrating their personal lives with the Eternal.

By logical extension, a few esoteric Taoists eventually seized upon the common conviction that balancing the positive and negative quality of foods was beneficial and amplified it. They were convinced that by ingesting certain commodities or combinations of them, they could render themselves immortal. The elixir they sought was opined to be a substance that would so perfectly integrate its consumer with the rhythms of the Ineffable that the dissonant experience of death could be evaded. Enterprising alchemists tried a variety of recipes in their search for the precious formula (frequently at very advanced ages). Popular ingredients were ginseng, mushrooms, gold, vermilion, and tea. (Tea was one of the more benign ingredients in the Taoists' *materia medica:* Retorting vermilion creates mercury—a lethal poison.)

The Chinese alchemists' use of tea is particularly interesting in the context of this research because it foreshadows later attempts to shift the tea ritual's function from the confirmatory to the transformatory sphere. The Taoists were neither using tea to confirm their conception of the cosmos nor their position in it. They were searching for a magical potion that would change their relationship to it. The difference between this and later developments in tea ritual was that the Taoists believed imbibing "the elixir of immortality" would transform them. As we shall see, later practitioners discovered it was the act of preparing tea, not drinking it, which brought about changes.

Tea-drinking acquires a Confucian element

By the middle of the T'ang, tea-drinking was not only integrated into Buddhist temple ritual and the metaphysical machinations of the Taoists but also widespread in the capital of Ch'ang-an. Scholars and literati enthusiastically celebrated the convivial virtues of tea in essay and poetry. As time passed, the etiquette associated with tea-drinking became more rigid. A strongly confirmatory, Confucian element was beginning to influence tea preparation and consumption.

This trend was initiated centuries before tea became a facet of life among elite of Ch'ang-an. During the late Chou dynasty (1122?–256 B.C.), the great teacher known in the West as Confucius (K'ung-tzu 551–479 B.C.) revolutionized Chinese philosophy by expanding the concept of *li,* (ritual etiquette) to include a component of sincere respect. The great sage suggested that by behaving correctly in social situations and performing traditional rites properly, a gentleman cultivated his spirit and promoted the smooth functioning of society. This he believed ultimately contributed to the harmonious functioning of Heaven.

Confucius was particularly concerned with the minutia of daily life. For him, a gentleman's duty to demonstrate a proper regard for *li* devolved from the assiduous maintenance of memorial rites from his ancestors directly down to the way his meat was cut (Legge 1893, 468–470), or his mat was placed ("He would not sit on a mat that was not properly laid," Chai and Chai 1965, 67). Such behavior may seem strange or fussy today, but there was an underlying rationale: Good men must assume responsibility for even their most trivial acts as even these affect their character, social relationships, and consequently the cosmic balance.

Regrettably, in the years that intervened between Confucius' lifetime and the widespread popularization of tea-drinking, the importance of manifesting virtue through moral conduct became predominantly construed as a matter of strictly observing etiquette. Tea preparation was easily integrated into this world view. Since some varieties of tea were obviously superior to others, it was considered *de rigueur* to present the best to the elite with elaborate ceremony.

The relationship between morality, etiquette, and maintaining the social status quo became tautological: A gentleman's social position and access to luxuries (such as tea) were considered morally justified because he observed etiquette appropriate to his social position. By the seventh century, this development had reached its logical apogee as far as tea was concerned. It became the custom to ceremoniously pay an annual tribute of new tea to the emperor.

The tea classic of Lu Yü

Lu Yü (d. 804) was an eccentric T'ang dynasty scholar whose approach to tea ritual both influenced and typified that of his social class and era. Born sometime early in the first half of the eighth century, he was raised by priests from Dragon Cloud Monastery of the Ch'an Buddhists (the precursors of Zen thought in Japan). Being tempermental, he rejected their calling and ran away to become an actor. Sometime around A.D. 760 he found himself living in Chekiang province. There it became his custom to take walks in the forest and to compose poems as he wandered. One day, overwhelmed by a poem he was chanting about a fallen tree, he went home for a refreshing cup of tea. It was then that he was inspired to write *The Classic of Tea* (Sen 1977a).[2]

In the *Classic of Tea*, Lu Yü made initial reference to tea-growing and tea's medicinal value. (He noted that the nature of the herb was "cold," a reflection of the Taoist element in his approach.) Then he described the utensils and processes necessary to the proper manufacture and preparation of tea.[3] This was the first indication that the physical and symbolic characteristics of utensils would play an important part in tea ritual.

Some of the objects Lu Yü described are still used in their original forms. Others have become obsolete—principally because of the shift from brick to powdered tea. The master's brazier is one of the utensils most likely to appear familiar to modern practitioners. It was not unlike the Korean-style *furo* (braziers) commonly seen in today's tearooms. Braziers in Lu Yü's time were of brass or iron and had three legs. His own was decorated with inscriptions and archaic characters. One inscription referred to harmonizing the five elements, an early example of the use of decorative symbolism in Tea. Trigrams from the *I Ching* also adorned Lu Yü's brazier. They were associated with pictures of the pheasant, a fire bird; the tiger, a wind beast; and a fish, a water creature. Lu Yü explained the presence of these motifs saying that wind can stir up fire and fire can boil water, a reference to Taoist belief in the complementary relationship between the elements (Lu Yü 1974).

Astonishingly, despite changes in the form of both processed tea and utensils, most of Lu Yü's recommendations regarding preparation remain relevant. (Only the advice related to brick tea can be totally disregarded.) The passages that emphasize the value of moderation in tea-drinking and lifestyle; close attention to detail, cleanliness, and form; and the careful consideration of the guest's comfort are particularly significant as each point evinces a Confucian regard for *li* and echoes the admonitions of modern tea teachers.

Lu Yü's work is significant because it represents an important digression from the developing bifurcation of religious and secular tea rituals. Lu Yü employed Taoist symbolism to highlight the individual's relationship to an ordered cosmos while his concern for proper etiquette bolstered the Confucian vision of social order. In addition, it is likely that the book owes something to Lu Yü's sojourn among the Ch'an even if it reflects only the Buddhist custom of meticulously codifying the procedures relevant to everyday life in monastic communities.

For Lu Yü, the ability to synthesize diverse religious

philosophies and relate them to tea resulted in official prefer-
ment and ultimately posthumous deification as the Chinese
"God of Tea." For Tea it meant that a literary tradition combin-
ing philosophy with preparation technique had been established and endorsed by the Chinese intellectual elite.

Tea and Ch'an

It is impossible to explain the relationship between modern tea
practice and religion without supplying at least a cursory introduction to Ch'an Buddhism. Siddhārtha Gautama, the Indian
prince who founded Buddhism, taught that those who desired
salvation from the endless cycle of reincarnation must completely reject secular life and follow Buddhist principles (the
dharma). Respecting the *dharma* supposedly enabled the spiritually adept to cast off all earthly illusions and enter *parinirvāna*
after death. *Parinirvāna* may be cursorily described as state of
salvation beyond human comprehension that lies between existence and nonexistence. This form in Buddhism is called "*Theravāda*" (the Doctrine of the Elders) and survives in India, Sri
Lanka, Burma, and Thailand.

After the historical Buddha died, some of his followers
began to envision him as a godlike entity. They believed salvation might be found in uniting their individual spirits with that
of the Buddha. As time passed, a few became convinced that a
small group of exemplary Buddhists (*bodhisattvas*) had freely
chosen not to enter *parinirvāna* in order to guide others along
the way. These *bodhisattvas* were conceptualized presiding over
intermediate paradises where the virtuous could hope to find
temporary respite from the cycle of reincarnation. This type of
Buddhism came to be called "*Mahāyāna*," the Great Vehicle,
because it was considered capable of carrying everyone to salvation. *Theravāda* Buddhism was known as "*Hīnayāna*," the
Lesser Vehicle, to Mahāyānists. Both kinds of Buddhism spread
throughout east Asia.

In China, the two kinds of Buddhism diverged further. The
bulk of Mahāyānists split into (1) two groups that were scholas-
tically oriented (the T'ien-t'ai and Hua-yen sects), (2) a form
that preached salvation by faith and good works (Ching-t'u or
Pure Land Buddhism), and (3) Ch'an.

Tu Wei-ming summarizes the essence of Bodhidharma
Ch'an as:

(1) a belief in the universality of the true nature shared by all
sentient beings,
(2) a commitment to the self-enlightening capacity of that
nature, and
(3) a preference for realizing that nature through the cultivation of the mind. (Tu 1985, 10)

Ch'an ideology was unique in that some of its followers were
convinced that enlightenment could be attained through a single flash of perception. Neither the study of religious texts nor
sitting in meditation were considered prerequisite to achieving
this state. Also fundamental to Ch'an was the idea that the philosophy's essential precepts could only be communicated
through direct mind to mind transmission.

In a related development, which will eventually be demonstrated particularly significant for tea ritual, Hui-neng (E'no,
638–713), one of the most important Ch'an patriarchs, asserted
that one could understand one's personal Buddha nature only
by transcending language and the existing structure of the
mind. Some analysts conclude that this approach to salvation
owes much to the Taoist vision of totally losing oneself in the
Way (Tu 1985, 16; Hucker 1975, 214).

The masters who followed Hui-neng taught that an enlightened state could be achieved at any time and in any place
—even in the course of performing the most mundane tasks. To
help their followers transcend intellectual striving and superficial perceptions of reality, adepts were subjected to hard physical work and rigorous mental training. Often *kung-an* (called
"*kōan*" in Japanese), seemingly paradoxical, were employed as
a teaching device.

Though followers of Ch'an theoretically rejected written
texts, objects of worship, and ritual, the strenuous routine of life
in their communities did not preclude the enjoyment of all the
customary prerequisites of Chinese monasticism. In fact, tea ritual was a well-documented feature of life in their communities.

Some historians believe that Ch'an monks drank tea out of
a large common bowl before an image of Bodhidharma (Tierney 1975). This custom of sharing a single bowl among the
assembled monastic community is reputed to have been mentioned in the *Pai-chang ch'ing-kuei* (called the "*Hyakujō Shingi*"
in Japanese), a code governing the organization of Ch'an
monasteries purportedly written some time during Lu Yü's era

by the Ch'an monk Huai-hai (also known as "Pai-chang," "Hyakujō Ekai," and "Rikū," A.D. 749–814) (Collcutt 1981; Fujikawa 1957; Hayashiya 1971b).[4] In contrast to this predominantly commensal offertory rite, the oldest known surviving example of Ch'an tea ritual (*charei*) involves bringing individual bowls of powdered tea into the room, placing them before the assembled guests, supplying hot water from a ewer, and then whipping the tea. While each type of ritual has different implications for the analysis of today's *chanoyu*, it is unlikely the two were mutually exclusive. The former was probably part of daily routine. The monks may have offered a bowl of tea to Buddha and subsequently shared a single bowl among themselves. The latter was most likely a special ceremony where one bowl of tea was presented to the Buddha and individual bowls were offered to guests of the temple. In the next chapter we shall discover that by the ninth century, the Japanese were among the monk's assembled guests, but first let us briefly review the Chinese contribution to tea in the context of the definitions of religion previously suggested.

ASSESSING CHINESE TEA RITUAL

The Chinese contributed significantly to the development of tea ritual. In China, Tea unquestionably became a supra-linguistic communications currency of the type described by Nancy Munn (Munn 1973); that is, the procedure both came to incorporate symbols from a number of philosophical systems and began to function as a dominant symbol. Nevertheless, compared to the full-blown cognitive synthesis later to be realized in Japan, Chinese tea ritual represented only preliminary stages in the total evolution of the Way of Tea.

The Chinese practiced three very different kinds of tea ritual: secular, offertory, and commensal rites. Lu Yü's predominantly secular tea ritual typified the Confucian response to Taoism. In the *Classic of Tea* everything and everyone had a designated job to perform. The implication was that higher-order satisfaction would result if these functions were discharged in an appropriate manner. Even the anecdotal material at the end of the *Classic of Tea* featured historical figures whose love of tea and proper conduct resulted in health, wealth, and prestige. This indicates the central function of Lu Yü's tea ritual may have been to supply an example of one aspect of life a gentleman could refine to perfection. For this reason, the process of making tea came to epitomize the type of integrated social and spiritual action deemed essential to the promotion of *li* and, by extension, to the harmonious integration of the *Tao*. It was definitely a confirmatory ritual.

In contrast to Lu Yü's egocentric approach to Tea, the commensal and offertory rituals celebrated among the Ch'an focused on collective goals. When monks offered a bowl of tea to Buddha and/or shared it among themselves, they reaffirmed their collective commitment to follow the *dharma*. Sometimes this included propitiating or attempting to commune with a spiritual entity. (I suspect the tea ritual practiced by the Ch'an owed more to Mahāyānist precedent than the group's own philosophical precepts.) Clearly, the rational for these rites was quite different from those conducted by either the Taoists or the Confucians; but, this must also be characterized as confirmatory ritual.

In retrospect, despite the fact that they combined a single, superficially similar, overt function (making tea) with some shared philosophy and symbolism; offertory, commensal, and social tea rituals were not integrated into a single system in China. All three converted the act of making tea into a symbolic gesture meaningful in the larger cultural milieu and all were intended, to some extent, to confirm the participant's status relative to the universal order. But, even though the process of synthesizing Confucian, Taoist, and Buddhist cognitive systems through tea ritual had begun, practitioners had yet to address the problem of salvation or use tea ritual as an effective vehicle for transforming their outlook on life. Tea ritual had not yet become "a cultural system of symbols . . . concerned with transforming, temporally or permanently, some 'significant ill' that is seen to be part of the cosmological or existential order of human life" (Girardot 1983, 6).

Chapter 3

Tea Comes to Japan

EARLY JAPANESE CONTACT WITH TEA

*B*eginning in the early seventh century, the Japanese periodically sent official delegations to China. One such group of diplomats and scholars left Japan in A.D. 804. When they returned, their party included a Japanese monk named Eichū (743–816) who had just completed thirty years of Buddhist study in Ch'ang-an. Eichū brought tea with him, probably in the form of leaves pressed into a small ball, a form then popular in China.

Eichū seems to have simultaneously acquired a taste for tea and Chinese philosophy. He may have been acquainted with Lu Yü's *Classic of Tea* or even the *Pai-chang ch'ing-kuei*. At any rate, the *Nihon Kōki* (a work preserved in the Imperial Depository of Nara) reports that Eichū offered tea to Emperor Saga (785–842) on the shores of Lake Biwa in A.D. 815, an event generally considered the beginning of the Japanese Tea tradition.

The Emperor must have enjoyed his bowl of tea because he ordered tea seeds sown in neighboring provinces and founded a government tea farm in Kyōto. The use of this small crop was probably confined to that of the nobles and priests. Aristocratic poetry of the era refers to the pleasure of casual tea-drinking in pastoral settings, but religious tea ritual conducted in the Chinese fashion also thrived.

Temple records indicate that even after the death of Emperor Saga in A.D. 842, and an ensuing deterioration of interest in things Chinese, tea-drinking remained part of monastic habit. Imperial visitors to Buddhist institutions were regularly offered tea during this era. In fact, extant inventories list utensils used at these rituals. They reveal that T'ang dynasty tea bowls were especially treasured and probably reserved for nobles. The monks themselves used Japanese copies.

Despite a long hiatus in official intercourse, Japanese priests continued to travel to China for religious education for the next several hundred years. One such traveling monk, Jōjin (1011–1081), is said to have personally recommended the Chinese Emperor include tea bowls on the list of trade items desired by the Japanese. Regrettably, Jōjin died before he had the opportunity to return to Japan with the precious utensils.

EISAI, RINZAI ZEN, AND TEA

In the twelfth century, the popularity of tea in Japan was greatly stimulated by Eisai (1141–1215), the monk who introduced Rinzai Zen to Japan. (Zen is the Japanese name for Ch'an.) Like Japanese ecclesiastics of earlier days, Eisai went to China to clarify his understanding of Buddhism, specifically that of the Tendai (called "T'ien-t'ai" in China) sect. His first trip was undertaken in 1168 and his second in 1187. When the peripatetic bonze returned from his last journey to the mainland; he bore powdered tea, tea seeds, and some revolutionary ideas about religion derived from Ch'an philosophy.[1]

Landing in Japan, Eisai immediately introduced the cultivation of tea to Reisenji in what is now Nagasaki Prefecture. A few years later (1207), he presented seeds from these plants to his good friend Myōe (1173–1232). Myōe planted them at Kōzanji at Toganoo, an institution he had recently founded. The leaves eventually produced there were of particularly high quality and came to be considered "the true tea" by connoisseurs.

A great advocate of the benefits of tea as medicine, Eisai sent some powdered tea to Minamoto Sanetomo (1192–1219, the *shōgun*) in 1214. Sanetomo was known to be in poor health, partially due to an excessive consumption of *saké* (Japanese rice wine). Good advice to the contrary, Sanetomo continued drinking and became increasingly ill. The next year Eisai was called to take part in prayers for his health. At that time, he gave the *shōgun* a copy of a work he had written called the *Kissa Yōjōki*.

The *Kissa Yōjōki* was the first treatise on tea to be written in Japan. It reviewed both the physical and spiritual benefits of tea. In a catalogue of virtues reminiscent of those included in the

Chinese herbals, the author recommended tea as a cure for lupus, beriberi, fatigue, thirst, bad digestion, diseases of the heart, and so forth. The Taoist influence became evident when he proclaimed: "Tea is a divine medicine which prolongs life" (Kida 1970, 48). Eisai was particularly adept in reconciling esoteric Buddhist and Taoist lore in his explanation of tea's effectiveness as medicine. Foreshadowing future developments in tea ritual, he also advised offering tea to both gods and buddhas.

The important thing to remember about Eisai's contribution to *chadō* is that he brought much more than tea from China. Eisai introduced an approach to Buddhism that offered the possibility of salvation to those not content to rely on *sutra* studies, esoteric ritual, or blind faith. Followers of Zen shared the conviction that anyone could be enlightened. Further, they believed this goal could be achieved through a personal commitment to cultivate one's mind. These ideas presented a dramatic challenge to the Buddhist groups already deeply entrenched in Japanese society.

Because the established sects had a vested interest in convincing the rest of the population that the scriptural and esoteric knowledge essential to salvation could only be attained through their mediation, some Buddhists were adamantly opposed to the introduction of Zen. In contrast, the newly powerful warrior class (the *samurai*) welcomed the new philosophy.

Many *samurai* faced death frequently and undoubtedly had genuine concerns about the fate of their souls. Clerics of the more orthodox sects (who were either convinced that warriors could not be saved from the Buddhist hells so graphically depicted in their temples or were, at best, willing to sell them respite in intermediate paradises) offered little in the way of spiritual sustenance. Moreover, when thousands of Tendai monks streamed down from Mount Hiei carrying their *naginata* (a long pike-like sword) and laid waste to the capital, these monks' commitment to even the most basic Buddhist precepts was called into question. Zen offered the *samurai* a satisfying spiritual alternative and it supplied their leaders with a potentially effective counter to the dangerous warrior monks of Mount Hiei.

The rituals Eisai introduced to his country most certainly imitated those of China's religious and secular elite. The conservative general populace, however, was in no hurry to cast aside the familiar spirits of their land for foreign gods. The Buddhist response was to declare the *kami* (native Japanese spirits) primitive manifestations of various *bodhisattvas*.

Eison (1201–1290), a Buddhist revivalist, was convinced that tea could help him introduce a fresh synthesis of Chinese and Japanese philosophies to the common people. In 1239, this eclectic bonze diplomatically offered tea to the popular *Shintō* god Hachiman. This may be the first known instance of tea being presented at a *Shintō* shrine (*kencha*). Given the fact that the etiquette of such institutions were well-established and required accommodation, the incident probably heralded the introduction of indigenous concepts and symbols into the tea ritual.

TEA COMPETITIONS

In contrast to the decorous Tea of the monks, were the tea competitions (*tōcha, cha kabuki,* or *cha awase*) of the nobles and *samurai*. The creation of *cha awase* were a logical development in the life-style of the Heian (794–1185) nobility and the *samurai* of the early Kamakura (1185–1249) period. Court routine revolved around attendance at ceremonials and strictly structured leisure activity. Diaries and novels written by ladies of this era chronicle the profound boredom of the privileged.

In order to pass the time, games called "*mono awase*" were frequently played. These involved comparing shells, incense, birds, insects, and various utensils. Some competitions required participants to complete poems or stories. Since, tea, incense, and fine ceramics were all precious new arrivals from China, the elite began testing their discretionary skills by competing in games relevant to these luxurious commodities.

Cha awase drew inspiration from the tea rituals of the monasteries, but its etiquette was influenced by the rules of courtly pastimes such as incense identification (*kō awase*). At tea competitions, guests sat in lines and were served *temmoku* tea bowls with powdered tea already inside of them. A retainer moved down the rows of guests with an ewer and whisk (*chasen*) whipping tea. Many cups of tea were served and prizes were awarded for identifying the type of tea involved and the area of its production.

An account included in the *Taiheiki,* a famous war chronicle, evokes the extravagant spirit that ruled Tea in the Nambokuchō era (the period of Northern and Southern Courts, 1336–1392):

Guests of the *shōgun* Ashikaga Takauji (1305–1358), beautifully dressed in satin damask and gold brocade, were seated in chairs covered with leopard or tiger skins. Scores of delicacies were offered to them and one hundred prizes were displayed in the room. All the guests received some token of the *shōgun's* largess such as rolls of cloth, *kimono*, bags of gold dust, rare incense, or armor. After comparing teas and winning additional prizes, the sated guests distributed all these treasures among their attendants.

FURTHER ZEN INFLUENCE ON TEA

This type of display could not help but draw the attention of those Japanese interested in promoting a less materialistic approach to life. Prominent Buddhists were striving to return an atmosphere of restraint to Japanese life in general and tea ritual in particular. Probably in reaction to the technical elaboration of tea technique, Dōgen (1200–1253), the first Japanese patriarch of Sōtō Zen and a student of Eisai, included regulations for the tea ritual in his *Eihei Shingi* (the Eihei temple rules for daily life).

Even so, tea ritual became increasingly intricate even within the Buddhist community. For example, when Nampo Jōmyō (1235–1307), yet another Zen monk, returned from China in 1267, he brought with him a Chinese tea stand (*daisu*) and a seven volume textbook on Tea.[2] Nampo's tea probably represented an attempt to reestablish the Chinese tea tradition that had become known as of the Ching-shan school. Unfortunately, we have little information regarding the rituals he conducted.

Nampo's contemporary Musō Soseki (1275–1351), a highly respected Zen priest, who taught three emperors, may have also practiced Tea in the Ching-shan tradition. However, Musō influenced tea philosophy much more significantly that he affected its technique. Musō promoted the idea that "Tea and Zen are One" (*Cha Zen ichimi*). He believed:

> From the viewpoint of Zen, mountain water and tea drinking, singing songs, reading poems, anything one does in one's daily life or experiences is a means of gaining *satori*, enlightenment, which is the only way to realize the way of the Buddha. (Musō Soseki in Nishibe 1976, 15)

Clearly, the "National Teacher" believed tea ritual could be more than a form of entertainment or arcane temple rite. He even succeeded in convincing the Ashikaga *shōgun* to support his vision by banning the most obvious misuses of Tea such as heavy gambling at *cha awase*. Unfortunately, the edict promulgated in 1336 was ineffectual and Musō's Zen approach to tea was not widely accepted.

NŌAMI'S ATTEMPT TO RECONCILE ZEN TEA WITH THE TEA OF THE ELITES

During the Muromachi period (1392–1573), native Japanese culture experienced a renaissance. Tea became slightly more relaxed and less dependent on borrowed Chinese aesthetics. Furthermore, *shoin*-style architecture (formal, palace-style rooms) became popular, profoundly affecting the environment in which tea ritual was practiced. Important features of *shoin*-style rooms were the presence of a *tokonoma* (an alcove suggested by a similar architectural feature in Buddhist temples) and *tatami* (thick straw mats), which covered a large area of floor. Decorating these elegant rooms with flowers and art objects became a professional specialty. The Ashikaga *shōgun* Yoshimitsu (1358–1408) even created a special class of attendants (*dōbōshū*) to arrange his *shoin* for social events and to curate his treasured possessions.

The style of tea gathering conducted during this period was very rigid. Anxious to enhance their status, the military rulers of the Muromachi period had given the responsibility for establishing rules of etiquette for indoor and outdoor social events to the Ogasawara and Ise houses respectively. Nōami (1397–1471), one of Ashikaga Yoshimasa's (1435–1490) *dōbōshū*, began his career practicing Tea according to the rules set down by the Ogasawara family but later developed his own Zen-influenced approach to tea preparation.

Nōami's innovations included simplifying the physical arrangements of the *shoin* and using the *daisu* with a matched set of Chinese bronze (*karakane*) utensils. This new *shoin*-style Tea became known as that of the Higashiyama school (named after an exclusive area of Kyōto). Today's most formal tea preparation procedures use utensils and procedures similar to Nōami's. Nōami is also often credited with the coauthorship of the *Kundaikan Sōchōki*, a lengthy aesthetic compendium he is thought to have produced in collaboration with Sōami (d. 1525), another *dōbōshū*.

The *Kundaikan Sōchōki* described and ranked paintings, calligraphy, and various other decorative articles. Objects were classified *shin* (formal), *gyō* (semiformal), or *sō* (informal) according to the style of Ogasawara etiquette. Subject matter as well as execution was taken into consideration in ranking objects. For example, *shin* paintings were identified as high quality works with Buddhist or *Shintō* subjects while *gyō* paintings merely showed respect for the gods. *Sō* paintings, in contrast, reflected completely secular points of view. The tendency to associate the aesthetic characteristics of certain kinds of art objects with specific social situations (also formal, semiformal, and informal) thus established remains an important aspect of modern tea practice.

MURATA SHUKŌ INTRODUCES THE *WABI*-STYLE

Murata Shukō (1422–1502) was a priest from the Shōmyōji near Nara. (This temple is associated with the "Pure Land" sect.) His encounters with Nōami and Zen master Ikkyū Sōjun (1394–1481) produced significant changes in tea ritual.

As the story goes: Shukō had trouble staying awake to read the Scriptures, so he consulted a famous doctor who recommended drinking tea. Providentially, Nōami was in Nara to escape the ravages of the Ōnin Wars. This gave Shukō the opportunity to study with a master of the *shoin*-style. Shukō added the tea-style of Ikkyū to his repertoire somewhat later, after traveling to Kyōto for further religious studies.

Ikkyū is said to have been the unacknowledged son of Emperor Gokomatsu (1377–1433). Like many young aristocrats, who could not legitimately succeed to their father's lines, Ikkyū was consigned to the priesthood at an early age. However, unlike many of his peers, this particular youth seized upon his calling with sincere enthusiasm. He studied Zen under a number of the well-known masters of the day and eventually became the *dharma* heir of Kasō Sōdan (1352–1428), the chief priest of Daitokuji. (Becoming a *dharma* heir means he was acknowledged as heir to his master's religious teaching not necessarily his ecclesiastical status.)

Not surprisingly, the total freedom of thought and action enjoyed by Ikkyū appeared eccentric to his contemporaries: Ikkyū lived a wandering life. Acquiring an entourage of talented poets, painters, and actors, he is said to have been a frequently *habitue* of Kyōto's brothels and drinking shops. There was, however, spiritual method to his madness: the good monk's iconoclastic style was firmly rooted in the conviction that all sentient beings were capable of enlightenment and that the self-knowledge prerequisite to this state could be acquired any time and anywhere.

Although no particulars of Ikkyū's tea-style survive, we can assume that it was based on that of the Ching-shan school. (Nampo Jōmyō had transmitted this variety of Chinese temple tea to Daitokuji through Musō along with the *daisu* he brought from China. Jōmyō's *daisu* was apparently neglected for many years as Shukō is credited with restoring it to use. Sadler 1962, 2). Ikkyū, however, was not one to leave precedent unchallenged. His approach to tea ritual must have been as extraordinary as his life-style. Once, in a gesture typical of Zen masters, Ikkyū gave a great shout (Katsu!) and smashed Shukō's tea bowl with an iron rod (*kanabō*).

The implications of the gesture were not lost on the younger monk. According to the *Yamanoue Sōjiki* (a respected tea commentary written in 1588), Ikkyū taught Shukō: "The Buddha *dharma* is also in the way of tea" (Nishibe 1981, 23). This advice is believed to have inspired Shukō to create the first truly original tea ritual; an inspired synthesis of Chinese temple tea, Nōami's *shoin*-style, and Zen.

Shukō taught that four values were central to tea practice. They were: (1) *kin*, reverence, (2) *kei*, respect, (3) *sei*, purity, and (4) *jaku*, tranquillity. *Kin* is a type of reverence that has aspects of sincerity and modesty to it, an attitude unlikely to be common among those who participated in tea competitions. The concept of *kei* is said to have been originally inspired by the respect Zen monks were encouraged to feel for their food. This sentiment incorporates feelings of gratitude and sincere appreciation. *Sei* is a uniquely Japanese idea. It can best be described as a physical and spiritual purity appropriate for those who approach sacred precincts. The final element of the quartet, *jaku*, is strictly a Buddhist term. It is an inner tranquillity that transcends individual desires (one of the two characters that compose the Japanese word, *jakumetsu*, for *nirvana*).

All these qualities were given concrete expression in the physical changes Shukō made in the tea environment. His innovations included practicing tea in a four-and-one-half mat teahouse (*yojōhan*) and hanging Zen calligraphy (a gift from Ikkyū) in the *tokonoma*.[3] Shukō is also credited with the reduction of the *tokonoma* from the multiple "bays" of the *shoin*-style room to the single bay of the *sōan* (small, informal tearoom). Each innovation reflected a reduction in scale and a more nativistic trend in Tea. All were calculated to redirect the practitioner's attention away from materialism and toward the more spiritual aspects of tea preparation.

 Shukō's modest Zen Tea is considered the forerunner of the modern *wabi*-style. *Wabi* is an elusive quality with both spiritual and aesthetic aspects. It has implications of material insufficiency, muted beauty, a tinge of loneliness, and a suggestion of spiritual aloofness.[4] Shukō attempted to characterize his approach to tea ritual in a letter sent to a disciple named Chōin (also known as Furuichi Harima, 1452?–1508) around 1488 (the *Kokoro no Fumi*). Shukō advised his friend to help dissolve the line between Japanese and Chinese utensils by focusing on the concepts of "chill" (*hie*) and "withered" (*kare*). (These ideas were borrowed from *renga* poetry, a literary form of which Shukō had mastered before he began concentrating on tea ritual). Shukō believed his new aesthetic approach would aid Tea adepts in endowing their practice with a more spiritual ambiance.

Associated with Shukō's approach to tea ritual was a new appreciation for native utensils such as those of the Bizen and Shigaraki kilns. Shukō did not, however, recommend the total rejection of Chinese ceramics. Such utensils actually continued to occupy a central place in his tearoom. Shukō apparently intended only to enhance the beauty of both Chinese and Japanese pieces by using them in combination. This he believed suggested the charming vision of "a fine steed tethered at a thatched hut," an aesthetic that created an atmosphere of profound subtlety (*yūgen*).[5]

Tradition has it that Nōami recommended Shukō's Tea to Ashikaga Yoshimasa. Yoshimasa, tired of the lavishness of *shoin*-style Tea, is believed by some to have traveled to Shukō's small hut to learn the Tea of the Buddhist recluse (Nishibe 1981, 24). Whether this is true or not, gambling and drinking finally began to disappear from the tearoom during Shukō's span of influence.

A BRIEF REVIEW OF JAPANESE TEA RITUAL
THROUGH THE ASHIKAGA ERA

Although tea was originally introduced to Japan by Buddhist monks, it soon became popular with the secular elite. While the priests attempted to replicate the ritual of the Ch'an monasteries, *shoin*-style ritual incorporated elements of court etiquette and the gambling games of the Heian aristocracy. Chinese utensils were highly prized by both religious and secular practitioners during this period. The expense of the utensils and the relative scarcity of tea itself conspired against its distribution among the general populace. Thus, the ability to practice Tea confirmed membership in the elite.

Mindful of the religious content and origins of tea ritual, Zen priests repeatedly attempted to restore religious meaning to the increasingly degenerate secular practice of Tea. As a result, they began to think of tea ritual not merely as a commensal or offertory rite but as a unique vehicle for enlightenment. Tea ritual's transformatory potential was beginning to be recognized. This trend was a logical extension of Rinzai Zen philosophy: that is, if all sentient beings have a Buddha nature and may approach enlightenment in an infinite number of ways, why not cultivate the mind through the practice of tea ritual?

Also characteristic of Zen, was the conviction that spiritual aspirants must constantly question their assumptions to free their minds from earthly delusions. Zen tea practitioners consequently became increasingly liberated from convention in their use of materials and techniques. By the end of the Ashikaga period, native Japanese utensils were beginning to replace Chinese prototypes and tea procedures were being simplified. On the whole, however, tea ritual remained the province of the elite. The Zen-based vision of Tea as a "Way" to salvation had yet to be fully realized.

Chapter 4

The Samurai *and the Merchant Tea Masters*

JŌŌ ESTABLISHES THE SAKAI SCHOOL

*I*f the previous centuries of Japanese tea history were the era of the priest and the aristocrat, the next few were those of the merchant and the warrior (*samurai*). Officially, merchants were members of the lowest class of Japanese society: they ranked below nobles, *samurai*, and farmers. Nevertheless, urban growth and the developing cash economy placed them in a position of economic, if not social, privilege. The costly Ōnin Wars further strengthened their situation because the contending feudal lords (*daimyō*) relied on them for both capital and military supplies.

With plenty of money but little access to elite society, the merchants began to establish their own cultural cliques. Tea became a prominent preoccupation among them. Sakai, a prosperous and independent port city, which had escaped the worst ravages on the ongoing civil wars, became the center of tea practice among the merchant class. For most of the sixteenth century, these men and their progeny would dominate *chanoyu*.

The ascent of the men of Sakai to preeminence in the Tea world began in 1525 when a successful leather merchant's son, Takeno Jōō (1502–1555), left Sakai to study poetry in Kyōto with Sanjōnishi Sanetaka (1455–1537), the leading *waka* (a form of poetry) master of the day. While he was in the capital city, Jōō encountered the Zen approach to Tea. Totally enraptured with *chadō*, Jōō entered the priesthood, training under Dairin

Sōtō (1480–1568), the chief-priest of Daitokuji. Soon thereafter, the young man withdrew to a modest dwelling in the lower part of Kyōto from whence he exercised a considerable influence on the tea practice of his day.

Even though he was said to have owned as many as sixty *ōmeibutsu* (a classification of famous tea utensils most of which were of Chinese origin and had important historical significance), Jōō dedicated himself to the respectful development of Shukō's *wabi* Tea. Perhaps inspired by the master's use of native utensils, Jōō became the first to hang the work of a Japanese poet in the *tokonoma*. The piece was a poem by Fujiwara Teika (1162–1240) written on a lightly colored piece of paper called "*shikishi.*" He also changed the decoration of the tearoom by substituting plain clay walls for the papered type preferred by Shukō, using bamboo for the lattice in his window, and replacing lacquer with plain wood on the bottom sill of the *tokonoma*.

Jōō is best known for his preference for wabi utensils. The famous recluse was the first to use an ordinary well bucket to hold water in the tearoom, a simple section of bamboo for a lid rest (Tanihata 1981c, 53), and a pilgrim's bent wood rice container for waste water. The creation of the *fukurodana*, an innovative tea stand (*tana*) with an enclosed shelf, was also among his achievements. It was the first alternative to the more formal *daisu* and as such it heralded a trend toward more relaxed tea gatherings.

Today, Jōō is generally thought of as a transitional figure between Murata Shukō and Sen Rikyū (1522–1591). The style of Tea Jōō founded is called that of the "Sakai school" because, despite his priestly calling, his tea was fundamentally representative of the wealth and cultural richness of his native place.

THE ERA OF SEN RIKYŪ

Introducing Sen Rikyū

One of Jōō's disciples was destined to have the greatest influence on *chadō* of any individual in its history. Although, in classic Japanese fashion, he was known by a variety of names throughout his lifetime; we know him best as Sen Rikyū. He is universally recognized as the most important tea master who ever lived.

Rikyū's impact on *chadō* was so dramatic that tea history now seems firmly divided into the events and developments that preceded his *seppuku* (ritual suicide) in 1591 and those which followed it. Unfortunately, the mystery that shrouds this well-known but little understood incident confounds most interpretations of tea ritual. With this in mind, I intend to introduce the historical context in which Sen Rikyū lived (and died) in this chapter, reserving discussion of the great tea master's teachings and the lingering repercussions of his suicide for the next.

Sen Rikyū (known as Yoshirō in his youth and later as Sōeki) was born into a family of fish wholesalers, one of the thirty-six powerful merchant families (nayashū) who virtually controlled Sakai. At an early age, perhaps as young as fifteen, Rikyū began the study of tea with Kitamuki Dōchin (1504–1562), a prominent exponent of the *shoin*-style. Sometime during his early years of tea practice, Rikyū also met Jōō. Impressed with Rikyū's commitment and ability, the master accepted the promising young man as his student (Nishibe 1981, 31).

The historical record reveals little more about Rikyū until he was about thirty years of age. Then his life began to change drastically. Hata Kohei suggests that sometime during this period he was introduced to the Ashikaga *shōgun* (Hata 1976, 50). As Rikyū was known as a collector of famous utensils and master of the *daisu* (a particularly appropriate type of utensil to serve those of high rank) this seems not unlikely. Speculation aside, it is known that in 1570 the tea master encountered a public figure who was to significantly affect his fate: The man was Oda Nobunaga (1534–1582), a provincial warlord of great ambition and ability.

Oda Nobunaga and Sen Rikyū

Following some of Nobunaga's early military successes, Ashikaga Yoshiaki (1563–1597) solicited his help to restore the waning authority of the shogunate. Not long after, the Emperor Ōgimachi (1517–1593) also sent a message requesting the general's aid in recovering stolen imperial property. Thus, nominally authorized, Nobunaga entered Kyōto in 1568 (the opposing forces had fled) and almost immediately formally installed Yoshiaki as *shōgun*. There was, however, little doubt regarding the identity of the individual who controlled the capital: The victorious warlord's seal bore the engraved motto "Rule the Empire by Force" (Sansom 1961, 278).

About this time, Nobunaga also began to (rather aggressively) collect famous tea utensils. Perhaps Nobunaga was genuinely obsessed with Tea. Or, he may have wanted to add a veneer of respectability to his notoriously uncouth public image. Most certainly, the warlord was aware of the advantages to be gained from associating with the merchants of Sakai. Whatever Nobunaga's motive—when the citizens of Sakai responded to his exorbitant demands for "arrow money" (a thinly veiled threat to lay waste to the city), they prudently decided to include some of their prized tea implements in the settlement.

Imai Sōkyū (1520–1593), a member of Sakai's ruling council as well as a munitions dealer and well-known tea master, was instrumental in negotiating the agreement between Sakai and Nobunaga. At his invitation (and that of other influential residents of Sakai), Nobunaga came to Sakai in 1570, ostensibly to "view" the city's treasures. Imai's fellow tea practitioner Rikyū was among the members of the local delegation selected to serve the important visitor.

The young man must have made a good impression on the *samurai* because he was soon appointed to Nobunaga's entourage. Not much later, the general installed Rikyū in Azuchi Castle, charging him with the construction of its tearooms. Meanwhile, Nobunaga continued to collect famous utensils, adding to Rikyū's responsibilities as their curator (Ito 1976, 7–8).

Tea not only provided Nobunaga with a good opportunity to meet military suppliers and moneylenders but it also allowed him to display his power without force of arms. He even had the temerity to hold a tea gathering featuring a piece of rare incense appropriated without permission from the Imperial Repository in Nara. The message was clear—only the Ashikaga *shōgun* Yoshimasa had previously dared such an affront to the emperor's dignity.

The aura of strength and polish Nobunaga attempted to project through tea ritual made its practice increasingly attractive to warriors of every rank. By manipulating access to this desirable avenue of upward mobility, Nobunaga gained a new method of controlling his retainers. Controverting the tea masters' right to freely accept students on their own initiative, Nobunaga forbade the public practice of Tea among *samurai* not personally authorized by him.

This development was to have important consequences for

tea history in general and Rikyū in particular. For, in 1578, Oda Nobunaga gave his vassal Toyotomi Hideyoshi (1536–1598) permission to practice *chanoyu*. The ambitious young soldier professed to be as delighted about this honor as he was about the gift of two provinces and a gold mine (Berry 1982, 76). Nobunaga pointedly advised his protege: "For tea companions, choose merchants from Sakai!" (Cort 1982b, 20)

Ironically, in 1582 Oda Nobunaga died in a fire that occurred when he came under attack after preparing tea at Honnōji in Kyōto. Hideyoshi acted swiftly to consolidate his power. Significantly, within a year he announced that he was appointing Nobunaga's tea masters, including Rikyū, to his own entourage.

Rikyū and Hideyoshi

A complex relationship is initiated   The Japan that Hideyoshi inherited from Nobunaga (a legacy not unchallenged by Nobunaga's offspring) was still a loose affiliation of warring factions. Hideyoshi had many battles to fight, both militarily and politically. In the course of doing so he cleverly manipulated the practice of *chanoyu* to serve his own ends. On the battlefield, Hideyoshi constructed a portable teahouse so he could practice in view of the combatants (Sadler 1963, 129). The sight of the general calmly preparing Tea was calculated to intimidate the enemy and instill confidence in retainers. It is also possible that these tranquil moments helped soothe Hideyoshi's own jittery nerves.

Even so, tea was more than a form of bellicose histrionics or personal therapy to Hideyoshi. The newly powerful warlord also used tearooms for quiet strategy meetings with his vassals. One of Hideyoshi's men, Kuroda Kampei Yoshitaka (1546–1604) objected, thinking it dangerous for *samurai* to huddle in a small place unarmed (not an unfounded suspicion). Hideyoshi's response was to invite the disgruntled officer to drink tea, quietly discussing confidential military matters. Kuroda diplomatically observed: "Now I see that a great general never likes anything without a very good reason!" (Sadler 1963, 139).

Hideyoshi obviously had more than one reason for liking *chadō*. And, as Kuroda must have noted, Nobunaga's canny successor was not reluctant to use *chadō* as a mechanism of social control. In fact, it was largely through the use of subtle means such as the manipulation of tea ritual that Hideyoshi almost completely pacified Japan. Then he began to exploit Tea on a grand scale.

Most notably, in 1584 Hideyoshi offered to prepare tea for the emperor. The occasion was Hideyoshi's appointment to the position of *kampaku,* the emperor's chief advisor. (Hideyoshi designed a spectacular, shrine-like "golden tearoom" especially for the event.) Extending such an invitation was unprecedented and more than a little presumptuous for a former foot soldier like Hideyoshi (Cort 1982b, 24).

Since Hideyoshi needed help in serving tea, the emperor formally invested Rikyū with a *kojigo* ("enlightened layman's title") for the occasion. This designation was bestowed on the tea master specifically to help circumvent the complicated problems of etiquette that would have inevitably accompanied the admission of a commoner to the imperial presence. (The tea master already held the priestly title of *koji* conferred on him by his Zen master after thirty years of practice.) At the same time, the merchant from Sakai was awarded the title of "Tea Master of Japan" (*tenka gosadō*) (Hamamoto 1985, 8).

The symbolic and political ramifications of this unique tea gathering were staggering. To begin with, Hideyoshi and his tea master (who had no choice in the matter) were to some extent assuming the prerogative of several ancient clans of *Shintō* priests who specialized in court ritual. For another, preparing tea for the direct descendent of the Sun goddess was more than a statement of social status or respect: The victorious warlord was clearly flaunting his ability to constrain the emperor's cooperation and simultaneously trying to symbolically confirm his legitimacy as the imperial guardian.

At the same time Hideyoshi was respectfully coercing the emperor, he was also employing his tea master in rather unorthodox ways. Rikyū's correspondence (skillfully analyzed by Beatrice Bodart in research based on Kuwata Tadachika's analysis of over two hundred and sixty letters written by the tea master) indicates that the tea master performed a wide variety of quasi-diplomatic and personal services for his lord. Various epistles make it clear that Rikyū managed some of Hideyoshi's money, transmitted secret messages and maps on his behalf, conducted sensitive negotiations for his lord, and even supervised Ōsaka Castle in the *kampaku*'s absence (Bodart 1977, 53).

Bodart suggests it was precisely because Rikyū was not a warrior that he became a valuable asset to Hideyoshi. Rikyū was intelligent and trustworthy but superfluous on the battlefield. Assigning major domestic responsibilities to the tea master freed a warrior to perform his primary function. Moreover, Rikyū occupied a structural position that made him an unusually valuable unofficial deputy. As a wealthy merchant and famous tea master, he had connections among the elite but was free of the crosscutting allegiances and personal military ambitions characteristic of most *samurai*.

Hideyoshi also depended on Rikyū in ways more consistent with the traditional functions of a tea master: The historical record shows that the *kampaku* quite effectively used his tea master's reputation to enhance his own social standing. For example, the proud old Shimazu clan ignored a piece of correspondence from Hideyoshi (who they saw as an upstart) but subsequently responded quite politely to similar letter written by Rikyū and Hosokawa Yūsai, 1534–1610, a distinguished literary figure and tea practitioner, who was the father of Rikyū's famous disciple, Hosokawa Sansai, 1563–1645, the Christian general.

Hideyoshi was not ungrateful for Rikyū's services. In a short period of time, the tea master's status as an advisor became so high that he was publicly recognized as the only non-*samurai* in the *kampaku*'s inner circle. Ōtomo Sōrin (1530–1585), the visiting representative of a group of powerful provincial lords, was astonished to discover that "there is no one other than Sōeki [Rikyū] who can even say a word to the *kampaku*" (Bodart 1977, 57). His assumption was confirmed when Toyotomi Hidenaga (1540–1591), Hideyoshi's stepbrother told him: "Confidential matters are known by Sōeki [i.e. Rikyū] and public matters by the saishō (Hidenaga)" (Bodart 1977, 57).

Obviously, Hideyoshi and Rikyū had developed a unique and complex relationship—one that confounded the customary role's of (1) lord and retainer, (2) merchant and *samurai*, and (3) student and teacher. The multitude of problems that resulted from the tea master's lofty but ambiguous position support Kuwata Tadachika's assertion that the Rikyū's fate had more to do with his structural status than his ritual practice. To show why, I will address the aforementioned relationship pairs individually.

Lord and retainer   According to the ethics of the age, Rikyū owed Hideyoshi unqualified loyalty, which the latter was obliged to reciprocate with his favor and protection. This affiliation was rooted in the rapprochement between the Confucian ethic and the native Japanese belief system. Specifically, the emperor was identified as both patriarch and sovereign of the Japanese people and placed at the apex of a vertically ordered social hierarchy. This was an effective device for resolving any potential conflict between filial piety, which was often interpreted as clan loyalty in Japan, and obedience to the state. Since Hideyoshi was the emperor's officially designated agent and protector, fealty due the emperor was also nominally due his representative. Hideyoshi's structural proximity to the emperor and Rikyū's analogous intimacy with the *kampaku* reinforced the obligation.

In addition, as a member of the *kampaku*'s advisory council, Rikyū was doubly bound by the code of *bushidō*, the "Way" of the warrior. Because the merchant tea master enjoyed the privilege of sitting among the highest ranking *samurai* and even the right to own a sword and armor (the emblems of the *samurai*), he was drawn by fiat into the tight fraternity of military men morally obliged to value their lord's interests over all others.

Rikyū appears to have responded to Hideyoshi's trust by trying to serve him sincerely and well in a multitude of capacities. After all, compared to Nobunaga, Hideyoshi was a man of reason and a great peacemaker. (The severed heads periodically displayed before the general also constituted a graphic reminder of the potential consequences of his displeasure.) Even so, given Rikyū's love of *wabi* tea and the *kampaku*'s obvious insensitivity to the true meaning of the aesthetic, one might well ask why the tea master did not plead age or ill health and retire to his tearoom? After all, the tea master had given years of loyal service to Hideyoshi and his correspondence reveals no pecuniary motive for staying. (Rikyū was very seldom rewarded with more than a robe or special food item and his estate included little he had not inherited from his father according to Bodart 1977, 50).

Rikyū probably maintained what he must have realized was a vulnerable position in Hideyoshi's inner circle for two reasons. First, the tea master had a consuming passion. As he himself wrote:

I strove with all my powers to create tea in the spirit of the
roji and thatched hut, which had never before existed in
either China or Japan. (Sen Rikyū in Hisamatsu 1987, 10)

Rikyū knew that, if he abandoned Hideyoshi before his
vision of *chadō* came to fruition, his opportunity to influence the
future course of the Way of Tea would devolve on his successor.
With no satisfactory heir to his practice in sight, the *kampaku*'s
tea master would have been understandably reluctant to retire.

Second, Rikyū was compelled to stay with Hideyoshi by a
strong sense of social responsibility (and probably more than a
modicum of pride). The tea master clearly thought of himself as
a great statesman. In a poem written to his daughter a few weeks
before his death he compares himself to Sugawara Michizane
(845–903), a Heian period (794–1192) minister and distinguished
literary figure who died in exile after being unjustly accused of
plotting against the Fujiwara regents (Bodart 1977, 74). Michizane was later deified as the "god of literature."

Both Michizane and Rikyū were undoubtedly influenced by
the Confucian model of the wise teacher/good counselor. This
probably inspired Rikyū to cultivate the peaceful side of Hideyoshi's personality through tea ritual. By providing the type of
subtle moral guidance inherent in *chadō*, the tea master might
have hoped to mediate some of his lord's increasingly violent
impulses and counter the bad counsel of the self-serving *samurai*
who surrounded him. (In fact, Hideyoshi's most savage acts, the
destruction of his nephew Hidetsugu and all his family, and the
persecution of the Christians took place after Rikyū's death.)

Student and teacher If either Rikyū or Hideyoshi had been
more malleable or less talented, history would have taken a different course. As it happened, however, one of the greatest
politicians Japan had ever known had elected to study *chadō*
with the greatest tea master in Japanese history. It was a heady
combination. Hideyoshi thought himself a better tea master
than he was and Rikyū overestimated his ability as a diplomat.
The subliminal enmity and sense of competition engendered by
the juxtaposition of statuses inherent in the pair's dual roles of
lord/retainer and student/teacher ultimately sealed the tea
master's fate.

Hideyoshi quite naturally chose to base his perception of
his status vis à vis his tea master's on the prevailing social

order, the military chain of command, precedents set by Taira and Minamoto leaders, Confucianism, and his own megalomania. Rikyū, who was a student of Zen and not a soldier, focused on the ethical responsibilities of his role as a teacher. His personal spiritual training compelled him to nurture his mercurial student's none too obvious propensity for introspection, at any cost. Such a perception of a tea master's moral obligation was entirely consistent with the Buddhist concept of hierarchy based on spiritually earned merit and the Zen tradition of the oral transmission of the *dharma* fundamental to the Way of Tea.

Chie Nakane has observed that the golden rule of Japanese social ethics is "No man can serve two masters," but Rikyū was trying to do just that (Nakane 1970, 59). As a dedicated teacher of a form of religious practice (*chadō*), he derived his authority from and actively promoted a hierarchy based on spiritual merit. At the same time, as one of Hideyoshi's senior retainers, Rikyū was deeply committed to a lofty position in a secular social structure predicated on the use of physical force.

The great tea master seems to have tried to resolve the problem of conflicting secular and religious obligations by rationalizing his dual loyalties to Buddha and Hideyoshi with the Confucian good teacher/wise counselor model. Rikyū may have been able to sustain this position indefinitely had Hideyoshi not grown paranoid in his old age.[1] Unfortunately, the warlord had spent most of his life ferreting out and profiting by the timely analysis of conflicting allegiances and the passage of time had not mellowed him. When Hideyoshi realized Rikyū could not be dominated or excelled in the tearoom, he must have felt vaguely intimidated—a dangerous and unwelcome sensation to a warrior.

The conflict between the two men was probably exacerbated by the deep respect Rikyū showed for his religious teacher Kokei Sōchin, the abbot of Daitokuji (1532–1597). Given what we know of his personality and values, Hideyoshi would have been hard-pressed to understand why his teacher was so much more impressed with Kokei's spirituality than his power. Unable to share or comprehend the friendship between the two men, the *kampaku* may have suspected a conspiracy or the threat of one. (Kokei was briefly banished to Kyūshū for unknown reasons only to be later reinstated at Daitokuji through the tea master's intervention.)

Independent religious sectarians continued to be a problem for the *samurai* even after Nobunaga slaughtered thousands of Tendai warrior-monks on Mount Hiei in 1571 and twenty thousand Ikkō (a Jōdo Buddhist sect) partisans in 1574. It is quite likely that Hideyoshi was suspicious of the special relationship merchants from Sakai had developed with the monks of Daitokuji, which was located uncomfortably near both his Jurakudai headquarters and the imperial palace (Nishibe 1981, 40). After all, brokers from Sakai had handled the finances of the rebellious Ikkō (Sansom 1961, 272). The *kampaku* knew from experience that militant action was impossible without capital. Like every astute secular authority of the era, Hideyoshi became wary when individuals of means started intimately associating with representatives of the religious hierarchy (as evidenced by Hideyoshi's and Tokugawa Ieyasu's (1542–1616) treatment of both militant Buddhists and the Christians).

Merchant and samurai   The forgoing suggests that Hideyoshi had another reason to consider his tea master an undefined threat—Rikyū was a merchant. In the early years of their association, the message of egalitarianism inherent in Rikyū's *wabi* tea would have appealed to Hideyoshi, for he was searching for ways to gracefully insinuate himself among Japan's proud hereditary elite. As he grew older, more confident of his own social position, and increasingly concerned about posterity, the tea master's message must have sounded a sour note.

Hideyoshi was a pragmatist, not an idealist. He had spent a lifetime clawing his way to the top of the social ladder. As his mortality began to weigh more heavily upon him, the *kampaku*'s thoughts turned to his heirs' future among the powerful, predatory lords that surrounded him. With poor health enhancing the urgency of the situation, Hideyoshi's patience with his tea master predictably began to wear thin. The old man's imposing presence must have reminded Hideyoshi that he had not been born to the status he was now demanding for his son and there were those who remembered.

There may be yet another reason. The proximity of someone from the merchant class would have irritated Hideyoshi: In the early days of the *samurai*'s ascent to power, he had been anxious to associate with anyone who could supply him with the wherewithal to finance his military campaigns. That was precisely why Nobunaga had recommended he practice tea with the merchants from Sakai. Unfortunately, financial partners have a way of becoming creditors when they are denied their share of the profits. As a *samurai*, Hideyoshi had a vested interest in keeping his former benefactors from becoming more influential as they collected their debts: The Japanese economy was rapidly shifting from an agricultural to an urban base but the *daimyō*'s wealth had been traditionally reckoned by the rice production of their domains. If the warriors were to retain power, it was imperative that they gain control of sectors of the economy formerly abandoned to the merchants.

To facilitate the consolidation of their power, the *samurai* were developing a primitive concept of the "public province," one which would allow them to control vital assets such as banking, transportation, trade, and communications (Berry 1982, 156–159). The merchants were obviously resistant to these encroachments on their sources of income and the increasingly obvious attempts by the authorities to suppress their class. In the highest echelons, the mutual antagonism was intensified by the reluctance of some financiers to support Hideyoshi's Korean campaign (Sansom 1961, 361–362). Tension was building and the *kampaku* was acquiring a sense of urgency regarding his long-range plan to freeze the social order. Rikyū, a partisan of the merchant's cause whom Hideyoshi had raised far above his nominal social station, was beginning to look more like a liability than an asset.

Even if Hideyoshi and Rikyū had personally been able to reach a tacit agreement to ignore the tea master's merchant status, the *samurai* surrounding them would never have sanctioned their disregard for conventionally prescribed rank. Most of these men owed virtually everything they had to their blood and the relationships thus engendered. The presence of a member of the lower class in high station must have been particularly irritating to the unproven but ambitious youngsters among them—youths trained to recite their pedigree before engaging in single combat.

Following the lead of the Japanese historian Asao Naohiro, Beatrice Bodart suggests that Rikyū fell victim to the ambitions of just this kind of young warrior—Ishida Mitsunari (1560–1600). Mitsunari, who is described as holding the tea master's position as Hideyoshi's right hand man ten years later, headed a political group that opposed another clique led by Tokugawa Ieyasu (1542–1616) (Bodart 1977, 68). As Hideyoshi's closest confident, Rikyū may have been perceived by Mitsunari as a barrier to his own rising ambitions.

The events surrounding Rikyū's death

The Great Kitano tea gathering, an extravaganza held in 1587 was the culmination of Rikyū and Hideyoshi's collective effort to develop tea ritual. Significantly, every tea practitioner in the country was commanded to attend. *Wabi* tea men were specifically informed they would be denied the right to make tea in the future if they failed to appear. The first day, Hideyoshi and his three tea masters served tea to some eight hundred assembled guests with their own hands. (The famous golden tearoom was the centerpiece of the event.) Then, for reasons as yet unsatisfactorily explained, the *kampaku* canceled the rest of the event.

In her excellent article on the Great Kitano Tea Gathering, Louise Cort suggests Hideyoshi was growing increasingly disenchanted with the merchants from Sakai, great tea masters like Rikyū and Imai Sōkyū whose presence dominated the event (Cort 1982b). Cort also mentions that Hideyoshi was frustrated by the late arrival of an important merchant Kamiya Sōtan (1551–1635) from the rival port of Hakata, a man the *kampaku* counted on to help him finance the Korean expedition. Hideyoshi was also likely to have been exhausted and not a little exasperated with the unfamiliar and overwhelming dose of egalitarianism that Rikyū had arranged for him.

As might have been expected, the *kampaku*'s feelings of hostility toward his tea master were beginning to escalate. Rather than withdrawing discreetly in the face of Hideyoshi's increasing instability, Rikyū seems to have become more involved in the risky intrigues of the day. For example, when Hideyoshi banished Rikyū's friend Kokei Sōchin to Kyūshū in 1588, the persistently independent tea master dared to hold a final tea gathering for his friend in the Jurakudai, Hideyoshi's personal residence. Rikyū even displayed a valuable scroll that Hideyoshi had left in his care for remounting. This was a dangerous way to flaunt authority; it is hard to believe that news of this affront did not reach the *kampaku*'s ears.

The last few years have seen a renaissance of speculation related to Rikyū's forced *seppuku* (ritual suicide). Some hold that

Rikyū came under suspicion as a secret Christian (Berry 1982, 225). Romantics say the tea master incurred Hideyoshi's wrath by denying the general his beautiful widowed daughter (Sadler 1962, 116–118). Still others conjecture Rikyū's alleged trade in tea utensils offended his patron or that the *kampaku* suspected a conspiracy to poison him with tea (Castile 1971, 74–76).

The most popular theory among Rikyū's contemporaries was that Hideyoshi became infuriated by a statue of Rikyū wearing leather snow *geta* (sandals), which had been placed in the upper level of the *san mon* ("mountain gate") at Daitokuji by the tea master's friend Kokei. It was apparently a rather typical gesture of thanks for Rikyū's patronage: The tea master had commissioned the gate's completion to commemorate the seventeenth anniversary of his father's death. The snow *geta* seem to have been the offending factor: their presence was interpreted as potentially insulting to Hideyoshi or any imperial messengers that might have occasion to pass below.

There may have been, however, a time lag of about a year between installation of the statue and Rikyū's suicide. During that period, letters indicate that Rikyū was still party to Hideyoshi's most secret plans and negotiations (Bodart 1977, 63). Bodart argues that the statue was not the underlying cause for Hideyoshi's fatal order. She musters evidence to support the theory that Rikyū was a victim of conspiracy within the upper ranks of Hideyoshi's entourage.

I believe that to Hideyoshi the statue symbolized what he perceived as Rikyū's insistence on his own superiority and by extrapolation, the merchants' insistence on social parity with the *samurai*. This made him susceptible to insinuations of a plot involving Rikyū made by a small faction of ambitious *samurai* intent on promoting their own interests and that of their class. Because Hideyoshi was frustrated by the merchants' reticence in supporting the Korean campaign and deeply concerned about the poor health of his treasured son Tsurumatsu (1589–1591, who was to die at the age of three only six months after Rikyū), the negative aspects of Rikyū's role in secret negotiations regarding a conflict between two powerful retainers, the affair of the statue at Daitokuji, and so forth could have been exacerbated by clever gossip and circumstantial evidence.

The fact that Masuda Nagamori (1545–1615) (who was one of Rikyū's students as well as an associate of Ishida Mitsunari) escorted Rikyū from exile in Sakai to his death in Kyōto supports this theory. It is reinforced by the knowledge that six hundred (or three thousand, depending on which account you read) soldiers commanded by Uesugi Kagekatsu (1555–1623), another Ishida supporter, surrounded the site of Rikyū's *seppuku*. (One wonders who ordered the guard and what they expected to accomplish. Did they expect an escape, a rescue, or an attempt to deliver a last minute appeal for stay of sentence?)

No matter what the immediate impetus, Rikyū's star had fallen. He lacked influential family or regional support; his protector Hidenaga had just died, and, for some reason, the tea master felt he must refuse the proffered support of Hideyoshi's wife and mother. Rikyū was first ordered hastily into house arrest in Sakai and then called back to Kyōto to commit suicide.[2] His *seppuku* took place on 21 April of 1591. On his last day, Rikyū prepared tea and wrote two death poems, one in Chinese and one in Japanese:

> Seventy years of life—
> Ha ha! and what a fuss!
> With this sacred sword of mine,
> Both buddhas and patriarchs I kill!
> I raise the sword,
> This sword of mine,
> Long in my possession—
> The time has come at last—
> Skyward I throw it up!
>
> (Translated by
> Daisetz Suzuki 1959, 319)

The first poem recalls ninth century Ch'an master Lin-chi's (d. 866, also known as I-hsüan, considered the first patriarch of Rinzai Zen) admonition to his disciples (a famous sermon surely familiar to Rikyū):

> Kill everything that stands in your way. If you meet the Buddha, kill the Buddha. If you meet the Patriarchs, kill the Patriarchs. If you meet the *arhats* [those who have attained *nirvana*] on your way, kill them too. (Lin-chi in Tu 1985, 22)

Interpreted in the context of Lin-chi's injunction, both of Rikyū's poems must be appreciated as declarations of awesome freedom, defiance, and perhaps even joy. Seven hundred years earlier the Ch'an patriarch had demanded his followers totally reject any potential impediment to enlightenment whether it be disguised as faith, scripture, sacrament, or metaphysics. Now, in the last hours of his life and after a lifetime of Zen training, Rikyū realized he could, at last, accept the master's challenge.

As noted previously, Rikyū's contemporaries were as mystified about the tragedy as we are today. Their attention focused on the apparently offensive statue at Daitokuji which was publicly "crucified" on the Ichijō Modoribashi (a bridge near the Jurakudai where the heads of traitors were customarily displayed) shortly before Rikyū's death. Although Hideyoshi reportedly refused to view his tea master's head as was customary in such cases, the head itself was displayed under the wooden image's feet (Kuwata, 1976). The statue's torso is believed to have been subsequently thrown in the river and lost, but its head was preserved by the tea master's old friend Kokei. This precious relic was later secretly returned to the Sen family where it may still be seen on a body of later manufacture in the Rikyūdō of Konnichian (Urasenke's memorial chapel).

Barring the discovery of new documentary evidence from the period, we will probably never have a better understanding of the cause of the famous tea master's death. Clearly, Rikyū had risen precariously high for a merchant's son from Sakai. It was a violent era and Hideyoshi's own ascent to power emphasized the potential of political intrigue. In the end, however, Rikyū demonstrated himself to be an individual whose spiritual stature and moral influence exceeded the limited horizons of his contemporaries.

Chapter 5

Sen Rikyū's Achievements in Tea

SOURCES OF INFORMATION

*I*n chapter 4, Sen Rikyū was introduced in the context of his historical milieu. I carefully detailed the interrelation between the structural ambiguity of the tea master's social position and his tragic fate because I wanted to make it absolutely clear Rikyū was not martyred. More likely, he was sacrificed to the totalitarian objectives of a tyrannical regime.

Rikyū's preeminence should not, however, be attributed exclusively to a misadventure with sixteenth century power politics. The *samurai* elite retained many tea practitioners and more than one died for apparently unjust reasons. Yamanoue Sōji (1544–1590), for example, was brutally executed by Toyotomi Hideyoshi in 1590 and Furuta Oribe (1543–1615) was required to commit *seppuku* by Tokugawa Ieyasu in 1615. Though both men were tea masters of great repute, neither attained a posthumous status even approaching that popularly accorded Rikyū. This suggests the latter is principally venerated for his unparalleled contribution to *chadō* not for the dramatic mode of his demise.

Most scholars and tea practitioners accept the premise that Rikyū significantly altered *chadō*. Controversy develops only when discussion is confined to the precise character of the great tea master's legacy. The problem is that, in the best Zen tradition, Rikyū personally recorded very little pertaining directly to either his philosophy or his practice. Fortunately, some of Rikyū's contemporaries had the foresight to preserve a few particularly revealing anecdotes for future generations. A work

entitled the *Kissa Nampō Roku* (*Recording on the Drinking of Tea
Which Comes From the South*), has dominated this genre for three
hundred years. It was purportedly compiled largely during
Rikyū's lifetime by one of his disciples, a Zen monk named
Nambō Sōkei (dates uncertain).

About a century later (in 1686), Tachibana Jitsuzan (1655–
1708), an Edo period (1603–1863) tea practitioner and calligrapher of note, claimed to have made facsimiles of the first five
sections of the *Nampō Roku*. As evidence of their authenticity, Jitsuzan cited notes on his copies indicating the originals bore the
imprint of Rikyū's seal. The first five sections of this remarkable
document contain: (1) memoranda on various aspects of tea, (2)
a record of the master's tea gatherings, (3) information concerning the proper use of tea stands, (4) advice on displaying tea
utensils in *shoin*-style rooms, and (5) recommendations regarding the proper use of the *daisu*.

In 1690, Jitsuzan supposedly secured two additional essays
said to have been written by Nambō shortly after Rikyū's
death. The last section was purportedly written for a secret
memorial service held just two years after the unfortunate
event. (Jitsuzan's copies surfaced in rather suspicious proximity
to Rikyū's one hundred year memorial services.) These supple-
ments describe preparation techniques and purportedly
include the monk's personal recollections of his famous teacher.

Some modern scholars think the author of the *Nampō Roku*
based his work on material more appropriately attributed to
the older Sakai tradition. The composition is also thought to
incorporate a considerable amount of creative input from Jitsuzan himself (Hirota 1980b, 32). Curiously, the *Nampō Roku*'s
questionable authenticity seems to be a matter of minor concern to modern tea practitioners, possibly because its contents
have been inextricably integrated into *chadō*'s oral tradition and
much the same material can be found elsewhere. (Although,
some of these sources may be equally apocryphal).

Left without a reliably authenticated written testament
from Rikyū, tea practitioners have created their own strategies
for organizing information culled from disparate secondary
sources, which range in quality from first-hand accounts such
as the *Yamanoue Sōjiki* to popular gossip of the era. The most
commonly employed cognitive model seems to be based on
simple chronological development. Not surprisingly given the

general pattern of Japanese social institutions, this structure superficially conforms to that of a genealogical tree. The image of Rikyū projected by this unsophisticated device is that of a safely orthodox tea master who combined Jōō's *wabi* Tea with Nōami's *shoin*-style Tea and, under the influence of Shukō's philosophy, mysteriously produced something that was more than the sum of all three. Rikyū himself is purported to have stated: "The transmission of the technique I received from Jōō ; the Way I received from Shukō" (from the *Kōshin Gegaki* [1662] quoted in Hisamatsu 1987, 11).

The problem with using this strictly linear paradigm as a basis for scholarly inquiry is that it limits analysis to a narrow temporal framework. To fully appreciate Rikyū's genius, we must place him in the context of tea philosophy as a whole. I believe this can best be accomplished by treating Rikyū's state of enlightenment as a matter of historical and ethnographic fact.

RIKYŪ'S CONTRIBUTION TO TEA PHILOSOPHY

Let us begin with the fundamentals of Rikyū's religious experience: He was probably ordained into the Buddhist priesthood at the age of sixteen by Dairin Sōtō, the ninetieth chief abbot of Daitokuji. Although this type of ordination usually assumes a subsequent return to secular life and is sometimes taken rather lightly, Rikyū appears to have persisted in his spiritual training. By the time the tea master was presented with the title of *kojigō* in 1585, his Zen master Kokei was able to proudly note: ". . . for thirty years, he has endeavored in Zen and tea" (Nishibe 1981, 33).

Rikyū's years of disciplined inquiry did not pass unremarked. His contemporaries (and/or near-contemporaries) attributed his charisma and creativity to religious conviction. The author of the *Nampō Roku* wrote:

> Layman Rikyū is a tea master of great awakening, one who has penetrated truth and whose acts are in accord with it. (From the "Metsugo" section of the *Nampō Roku* quoted in Hisamatsu 1987, 16)

The unfortunate Yamanoue Sōji put it even more bluntly: "Sōeki [Rikyū] takes the Dharma of Zen as eye (from the *Yamanoue Sōjiki* quoted in Hisamatsu 1987, 10).

Clearly, Rikyū's intimates perceived him as someone who

had realized a state of awareness beyond the ordinary plane of discrimination and differentiation—a concept fully recognized and thoroughly integrated into the cultural experience of the Momoyama intellectual elite. The Zen term for this phenomenon is *satori*. *Satori* can vary in quality and duration and may be experienced more than once by the same individual. True *satori* is supposed to inspire a profound personality change characterized by a mature compassion for all things and a sense of "original wholeness, health, or holiness" like that described by Norman J. Girardot (Girardot 1983, 7). Zen masters emphasize the fact that *satori* is not the end of spiritual training but the beginning.

Interestingly enough, an account of the precise mechanism through which Rikyū is supposed to have attained *satori* has been preserved in the oral tradition. This flash of profound intuitive awareness is said to have occurred after Kokei gave the tea master the *kōan* "Drink down all the waters of the River Hsi in a single gulp." It was a phrase credited with eliciting a similar response from a Chinese Zen layman called P'ang Yün (Hamamoto 1985, 8). P'ang Yün (d. 808) responded to his *satori* by retiring from office, throwing his belongings in the river, and withdrawing to a corner of his estate where he lived an exemplary life with his wife and children. Rikyū, in contrast, chose to stay with Hideyoshi, rededicating himself to the transformation of *chadō*.

Having experienced *satori*, both P'ang Yün and Rikyū encountered the classic Zen problem of deciding how to manifest their new understanding. For various reasons, neither elected to conform to the orthodox ecclesiastical model and become a monk. P'ang Yün ultimately decided to emulate the Theravādic ideal in lay fashion. He became a humble recluse. Rikyū took a more Mayāhāyanist stance and elected—*bodhisattva*-like—to remain in secular society and help others along the Way.

In a poem he supposedly wrote soon after attaining *satori*, Rikyū simultaneously revealed the anguish of his liminal position and his very Buddhist resolution to the problem. The subject matter is the bamboo ladle used to transfer water between the cold water jar and the boiling kettle:

> Even the ladle
> That goes between
> The hells of cold and hot:

> If it has no mind
> It has neither suffering.
> (Attributed to Sen Rikyū
> in Nishibe 1981, 34)

The active, pragmatic character of Rikyū's realization not only distinguished him from his predominantly priestly forebears in Tea but also definitively established *chadō* as a fully developed lay approach to Rinzai Zen. Shukō maintained that "the Buddha *Dharma* is also in the way of tea" (from the *Yamanoue Sōjiki* quoted in Nishibe 1981, 23). Rikyū went one step further. Insisting that *practicing* the Way of Tea was a potentially effective method of pursuing enlightenment, he said, "Through concentrating on *chanoyu* both guests and host can obtain salvation" (Rikyū from the *Nampō Roku* in Tanikawa 1981a, 41), and:

> *Chanoyu* is above all a matter of performing practice and attaining the Way in accord with Buddha's teaching. (Rikyū from the *Nampō Roku* in Nishibe 1981, 34)

One might think that Rikyū's prestige as an enlightened layman and national recognition as an exemplary Buddhist would elicit a modicum of support for his arguments. But suspicions about his political role combined with the general skepticism of his somewhat jaded contemporaries to mediate against the tea master's chances of stimulating sweeping changes in Tea solely on the basis of ascribed religious status. Deeply ingrained behavioral patterns such as those Rikyū somewhat idealistically hoped to modify are difficult to manipulate even with the aid of sophisticated modern communications systems. In sixteenth century Japan, only a few potential avenues of influence were available to aspiring proselytizers. Of these, Rikyū successfully employed: (a) conventional oral didacticism, (b) symbolism, (c) personal example, and (d) visual aids.

RIKYŪ AS A TEACHER

The oral component in Rikyū's message

If the dialogues, which survive in the anecdotal material are truly representative, then a sophisticated comprehension of the power of words and a blunt speaking style distinguished Rikyū's use of language. The great tea master clearly understood the art of changing perceptions through the select use of appropriate vocabulary. For example, when he wanted to establish the primacy of the religious elements in tea ritual, he began using the term *chanoyu* (literally "hot water for tea) to signify the whole behavioral complex. Rikyū and Jōō are popularly believed to have derived this term from a Buddhist phrase "Ten Cha Ten Tō" used to designate "the tea offering made before Buddha, ancestral spirits, or the dead" (Sadler 1962, 3). ("Yu" is the Japanese reading of the Chinese character for hot water "tō.") Previously, tea ritual had been called *"cha e"* (tea gathering or party) a name with more secular connotations.

In much the same manner, Rikyū significantly influenced tea values by changing a single character in Shukō's normative mnemonic "Kin Kei Sei Jaku" (reverence, respect, purity, and tranquillity). By substituting *wa* (harmony) for *kin* (reverence), the tea master encouraged a more egalitarian approach to Tea. Given Rikyū's admiration for Shukō, it is unlikely that this modification was made lightly. *Kin* connotes a respectful awareness of status differences between individuals while *wa* evokes the Confucian ideal of harmonious social interaction extolled in Prince Shōtoku's (572–621) Seventeen Article Constitution (See Tsunoda et al. 1964, 47–51). In essence, the former implies a social debt to one's superiors while the latter is charged with strong implications of *mutual* social obligation.

For all his linguistic erudition, Rikyū appears to have expressed himself with the crystalline simplicity and directness characteristic of Zen masters. There is no evidence that he flattered, minced words, or encouraged exclusivism that comes with an emphasis on esoteric "secrets." For example, when asked why the informal tea of the small room should represent a higher spiritual attainment than the more formal tea of the *shoin*, he responded:

> The practitioner brings water, gathers firewood, and boils the water. Making tea, he offers it to the Buddha, serves it to others, and drinks himself. He arranges flowers and burns incense. In all this he takes for model the acts of the Buddhas and patriarchs. (Rikyū from the *Nampō Roku* quoted in Hirota 1980b, 33)

And, when someone requested the "secrets" of *chadō*, Rikyū explained, "In summer, impart a sense of deep coolness, in winter, a feeling of warmth; lay the charcoal so it heats the water, prepare the tea so that it is pleasing: these are the

secrets." Not satisfied with such a simple response, his incredu-
lous listener sniffed: "That is something everyone knows." "If
so, try performing in accord with what I have stated. I will be
your guest, and perhaps become your student," the master
pointedly replied (from the *Nampō Roku* quoted in Hirota
1980b, 36).

Rikyū's use of symbols

As will become increasingly obvious, it is even more important
for ritual practitioners to become adept at the symbolic idiom
than the spoken one. Rikyū was a peerless master of the genre.
Under his influence, *chanoyu* became a seamless tapestry of
cleverly integrated symbolic elements from virtually every religious, intellectual, and cultural tradition the Japanese had
encountered to date.

Predictably, given the Ch'an influence in Tea and the intensity of the Heian elites' dedication to Chinese geomancy and
calendrical symbolism, there was a strong Taoist influence in
Rikyū's practice. According to the *Nampō Roku*, he said:

> It is only after years of practice you will grasp in its details
> the fact that everything from the hundred thousand ways of
> displaying utensils to the straw-thatched *wabi* tearoom, is
> governed by the measurements, based on *yin* and *yang*,
> applied in using the *daisu*. (From the *Nampō Roku* quoted in
> Hirota 1980b, 42).

Buddhist symbolism, in contrast, was most conspicuous by its
absence. It is true that Rikyū preferred to use inspirational
scrolls written by Zen priests and he also identified the garden
path (*roji*) with the way to the "Pure Land" mentioned in the
Lotus Sutra. But, for the most part, he avoided Buddhist
iconography. This was entirely in keeping with his religious
training. Zen adepts theoretically reject the mediation of esoteric symbols, relying instead on direct experience. If one assumes
the entire tearoom is ordered by the *dharma*, reiteration is
superfluous.

Nevertheless, Zen is comprehensive as well as experiential
by nature so Rikyū freely reinforced his message with a host of
symbols gleaned from a wide variety of sources. Symbols pertaining to the social order, like ranked seating arrangements,
represented the Confucian contribution to Rikyū's tea. *Shintō*

beliefs were most evident in the use of water for purification and natural materials for utensils.

Further, since three of Rikyū's seven principle disciples were Christians (Oda Uraku [1547–1621], Gamō Ujisato [1556–1595], and Takayama Ukon [1552–1614] according to Sadler 1962, 118) and Mass was celebrated in the tearoom during Nobunaga's lifetime (Sadler 1962, 92), Rikyū may have been incorporating some characteristics of Catholic ritual into his own practice.[1] (I believe his long practice of Zen mediates against the possibility of the tea master himself being a secret Christian.) If so, these elements are most likely to be the use of the silk cloth for purification and the shared cup of thick tea.

Rikyū is, in fact, credited with introducing (or reintroducing) the shared cup of *koicha* (thick tea) to the lay practice of *chadō*. (The tradition had been preserved only in temple practice.) According to Chikamatsu Shigenori (1695–1778), Rikyū began presenting a commensal bowl of thick tea because preparing individual portions was a lengthy and tedious process (from the *Chanoyu Kojidan* quoted in Tsutsui 1981, 45). This explanation, however, seems suspiciously simplistic: The Japanese elite have historically been quite reluctant to share eating utensils; Rikyū would have been well aware of this prejudice. It is improbable he would have challenged his guests' deeply ingrained standards of hygiene (which were thoroughly grounded in the *Shintō* concept of purity) without a compelling philosophical justification. More likely, Rikyū was inspired by Buddhist or Roman Catholic commensal symbolism (or a combination of both). (Roman Catholicism was introduced to Japan by Francis Xavier and two fellow Jesuits in 1549.) If Christian influence was a factor, the information undoubtedly would have been suppressed by his family and followers during the anti-Catholic purges, which occurred soon after his death.

Teaching by example

Rikyū's most effective mode of communication was probably simple behavioral illustration. For example, he once gave a tea gathering for another merchant that was interrupted by the unexpected arrival of a powerful *daimyō*. Feeling it wrong to displace the guest of honor for an uninvited visitor, the tea master ignored precedent and offered the newcomer a less prestigious seat in the tearoom. The gentleman, to his eternal credit, graciously accepted the lower position and the event proceeded smoothly (Sadler 1962, 228–229).

On this particular occasion Rikyū quite audaciously challenged the established hierarchy to teach an important lesson in values. (One wonders if a less important figure than the *tenka gosadō* would have been as successful.) By tactfully managing his guests, he almost wordlessly made a radical statement redefining the tearoom as a special environment where genuine consideration of others was more highly valued than conventionally prescribed social status.

A similar anecdote describes a situation that developed when Rikyū and some companions arrived unannounced at the home of a well-known tea-grower. Overjoyed to welcome such illustrious guests, the host prepared to serve tea. Unfortunately, being extremely nervous, the poor man made a number of clumsy mistakes. Nonetheless, Rikyū astonished the assembled group by complimenting his host quite lavishly. When his puzzled students later inquired why he had praised such a poor performance, Rikyū explained that he considered sincerity more critical than technique (Tanikawa 1980b, 9).

Both vignettes emphasize the role of the teacher as moral exemplar. Like Confucius, Rikyū tried to teach by example, striving for perfection in every aspect of his personal existence. As we shall discover in subsequent chapters, nothing related to Tea eluded his attention from the position of stepping stones in the garden to the rhythm of the host's breathing.

The visual elements in Rikyū's tea

Rikyū's high standards and attention to detail were probably most obvious in the visual elements of his practice. His taste virtually redefined Japanese aesthetics. As with other aspects of the great tea master's practice, there are scores of stories about his artistic sensitivity. Among other things, he was renowned for determining the proper "fit" of a utensil to within fractions of an inch (Sadler 1962, 112–114), creating beautiful utensils from common materials (Chikamatsu 1982, 40–42), selecting particularly subtle colors for tearoom use (Kurokawa 1983, 36), and manipulating light in novel ways (Itoh 1983, 27).

The environment in which Tea is made was radically altered under his influence. The room, the *ro* (hearth), and the *tatami* were made smaller (Nakamura 1970, 38) to reflect

Rikyū's *wabi* ideals. He also created the *nijiriguchi* (a very small sliding door supposedly inspired by the hatch on a river boat), employed rough-textured walls and ceramics, and used a considerable amount of bamboo to enhance the intimate atmosphere of the tearoom. In addition, he skillfully relocated the windows so subdued light infused tea gatherings with a feeling of tranquillity (Itoh 1976, 14) and eliminated *shoin*-style formality by avoiding the use of the *daisu* in many tea procedures.

Visual impact aside, the most fascinating thing about Rikyū's art was its profound and consistent integration with his philosophy. For example, creating the *nijiriguchi* and placing a sword rack (*katanakake*) nearby forced proud samurai to enter the tearoom humbly. The great tea master's creations manifest a deep respect for individuals and for the natural environment, which has made artistic integrity a cherished value in Japanese aesthetics. Everything Rikyū is known to have designed or preferred seems to have been selected not only for its practicality but also with a subtle appreciation for the inherent beauty of its constituent materials.

Rikyū's art also reflected his values. By demonstrating his preference for modest tea bowls made by the descendant of an immigrant Korean tile-maker (Chōjirō, 1516–1589), the *tenka gosadō* made an important statement about ethnic and class prejudice. By using ordinary bamboo or basketry for flowers instead of rare Chinese bronzes or celadon, he taught a lesson in restraint and the appreciation of nature. When he patronized local kilns, he taught the elite to appreciate the products of their own working class.

RIKYŪ IN RETROSPECT

Rikyū's perfectionism sometimes made him difficult to tolerate. According to one trivial but revealing anecdote, he was on his way to pick flowers in the hills above Kyōto when he thought to ask whether his companion had put the kettle on the fire before leaving. His friend replied that he had not. Rikyū immediately sent him home to rectify the matter, warning that one never knew who might drop in for tea in the evening (Birnbaum 1981, 52). The tea master is also known to have sustained long running feuds with Imai Sōkyū (1520–1593) (Tanihata 1981c, 54; Sadler 1962, 102), and his own son Dōan (1546–1607) (Sadler 1962, 110). On the whole, however, Rikyū appears to have been a modest and magnanimous individual. Nambō, who was one of his most devoted students, supposedly wrote:

> Because he sincerely wished to spread the true *chanoyu*, he did not hide his own failures; and he admired anyone who could do things better than he could, even a beginner. And because he was fair and kind, those who associated with him were fond of him. (from the *Nampō Roku* quoted in Tanikawa 1980b, 13)

Although years of quasi-deification have tended to conceal his real personality, Rikyū was forthright about his own shortcomings. He admitted "at times I still sully the water" (Hirota 1980b, 43), and also "I have experienced *chanoyu* true to my ideal only two or three times in my lifetime" (from the *Chadō Shiso Densho* quoted in Tanikawa 1981b, 48).

For all his perfectionism, Rikyū always seems to have demanded more of himself than he did of his students. Moreover, he appears to have had the rare ability to sustain his capacity for penetrating awareness throughout his long career. One of his contemporaries, Kusabeya Dōsetsu (dates unknown), observed: "Rikyū is sixty-six years old but he serves everything by himself. His service is not at all *nurui* [lukewarm]" (from the *Chadō Shiso Densho* quoted in Tanikawa 1980b, 20).

In sum, Rikyū's real contribution to *chadō* was not the notoriety associated with his violent death or his political prominence. It was an impeccable set of moral and artistic standards meticulously integrated with ritual through the realization that *chadō* is a road to salvation anyone can follow. Rikyū envisioned Tea as a transformatory ritual and, as we shall see, the transformatory elements in modern tea practice are very much his legacy.

Chapter 6

Sen Rikyū's Legacy

TEA AS AN ADAPTIVE MECHANISM

*C*asual observers of modern tea ritual, initially impressed by its obvious archaism in dress and environment, are often overwhelmed by what they perceive as an "other-worldliness"—a sense of immutability and distance from real historic processes. But, while the tearoom is a world apart spiritually, it has never been immune to change or insensitive to its social environment. As indicated in previous chapters, over the centuries *chadō* has become an increasingly efficient mechanism for helping individuals cope with the social and political maelstroms swirling about them. Under Rikyū's influence, it ultimately became a fully realized "cultural system of symbols ..." concerned with a means of transforming, temporally or permanently, some 'significant ill' that is seen to be part of the cosmological or existential order of human life" (Girardot 1983, 6).

As the case of the great tea master's personal torment readily illustrates, the chaos from which the religiously inclined seek salvation can have both historical and spiritual components. It follows that a successful ritual practice must have both a message and a structure responsive to alterations in the ambient social milieu. *Chadō* is obviously one of the most consistently effective and long-lived representatives of this genre. In this chapter, the personalities, organizational mechanisms, and shifts in ideational emphasis, which allowed Tea to survive from the sixteenth to the twentieth century, will be considered.

HIDEYOSHI'S FINAL YEARS

Hideyoshi may have regretted the death of his tea master: In later years he commanded his private apartments decorated "in a style pleasing to Rikyū" (Sansom 1961, 364) At the time of his tea master's death, however, the old warrior had been under tremendous strain. His succession was threatened by the imminent loss of Tsurumatsu and he was becoming increasingly dissatisfied with the nephew (Toyotomi Hidetsugu, 1568–1595), expected to succeed him. The *taikō* (Hideyoshi was elevated to *taikō*, retired regent, in 1591) was also intent on consolidating his grip on Japan before embarking on a campaign of conquest, which he was confident would eventually lead him to Beijing.

As suggested in chapter 4, purging Rikyū from the top ranks of his advisors was probably a minor aspect of Hideyoshi's comprehensive plan to reorganize Japanese society, placing the Toyotomi at its apex in perpetuity. The spear-carrier's son went about the process systematically, conducting a census and cadastral survey, extracting oaths of allegiance from provincial *daimyō*, appeasing the nobles with increased financial support, and pacifying the religious sects with new temples.

By 1588, Hideyoshi had also disarmed the peasants under the pious pretense of collecting weapons to melt into rivets for a massive wooden Buddha. Three years later (just a scant five months after Rikyū's death), he made another move toward totalitarianism, issuing a remarkable directive tying cultivators to the land and freezing mobility between the social classes. By firmly separating military men from the farmers and creating sumptuary legislation, which symbolically enhanced the former's prestige, Hideyoshi forced *samurai* into a situation of economic dependency on the *daimyō*. This focused attention on their mutual class interests—strengthening the *taikō*'s carefully wrought, pyramidal structure of regional alliances and undermining provincial factionalism.

As might be expected, *chanoyu* still had a political function. Hideyoshi continued to practice Tea without Rikyū. In fact, he soon installed Rikyū's student *daimyō* Furuta Oribe as his new tea master, commanding him to revise *chanoyu* to reflect "the formal decorum that is important to the *samurai* class" (Tanikawa 1980b, 13). Hideyoshi clearly wanted to return Tea to its pre-Rikyū confirmatory character.

During the several years preceding and following Rikyū's death, virtually all Hideyoshi's tea advisors had passed away. Oribe was a distinguished *samurai* who had served Nobunaga before Hideyoshi. Under Rikyū's tutelage, he also developed into a very talented tea practitioner. So, although he was rumored to be a poor connoisseur of utensils and comparatively inept at tea procedures, Hideyoshi's comrade succeeded Rikyū.

Oribe had long been at work on a flamboyantly decorative tea style characterized by a deep regard for rank. His most famous tearoom "Ennan" featured a special section for the guest's attendants. The mat covering this area could be removed to reveal a hardwood floor. This device permitted the status of lower-ranking guests to be clearly distinguished from that of those ensconced higher and more comfortably on *tatami*. (*Tatami* are about two-and-one-half inches thick.) Oribe also placed a two-tiered sword rack conveniently near his teahouse's *nijiriguchi* (crawling-in entrance) leaving little doubt about the class of the guests he intended to serve.

Despite Oribe's careful ministrations, the *taikō* seems to have lost some of his enthusiasm for Tea. In fact, he advised his heirs to follow his example in all things except "addiction to tea, a love of falconry, and a craze for women" (Sansom 1961, 366). The ailing old man became increasingly violent and paranoid as time passed. Hideyoshi's final tea gathering was held in 1598 under the blooming cherry trees in a park he had constructed near Daigoji in Kyōto's southeast quarter. It was an exclusive event that contrasted dramatically with the wonderful freedom of the Kitano gathering—armed men prevented uninvited guests from intruding. Hideyoshi died that same year leaving his late-born, five-year-old son Hideyori (1593–1615) in the care of a council of *daimyō* led by Tokugawa Ieyasu.

ESTABLISHING THE SEN FAMILY SCHOOLS OF TEA

Rikyū's family left Kyōto soon after his death. It was, after all, not unknown for a vindictive lord to climax an execution with the annihilation of the victim's entire family. Their prudence was apparently justified as Ishida Mitsunari may have tortured the tea master's wife and daughters (Bodart 1977, 72). Fortunately, some of Rikyū's influential friends (Kanamori Nagachika, 1524–1607, and Gamō Ujisato) helped to ensure his family's survival, holding them under nominal "house arrest" in their own territories.

Though most of Rikyū's property was confiscated at the time of his death, the tea master's reputation endured, an intangible legacy of great potential value. Identifying his heirs remains a complicated affair: Sen Rikyū had a son Dōan and some daughters born to his first wife who died in 1577. Dōan learned his father's tea style but apparently favored the newly influential *daimyō* style (Nakamura 1980, 25). Since Dōan's wife died young and his relationship with his father was strained, he left home and traveled about the country teaching tea to various provincial lords.

Rikyū's second wife was a woman named Sōon (d.1600). She had a son, Shōan, (1546–1614) by a previous marriage.[1] The tea master subsequently adopted his wife's son, wedding him to a daughter from his first marriage. This union produced Sōtan (1578–1658), Rikyū's grandson. It is not known precisely why Shōan (not his eldest biological son, Dōan) was recognized as the tea master's heir. Some say the issue was a conflict in tea philosophy. Others suggest that Dōan was so unattractive— either grotesquely obese or lame—that he would have been objectionable to the elite Rikyū served and, thus, a poor candidate to succeed him.

Whatever the reasoning, Shōan was selected as Rikyū's heir, but it was not until 1594 that he was officially recognized as head of the Sen family. (Dōan later died in Sakai.) At that time, the surviving family members were allowed by Hideyoshi to return to Kyōto and their property was restored (Haga 1981, 9). This change in fortunes resulted from the intercession of Tokugawa Ieyasu and others.

When the family returned to Kyōto, Sōtan was recalled from the temple where he had been studying Zen during these turbulent years. With the help of Sōon, Shōan undertook the responsibility of training the young man in *chanoyu* (Iguchi 1976, 10). Around age seventeen, Sōtan married and soon had two children, Sōsetsu (1592?–1652) and Sōshu (also known as Ichiō, 1593–1675). He later became divorced from his wife by mutual agreement. Shōan retired in 1598 when Sōtan was able to assume responsibility for the family.

Possibly as the result of his Zen training, Sōtan never compromised with the *daimyō* tea masters. Known as "*wabi* Sōtan," he consistently refused potentially lucrative invitations to teach tea in Edo, escaping one summons by feigning sickness. Sōtan preferred to remain in Kyōto, fostering his conviction that "Tea and Zen are One" (*"Cha Zen ichimi"*) and practicing tea with old friends from the Buddhist community. He associated with only few select members of the elite such as the Empress Tōfukumon'in (1607–1678) and the regent Konoe Nobuhiro (1599– 1649).

Even so, Sōtan recognized the need to provide for his sons' futures. Therefore, Sōsetsu was sent to Kaga as tea master to the *daimyō* Maeda Toshitsune (1593–1658) and the Yoshioka, a family of lacquer-makers, accepted Sōshu as their heir. Sōtan's second marriage (his wife Sōken was a waiting lady of the Empress Tōfukumon'in) further complicated the Sen lineage. It resulted in two more sons Sōsa, also known as Kōshin (1613–1672), and Sensō Sōshitsu (1622–1697).

Maintaining his strategy of securing appointments for his sons as tea masters of *daimyō*, Sōtan sent Sōsa to serve a branch of the Tokugawa family and Sensō to fill the position with the Maeda, which had been vacated by Sōsetsu. (The unhappy Sōsetsu, reported to have broken with his father over both *chanoyu* and his second marriage, abandoned his position in Kaga to travel around the country. In 1652, he contracted a fatal disease. Since Sōtan visited him just before his death and the two were eventually buried in adjoining graves at Daitoku-ji's Jukō'in sub-temple, their quarrel may have ultimately been reconciled.)

At the age of seventy, the old master decided to solve the problem of his surviving sons' inheritance by dividing his property into three parts: Sōsa was given the front part of the family home, which became Omotesenke (the "front Sen house"). Sōtan retired to the back portion of the parcel with his youngest son, Sensō. This was called "Urasenke" ("the back or inner Sen house").

At about the same time, Sōshu, Sōtan's surviving son from his first marriage, left the lacquer business to his daughter (who married Nakamura Sōtetsu I, establishing a famous lineage of lacquer artisans) and resumed teaching tea. From his father, Sōshu received another piece of land in the neighborhood, which became the home of the third Sen family, Mushanokōjisenke (named after the name of the street where it is located). All three branches of the family remain actively involved in advocating Sen Rikyū's tea.

TEA DURING THE EARLY TOKUGAWA PERIOD

With Rikyū gone and his heirs leading quiet lives in Kyōto, public supremacy in the tea world passed to *daimyō* such as Furuta Oribe and Kobori Enshū (1579–1647). Enshū was also a member of the warrior class but he is better known as a bureaucrat, garden designer, and architect. He was chiefly distinguished for his ability to function creatively within the system.

Both men served Tokugawa Ieyasu, who eventually cast aside his role as Hideyori's guardian and consolidated his personal position, defeating his former ward's supporters at the famous battle of Sekigahara in 1600. (Ishida Mitsunari, the ambitious *samurai* suspected of engineering Rikyū's downfall figured prominently among Hideyori's clique. He was decapitated in Kyōto after Sekigahara for his part in the plot opposing Ieyasu.)

Ieyasu, who was named *shōgun* in 1603, was a tea practitioner in the tradition of Hideyoshi and Nobunaga. But, unlike his predecessors, he was never obsessed with tea. He had an inquiring mind, concerned not only with the exercise of power but also the moral justification for it. Like many Japanese intellectuals, he found satisfaction in synthesis. One of his contemporaries, Ikeda Mitsumasa (1609–1682) observed:

> According to the view of Lord Gongen [Ieyasu], *Shintō*, Confucianism, and Buddhism should all three be used. Shintō is the way of inner truth and of inner purity. Confucianism is the way of sincerity, love, and benevolence. Buddhism emphasizes selflessness and desirelessness, teaching forbearance and compassion (Ikeda in Hall 1959, 291.)

Even so, Confucianism began to dominate Japanese philosophy under Ieyasu. The fact that the *samurai* were, at last, in firm control of the country probably stimulated the trend. There was a diminishing requirement for the skills of war and a corresponding increase in the need for diligent administrators. As Yamaga Sokō (1622–1685), one of the most important exponents of the increasingly rigidly defined Code of the Warrior (*bushidō*) succinctly explained: "One cannot succeed in applying military principles alone but must achieve complete self-cultivation, rectification of the heart, regulation of the state, and pacification of the world" (Sokō in Hall 1959, 275).

Also, Confucianism provided the ideal rationalization for preserving the status quo. Hayashi Razan (1583–1657), a young scholar who was a favorite of Ieyasu, brilliantly suggested equating the separation of Japanese society into four classes (*samurai*, farmers, artisans, and merchants) with the Confucian five relationships (ruler-subject, father-son, husband-wife, older-younger brother, and friend-friend), saying both were "part of the principles of heaven and is the Way which was taught by the Sage (Confucius)" (Hayashi in Totman 1983, 121).

Giving primacy to *Shintō* beliefs would have drawn attention to the relative incongruence in the emperor's position. Moreover, the nihilist strain in Buddhist philosophy, which had threatened secular authority in the past, had not been completely eradicated. The Confucians, on the other hand, were quite ready and able to serve the elite. They were convinced that "the *Shōgun* receives authority over the people of Japan as a trust from Heaven" (Hall 1959, 290) and were, consequently, cordially received in the corridors of power.

Rikyū's egalitarian ideals were largely forgotten as tea practitioners concentrated on demonstrating their Confucian respect for the social hierarchy. (Remember that Confucian concepts had been integrated into tea philosophy even before *chanoyu* came to Japan.) As Hayashi pointed out: "To say that there is no distinction between high and low is to be ignorant of the law of Heaven [*li*]" (Hayashi in Hall 1959, 274).

By the time of the third Tokugawa *shōgun* Iemitsu (1604–1651), Hosokawa Sansai, the only surviving tea master who had studied directly under Rikyū (and the one said to have most faithfully preserved the details of his practice), was beginning his lessons with this advice:

> You must remember that it is your military prowess that has obtained your fiefs and honors. Do not then neglect this your main business. It may be well enough to occupy any spare time you may have with *chanoyu*, but never let a diversion take the place of the serious work of life.(Sadler 1962, 160)

As the Tokugawa intensified their insistence on a spartan *samurai* life style, leadership in *chanoyu* began to devolve back upon the merchant tea masters. In addition to instructing the *daimyō*, the Sen family (and various others) taught the town's people, refined tea procedures, and collaborated with local artisans to design utensils.

Sensō, who became the fourth household head in the Urasenke line (I now confine myself primarily to the history of Urasenke), continued to serve the Maeda family, journeying often from Kyōto to Kaga. He was also notable for encouraging Chōzaemon (1629–1712), an outstanding potter from the Raku studio to establish the famous Ōhi kiln. Moreover, late in life, Sensō had the satisfaction of initiating public rites honoring Rikyū's memory (Iguchi 1976, 12). An increasingly elaborate ancestor cult subsequently developed, creating a mechanism still effective in nurturing the Sen family's identification with their famous forebear.

In the late seventeenth century, the diminishing political sensitivity of *chanoyu* fostered a surge of renewed interest in Rikyū's teachings. However, other than the discovery (creation, or compilation) of the *Nampō Roku*, little dramatically impacting Tea history occurred during the peaceful years that followed. Sensō's son Jōso (1673–1704) succeeded his father. He served the Maeda, created utensils, and became an excellent calligrapher before he died at age thirty-one.

Rikkansai (1694–1726), the sixth generation master, was only ten when the responsibility of preserving the family traditions fell upon him. Fortunately, the patriarch of Omotesenke, Gensō (1678–1730), was able to guide him. Rikkansai was just establishing a reputation for artistic creativity when he died at thirty-two. He was succeeded by Gensō's seventeen year old son, Chikusō (1709–1733), a young man who tragically died at age twenty-four.

By the time Ittō (1719–1771), Gensō's third son, became the Urasenke's eighth generation grand master at the age of fifteen, the Urasenke heritage was a heavy burden. The family was disorganized and in severe financial straits as the result of lacking mature leadership for so many years. It was probably in response to this critical situation that the eighth generation grand master began developing a new approach to preserving Rikyū's legacy in collaboration with his older brother Joshinsai (1706–1751), the grand master of Omotesenke.

Joshinsai elected to restructure the family's instruction in *chanoyu* by establishing an *iemoto* system. *Iemoto* are family-based schools of the traditional Japanese arts. The custom of confining the transmission of particular art forms to specific lineages probably began among poetry specialists at the beginning of the thirteenth century. By Joshinsai's time, the Yabunouchi school of tea (founded by one of Jōō's disciples, Yabunouchi Kenchū (also known as Sōchūsai, 1536–1627) had already long been organized along these lines (Plutschow 1986, 164).

The *iemoto* system is based on the idea that a single lineage may claim to be the only true authority on the artistic technique and related philosophy of a focal ancestor or famous teacher. The integrity of the message is preserved by strict training. Unauthorized communication of information is usually controlled by a convention limiting instruction at certain levels to oral transmission alone. The unspoken implication that school leadership has access to secret documents pertinent to the tradition reinforces its exclusiveness.

To aid prospective students in identifying its authentic representatives and to ensure consistency in the education of adherents, the lineages began to certify teachers and students at various levels of experience. Since instructors were financially recompensed according to the level of their expertise, fees related to these documents developed into a source of income for the families that originally issued them as well as for those below them in the hierarchy.

Joshinsai restructured the tea instruction available through Omotesenke, identifying its grades of proficiency (the *kyōjō*) with the seven stages of training considered critical for the spiritual development of Zen monks. Moreover, since both Joshinsai and Ittō were concerned about a potential loss of spiritual rigor in their expanded system of tea education, they developed seven ritual exercises with the aid of their Zen master Mugaku Sōen (1721–1791) and some fellow practitioners. These drill-like procedures (the *shichiji shiki*, "Seven Exercises") were intended to promote concentration and collaboration through their very complexity.

Just when it appeared that the Sen family fortunes were going to recover as the result of more efficient tea school organization, bad luck struck again. This time the misfortune was the great Tenmei fire that swept Kyōto in 1788. Ninety percent of the city was destroyed. Ittō's successor Fukensai (1746–1801, the ninth generation grand master) was forced to take refuge with his family and the few treasures they could carry in Daitokuji. The family compound was seriously damaged and the famous tearooms bequeathed by Sōtan needed extensive and expensive repair. Happily, the tearooms were restored in time for Rikyū's two hundredth year memorial service in 1790.

TEA IN THE LATE EDO PERIOD

Fukensai's son Nintokusai (1770–1826) succeeded him. Regrettably, all his sons predeceased him, requiring an heir to be adopted. The selection of a young man from the Matsudaira family of Aichi Prefecture was felicitous because Gengensai (1810–1877, the eleventh generation grand master) became a particularly innovative and productive tea master. He put his fine classical education to good use creating utensils, remodeling tearooms, and generally enhancing the prestige of the family. He even succeeded in adding a branch of the Tokugawa family to the list of family patrons. Lamentably, the Meiji restoration forced Gengensai to look even further afield in search of financial support. Since the Sen family and many of their *samurai* supporters lost their governmental stipends, he wisely made an innovative appeal to the business community.

One significant effect of the Meiji Restoration was a decline in the respect afforded to the traditional Japanese arts. Thus, Gengensai's most important contribution to *chanoyu* may have been a letter he wrote to the Japanese government on behalf of the entire Sen family. In it, he defended Tea as a way of life and a spiritual discipline. This helped establish Tea as an important symbolic component of Japan's emerging national identity. Anticipating other dramatic changes which occurred during the Meiji, Gengensai also devised a tea procedure (*ryūreidemae*, "standing bow" procedure) that permitted guests to sit at tables in western clothes rather than on *tatami*. He introduced his new technique at an international exhibition in Kyōto in 1872 (Sen 1979b, 48–49).

Gengensai's only son did not survive him. His son-in-law, Yūmyōsai (the twelfth grand master, 1852–1917) succeeded him. This young man was adopted from the Suminokura family just six years before Gengensai died. Preferring the contemplative life, Yūmyōsai retired to Daitokuji as soon as his son Ennōsai, (the thirteenth grand master, 1872–1917) was old enough to assume responsibility for the family. Yūmyōsai's wife, however, established a tradition among Sen family women, promoting Tea as a basic requirement in girls' schools throughout the country. Ennōsai supported his mother's effort, setting up intensive training seminars for tea teachers in Kyōto and founding a magazine (now called *Tankō*) to encourage wider interest in *chanoyu*.

With the help of his resourceful wife Kayoko (d. 1980), the fourteenth generation grand master Tantansai (1893–1964) shepherded Urasenke through the difficult era of World War II. Besides being a time of great economic hardship, all the male members of the *iemoto* except Tantansai and one senior instructor (*gyōtei*) were drafted. Sen Kayoko solved the problem of staffing by asking Hamamoto Sōshun (d. 1986) to become the first female senior instructor in Urasenke history.[2]

Tantansai's heir, the current (*o*)*iemoto* Sen Sōshitsu (Hōunsai, b.1923), was drafted into a naval attack unit near the end of the war. These units (*tokkōtai*) were better known in the West as *kamikaze* squads. Thirteen of these units were composed of volunteers, but the fourteenth was made up of the first conscripts from the universities.

In a fascinating article published in the *Asahi Shinbun*, 15 August 1980, Sen Sōshitsu (as the present grand master, Hōunsai, is best known by his generation title) described preparing tea for his fellow cadets and then listening to the radio signals that indicated they had attacked their targets and died. According to his own account, the experience caused the future grand master to ponder his feelings about war and militarism. Consequently, he became deeply committed to the idea of fostering peace and international friendship through tea ritual (*Urasenke Newsletter* [Autumn 1980], no. 22).

After the hostilities ended, Tantansai became the first Urasenke grand master to visit China and to travel in the West (including visits to Boston and Hawaii on his itinerary). He supported modern teaching methods, lecturing on the radio and creating a national organization for tea teachers called the "Tankōkai" (*Urasenke Newsletter* [Winter 1976]) During his tenure, Urasenke's first international chapter was also established in Hawaii.[3]

The contributions of the present grand master of Urasenke, Sen Sōshitsu cannot yet be fully evaluated. He is so active that his achievements seem to multiply on a daily basis. He will probably be best remembered for his support of *chanoyu* outside

Japan, and for his sophisticated use of both modern media and organizational methods. He has also substantially enlarged Urasenke's following while simultaneously improving the quality of its instruction. Sen Sōshitsu may eventually be recognized as one of the most significant figures in tea history because of the renewed emphasis he has placed on Rikyū's egalitarian ideals. His commitment to promoting the international practice of *chadō* indicates a profound awareness of tea ritual's religious function and its potential for serving universal needs.

CONCLUSION

Chanoyu's long history provides an extraordinarily well- documented example of interplay between the "confirmatory" and "transformatory" elements in ritual: The Taoists sought to transform their relationship with the Ineffable by compounding and imbibing the "elixir of immortality." At the same time, Lu Yü touted the idea that a Confucian gentleman could confirm his place in the universal order by properly preparing tea. Similarly, the Ch'an conducted commensal tea ritual to reaffirm their communities' dedication to the lofty principles of the Buddha *dharma*, while Heian courtiers sipped tea in luxurious surroundings to verify their collective position of privilege and reinforce their self-identification with the resplendent accomplishments of Chinese civilization.

However, just as the transformatory element in *chadō* was about to be subrogated to the confirmatory urges of the Momoyama social and clerical elite, a small group of Zen priests decided to revive the active principle in tea ritual. Musō Soseki, Murata Shukō, and Ikkyū Sōjun suggested the possibility of experiencing the type of profound reordering of individual perception they called *"satori"* while practicing tea. Inspired by these luminaries, Sen Rikyū envisioned a transformatory tea ritual (he called it *"wabi cha"*) that would function as a catalyst for enlightenment. Regrettably, at about the same time, Toyotomi Hideyoshi and Tokugawa Ieyasu concluded Tea would be an ideal normative buttress for the status quo (still a dominant concept in *chanoyu*).

Rikyū's descendants' struggle to preserve both the confirmatory and transformatory elements in their legacy has influenced virtually every tea ritual conducted in the last four centuries. Observing *chadō*'s current popularity (there may be as many as twenty million practitioners distributed through more than ten schools of Tea), it is difficult to remember that even a few decades ago, there was a very real chance of the tradition disappearing.

Today's tea practice can only be comprehended in its historical context. This includes appreciating the contributions generations of tea practitioners have made to its preservation and being aware of the complex character of tea ritual's structural development. With these themes in mind, let us examine some of the components of modern *chanoyu*.

Part II

Organization in the Tea World

Chapter 7

Tea School Structure

HISTORICAL INFLUENCES ON SEN FAMILY STRUCTURE

*I*t has become axiomatic for anthropologists analyzing Japanese culture to note that the patrilineal kin group supplies the model for virtually every social institution from the nuclear family to the nation. In the case of the Sen family schools of Tea, this structural bond has been nurtured and reinforced with particular intensity. A careful examination of tea history makes it evident why this should be so. For four hundred years, Rikyū's descendants have depended on identification with the great tea master for social status and economic survival. Yet, their right to Rikyū's legacy has required constant protection and nourishment.

As mentioned previously, there appear to be no available documents, corroborative contemporary accounts, or even suggestive anecdotes to indicate that Dōan, Rikyū's eldest son, was intended to exercise primogeniture. He was given only the family assets which remained in Sakai. While such tales may be apocryphal, the acrimony between father and son is reported to have been the stuff of general gossip during their lifetimes. In contrast, there is much evidence to suggest that the relationship between Rikyū and his son-in-law was felicitous. Even so, Shōan's position as an heir was unequivocally confirmed only when Rikyū's Kyōto property was entrusted to him several years after the tea master's death (and then only in his capacity as Sōtan's father).

Considering the circumstances surrounding his demise, it would not be surprising if Rikyū had purposely refrained from

publicly designating an heir. Once *seppuku* had become
inevitable, openly acknowledging such a relationship would
have been extremely dangerous given Hideyoshi's demonstrated proclivity for extending his vengeance to include the kin of
his perceived enemies.

Seen from a historical perspective, the valuable part of
Rikyū's legacy was not his real property (which was forfeit, at
any rate), but the prestige associated with being recognized as
his heir in *chanoyu*. Hideyoshi, of course, unhesitatingly
appointed Furuta Oribe as his new tea master, making him
Rikyū's nominal successor—in status at least. Unimpressed,
Hokosawa Sansai and other former disciples of the master
reacted by emphasizing their own strict dedication to his tradition. As time went on and Rikyū's reputation grew, more
claimants to his legacy emerged, most of whom insisted on
being recognized as the exclusive repositories of his "true"
teachings. Prominent among them was the founder of the
Yabunouchi school.

Succeeding generations of the Sen family were forced to
contend with powerful challenges to their right to the status
and patronage due those perceived as authentic custodians of
their illustrious ancestor's style. But, as the last chapter indicated, Urasenke's survival and current position as the largest and
most influential tea school in Japan did not result solely from
possession of a famous surname. Its success must be at least
partially attributed to the family's judicious management of
human resources.

At Urasenke (and most other tea schools), three traditional
Japanese social structures, the *ie, dōzoku,* and *iemoto* mediate the
interpersonal relationships essential to the preservation and
propagation of *chadō*. An awareness of the way these institutions function and interact is prerequisite to an understanding
of the Way of Tea.

IE, DŌZOKU, AND IEMOTO DEFINED

While precise definition may depend somewhat on context (rural
or urban, upper or lower class, pre-Meiji or post-Meiji), the *ie* is
generally understood to be a group of people, many but not all of
them kin, the majority of whom reside nearby and share social
and economic activities. The group is characterized by a collective monopoly on the social control of resources. The ultimate

decision-making power is held by the household head, a patrilineal prerogative which gives the whole temporal continuity.[1] Akitoshi Shimizu also notes that the *ie* includes ancestors as well as living persons, and thus has a symbolic as well as cultural identity. For example, if all the living members of an *ie* were to die out, the entity would continue to exist provided a related *ie* accepted responsibility for conducting the proper memorial services. The original *ie* could be revived at any time if assigned living members by the sustaining *ie* (Shimizu 1987, S86).

One feature that seems to be common to all but the most casual definitions of the *ie* (such as those based on common family crest or surname) is the central authority of the household head. The modern patriarch may retain only nominal (not legal, financial or decision-making) responsibility for family members or be totally in charge of their conduct and financial support. In either case, the *ie* can be operationally defined as those who owe their primary social debt (*on*) to the head of the household.

Since this obligation is not nullified by the death and the subsequent installation of a new *iemoto*, the moral contract is made between an individual and an institution—not between two people. The feature that distinguishes the *ie* from fictive kinship organizations modeled on patrilineal structure such as those of unions or businesses is that at least a core of its members are legal kin (adopted sons and new brides are *ie* members but not biological kin). In Japan, fictive and biologically based systems frequently overlap.

The *ie* developed out of the natural tendency of biological families to outgrow a finite set of economic resources. Prior to the imposition of a new civil code by Occupation Forces in 1948, the house coped with these circumstances in several ways: (1) if they were economically nonessential, it sent sons, who were not potential heirs, to other households for adoption; (2) a family lacking a male heir might adopt a spouse for a daughter; (3) a wealthy house might create a branch family by allocating resources to a younger son or employee; (4) a poor house might subjugate itself to a rich one; or (5) failing to employ any of these strategies, the *ie* had the potential of becoming nonexistent.

A social organization generally called a *"dōzoku"* in the anthropological literature was created in the third case, that is, when branch families were established by the main house.[2] Just as an individual owes a moral debt to his *ie* for his biological existence, economic sustenance, social position, or jural advocacy, the branch house (*bunke*) owes the main house (*honke*) its support. This support ideally finds expression in shared ceremonial functions, economic support, social interaction, and ideational respect.

The *iemoto*, in contrast to the *ie*, is an educational system with economic functions. It relies on the house to supply the upper echelons of its authority structure. As previously indicated, *ie* sometimes includes non-kin such as apprentices and/or employees. The iemoto extends its membership to instructors and their students as well. The two differ in that the *ie* exists to perpetuate itself biologically and economically, while the *iemoto*'s main function is to preserve an art form. Integrated *ie* and *iemoto* usually maintain a symbiotic economic alliance.

A document written by Nishiyama between 1811 and 1855 identifies three main characteristics of the *iemoto* system as they relate to professional training in the arts: (1) An *ie* claims the exclusive right to preserve a traditional art form and to control its transmission; (2) the system is sustained by the exclusive nature of the information communicated by teacher to student; and (3) the transmission has spiritual as well as a technical content (Ortolani 1969). This succinctly describes the system Ittō and Joshinsai applied to the Sen family's *chanoyu*.

URASENKE AS *IE*

Group membership

As previously noted, the *ie* is generally agreed to include biological kin living in or near the main house, kin temporarily living away but sharing the house's economic and ritual base, spouses of *ie* members, and the ancestors of the lineage. However, not everyone considered a member of the house need be kin. In the case of Urasenke, the *gyōtei* (senior instructors) and *mizuya sensei* (advanced teachers training in hopes of becoming *gyōtei*) might be considered part of the house structure.[3]

Gyōtei and *mizuya sensei* are intensively trained by the (o)iemoto personally and they are usually supported by the house for at least part of their lives (particularly in the early part of their training). Senior *gyōtei* are particularly close to the family as they have known its members since they were babies and assisted in the training of succeeding generations of (o)iemoto. *Mizuya sensei* are close because they are in daily contact with the family—they work seven days a week in Konnichian (the complex of tearooms and support facilities in Kyōto, which is the traditional home of the Urasenke grand master), starting with drawing water and arranging flowers before dawn. They clean the tearooms, serve tea to guests, and do whatever tasks are necessary to keep this complex institution running.

Since *mizuya sensei* are financed to study Tea for at least part of their youth and are present in the Sen home for most of their waking hours, it is not surprising that their personal needs become the concern and responsibility of the *ie*. They are, in fact, ill-advised to marry without the permission of the (o)iemoto. The system may seem archaic to outsiders, but it should be remembered that many *gyōtei* and *mizuya sensei* come from families that have historically served Sen tea masters. They share the value system of the organization and hope to acquire access and expertise that will eventually allow them to earn a living by pursuing *chadō*.

The old term *ichizoku rōtō* (one family group and its retainers) might be applied to a slightly larger group serving the *ie*. It includes teachers and staff at Urasenke Headquarters who are not *gyōtei* or *mizuya sensei*, full-time students in training programs for either Japanese or foreigners, administrative staff, and some temporary visitors. All these people have a special relationship with the (o)iemoto and are directly dependent on him.

What all this suggests is that, at least in the case of Urasenke, the *ie* has made a successful transition from the traditional to the modern Japanese economic structure, with little need to dramatically change its form. The presence and involvement of non-kin are essential to performing the Sen family's multitude of functions and the classic *ie* structure has been found to be an efficient organizing principle. Some of the roles played by members may have been expanded by modern contingencies but they stand in the same hierarchical relationship and are sustained by familiar rituals of etiquette.

Membership in this group and its slightly medieval character are reaffirmed once a month when many *gyōtei* and higher-ranking *mizuya sensei* gather with students from Urasenke's full-time program of tea-related studies to greet and be greeted by the (o)*iemoto* or a representative such as his heir or wife. Everyone wears formal *kimono*. They sit in one great hall in lines that reflect their status. On a command from an administrative functionary, everyone takes a position of respect, sitting with knuckles on the *tatami* (a position also assumed for nobles during certain portions of the tea procedures especially designed to serve them). When the (o)*iemoto* enters, everyone simultaneously makes a full formal bow.

Afterwards, the (o)*iemoto* delivers a short inspirational lecture and walks down the rows of students and staff saying a few words of thanks or encouragement to nearly everyone. Attendance at this ceremony is a privilege for all those non-kin whose lives are intimately connected with the functioning of the *ie*. In addition to reaffirming group membership, it provides a learning situation for students who may someday have to perform in similar social situations. Similar events are held for visiting tea teachers and staff employees.

A final group of people with a very special relationship to both Urasenke and the Sen family at large are the Senke Jūshoku, ten families designated during the Meiji era as the preeminent creators of preferred tea utensils (*konomi*) to the *ie*.[4] These houses have served the Sen's needs for many generations and have occasionally become associated by marriage. Their status as traditional craftsmen is high in Kyōto and Japan as a whole. The masters of these households are often invited to the family's most important ceremonial gatherings.

The responsibilities of membership in the ie

The first responsibility of each *ie* member is to consider the interests of the group paramount to his own individual desires. He or she contributes to the group in the manner in which the head of the family has decided is appropriate. In addition, the group member is charged with responsibility for preserving the reputation of the family, setting an example for inferiors within the *ie* hierarchy, respecting family traditions, being frugal with collective resources, and cooperating with other *ie* members.

As the focus of the *ie* and its chief representative in the outside world, the (o)*iemoto* has special obligations. He must set normative standards, which allow the group to function smoothly internally and among their neighbors. He is responsible for securing consensus within the family and expressing it to outsiders. In addition, he carries the heavy burden of ultimate financial responsibility for family survival and the preservation of its physical assets.

To this end, the head of the house must find satisfying and meaningful ways for group members to contribute to the well-being of the whole. If he succeeds, credit for the achievements of the group generally accrue to him (as a symbol of the house as well as personally). Reciprocally, the head of the family must accept the blame for any inappropriate behavior or failure on the part of house members. Further, because the *ie* has a temporal dimension, he must see to it that the special skills, which form the basis of the family economy, are preserved or improved upon. This may include training a successor to both his work skills and his leadership role. Finally, the family head must account for his decisions not only to living generations, but to his ancestors.

URASENKE IN THE CONTEXT OF THE *DŌZOKU*

As mentioned earlier, in times of financial success an (*o*)*iemoto* will sometimes create a subsidiary house (or houses) to accommodate his *ie*'s growing size and exploit whatever opportunities might exist within its ambient economic environment. Classic definitions of the *dōzoku* (Befu 1971, 57; Dore 1958, 105; Brown 1966,1130) require that the affiliation between lines be based on the primacy of the main house, and include shared economic and/or ceremonial functions. In the case of the Sen family, however, the three branches appear to function as separate and more or less equal units.

Most anthropologists familiar with Japanese extended kin organizations consider the division of responsibility for ancestor worship a particularly significant indicator of group structure (Smith 1974, 163; Befu 1971, 60). They have observed that within a conventionally organized *dōzoku*, the main line keeps the tablets of the shared ancestors and branch families assist in the ceremonial activities that honor them. However, in the case of the Sen family, the circumstances which surrounded the lives of the first few generations were far from ideal. Precedents for the current rather unconventional arrangement may have been set as early as the beginning of the seventeenth century.

First, Sen Rikyū could not be publicly honored for one hundred years after his death because he was officially in disgrace as a criminal: Even though the Tokugawa spared no love for the Toyotomi, the behavior of retainers suspected of plotting against their lords could not be officially sanctioned. This meant the generations which immediately succeeded Rikyū were not free to publicly reaffirm their structural relationships to their famous ancestor through memorial rites. This led to confusion a century later when both kin and non-kin claimants to Rikyū's tradition had multiplied and identification with the tea master had become crucial to the economic survival of his descendants.

Second, Shōan (while generally recognized as second generation in the Sen line) was an adopted son-in-law who relinquished his position as household head early. He was never recognized as a particularly talented tea practitioner although he was apparently quite faithful to his father-in-law's teachings. Stressing Shōan's position in the lineage would have underscored Rikyū's failure to endorse him as his heir in Tea, making it awkward for their mutual offspring to identify themselves as heirs to his tea tradition as well as his blood.

To complicate matters further, Sen Sōtan, who was an outstanding tea master, was an egalitarian like his famous grandfather: When he divided the Sen family property into three parts and allowed all his surviving sons to carry on the family name, he apparently elected not to establish a conventional *dōzoku* with a dominant main house and two subsidiary branches. Most likely, kindhearted Sōtan pursued this strategy because he considered all of his sons competent to carry on the family tradition. It may also be pertinent to note that his second wife came from a considerably higher ranking family than his first, a situation that may have made disfranchising his two younger sons in favor of his surviving oldest one diplomatically inappropriate as well as domestically disruptive.[5]

Finally, the patriarchs of the Sen family were distinguished among their contemporaries, not for the degree to which they complied with the ceremonial precedents of others, but for their creativity in developing original rituals. Given the fact that the entire family had suffered greatly from Rikyū's public prominence, it is not surprising that, for a time, his descendants prudently sought original and comparatively private ways to honor him.

The status of the Sen family as members of the urban elite and patrons of Daitokuji coupled with the Japanese custom of creating multiple ancestor tablets conveniently resolved the problem of responsibility and precedence.[6] Each of the Sen families honor their ancestors both in household shrines and at the Jukō'in sub-temple of Daitokuji (founded in 1566), where the graveyard of all three families (and Rikyū's gravestone) are located.[7] Memorial services for Rikyū are conducted on the twenty-eighth of each month; they are sponsored and attended in rotation by all three houses. All three houses hold periodic personal services for focal ancestors throughout the year.

Urasenke's private memorial chapel is called the "Rikyūdō." The original was built in 1690 by Sensō, the founder of the branch, to commemorate the one hundredth anniversary of Rikyū's death. It has also functioned as a repository for the wooden head of the ill-fated statue that so infuriated Hideyoshi. The same relic is displayed in the extant Rikyūdō, a three mat room within the famous Konnichian complex of tearooms. (A mat is approximately three feet by six feet in area.) Another altar in an adjoining room houses all private family memorial tablets.

One of the major responsibilities of the (o)iemoto is to offer tea in both these locations each morning. Interestingly enough, the present grand master also often offers tea to tablets of previous (o)iemoto, to his late Zen master, and to all deceased followers of chanoyu at a meditation hall on top of the new Chadō Research Center, which is located near Konnichian.[8]

Because the three main Sen lineages have lived within close proximity to each other and shared the same economic base (teaching chanoyu) since the early seventeenth century, they have found it essential to develop a system of symbolic and organizational devices that enforce their mutual ideational and economic separation. Each house visibly reinforces its own distinct personality (and attendant values) through a process that involves creating and using different crests, emblems, utensils, and ritual procedures.

By exploiting these minor distinctions between their styles of tea preparation, the three lineages simultaneously avoid the awkwardness of direct competition and convince prospective students that identification with them has special advantages and meaning—even if they are not kin. During the pre-Meiji era, this helped them secure the patronage of different daimyō and enabled them to associate with and serve disparate groups within the same community (*samurai* as opposed to town's people, for example).

For all their carefully maintained individuality, the three main branches of the Sen family do sometimes interact. All regularly include each other's representatives in events such as the New Year's celebration, marriage ceremonies, and funerals.[9] Further, when a house lacks an heir, a son may be (but is not always) adopted from another line. In addition, several important ideas related to the future of *chanoyu* (such as the concept of the *iemoto*) have been cooperatively developed. Finally, issues that affect the structure of the entire lineage (such as the creation of subsidiary houses) are occasionally submitted for collective approval.[10] Note, however, that none of these shared activities assume a hierarchal relationship between families based on either genealogical or economic primacy. (Perceptions of this situation may, of course, vary from line to line and generation to generation.)

The lack of *dōzoku*-like relationships among the three main houses does not mean such structures are entirely absent from their social network. Urasenke, for example, clearly functions as the *honke* for subsidiary lines of its own: The Ōtani, Naya, Izumi, Iguchi, Shiotsuki, and Sakurai families are consistently described in English publications as "members of (o)*iemoto*'s family." (Other schools probably have similar arrangements.) Subsidiary houses such as these usually assist the main house with major ritual responsibilities (such as those associated with the New Year's celebration and memorial services), and probably maintain close financial ties to the main line.

There is an excellent rational behind the proliferation of branch families among the *iemoto:* In an effort to break up the *zaibatsu* (giant family-owned business concerns) after World War II, Occupation authorities promulgated a new Civil Code requiring equal inheritance for all children, including females. Unfortunately, these laws were potentially devastating to the *iemoto* as well as the *zaibatsu* because the former also counted on the judicious management of collective capital for their economic survival.

In the past, sons other than the prospective (o)*iemoto* could be adopted out with no financial loss to the group. But, under the new law, such individuals' patrimony would eventually go to other *ie*. Consequently, it became economically advantageous to create a branch family for a second son—at least theoretically retaining his capital for cooperative use.[11] Similar considerations apply to daughters. Because they eventually inherit a significant portion of the family assets, it is more astute than ever to encourage marital liaisons with families whose business connections and/or social position complement or enhance those of the *iemoto*.

THE IEMOTO

Membership

Since the line between kin and non-kin is not as distinctly drawn in Japan as it is in some other societies and the precedent for extending the social institution beyond those living in close physical proximity already exists (the *ichizoku rōtō* described by Nakane 1970, 7), it is not surprising that the concept of *ie* was extended to create the *iemoto*. As the experience of the Sen family has shown, kin are not the only individuals with the potential to develop a sense of shared destiny and mutual identity necessary to efficient group functioning. When the demand for the specialized services outstrips the ability of the kin group to biologically produce specialists, it becomes necessary to develop a structure that preserves both the prerogatives of the family and the integrity of its artistic tradition.

This ideal was most broadly realized when Tantansai created the "Tankōkai," an organization for Japanese tea teachers trained by indirect representatives of the Urasenke rather than at Konnichian in Kyōto. Once the Tankōkai had been created, the pyramidal structure of the tea school was divided into two slightly different organizational structures and the functions of *ie* and *iemoto* began to diverge more dramatically.

Major divisions

Students enrolled in the full-time, professional Tea program in Kyōto (the Urasenke Chadō Senmon Gakko) study under many teachers, often including *gyōtei*, the *(o)iemoto*, and his heir (the *waka sōshō*). In contrast, teachers trained through the Tankōkai have, at least ideally, been trained by a single instructor. Their instruction takes longer and is usually of a more avocational nature. Graduates of both teaching hierarchies learn the same *temae* (ritual procedures) and progress through the same series of certificates, however, the networks, which they utilize once they become teachers, are likely to differ.

For example, a graduate of the full-time program ordinarily activates contacts developed through the *senpai-kōhai* (senior and junior) student hierarchy of the Gakuen. Such individual's access to advanced teachers and various activities at headquarters is enhanced by previous acquaintance. Non-Japanese, who graduate from the special program created for foreigners (Midorikai) and the Gakuen, have the opportunity to exercise a different set of options. They are sometimes appointed to direct the overseas *shutchōjo* (representative offices) of Konnichian and serve the (o)*iemoto* as his personal emissaries or remain at the *iemoto* and teach.

Students who earn their credentials through Tankōkai teachers usually lack the vertical access of Konnichian students but tend to develop more diversified contacts in the Tea world. Individuals in this category initially relate to instructors and students outside their immediate circle of co-practitioners (*shachū*) only through their own teacher. Even so, their circle of acquaintances inevitably expands—most often through participation in larger associations (*shibu* or *dōkōkai*) established with the encouragement of the (o)*iemoto*. The fact that such students are not geographically dispersed after their initial training period gives them time to make a multitude of horizontal connections in the Tea world. (Vertical access is also available through the teacher or the teacher's teacher as well as local Tankōkai or *shibu* organizations. Special intensive training courses are also regularly conducted at Urasenke headquarters or given locally by visiting gyōtei.)

The role of the (o)iemoto

As the tea school has more diverse functions than the *ie* itself, the role of (o)*iemoto* adds considerably to the responsibilities of the head of the family. In addition to setting normative standards, attempting to promote consensus within the group, training a successor, balancing the budget, and preserving the tradition, an (o)*iemoto* must teach, evaluate, and encourage his instructors, grant certificates, create tea procedures, design and authenticate utensils, fulfill a myriad of social obligations related to his position within the community and the world at large, locate and cultivate financial backers, and manage the organization's non-teaching personnel.[12]

Moreover, since Urasenke's (o)iemoto have trained in Rinzai Zen since the time of Rikyū, a priestly function must be added to their repertoire: The waka sōshō is officially recognized as the grand master's heir only after he has participated in a ceremony where he is given a certificate (tokudō shiki) and new names signifying his initiation into the Buddhist priesthood. This marks the conclusion of a short but rigorous period of Zen monastic training and the beginning of a genuine, on-going commitment to both religious training and practice. The present grand master, for example, has studied Zen for many years under both Gotō Zuigan Rōshi of Daitokuji and Kajiura Itsugai Rōshi of Myōshinji and is qualified to function as abbot of "Kyōshinan," a Zen training hall located in Urasenke's Kyōto headquarters.

To complicate matters further, the duties of the grand master have been recently augmented by the availability of mass communications and quick transportation: Besides taking an active part in civic groups and various international organizations, Sen Sōshitsu XV holds professorships at several universities. In this capacity, he lectures widely to academic groups interested in Tea as well as sponsoring forums for such discussions. He also writes and edits works on Tea in conjunction with the publishing activities of the Urasenke Foundation (the name by which the iemoto is known overseas) and appears on educational television.

THE UTILITY OF FAMILY-DOMINATED TEA SCHOOLS

When social commentators turn their attention to modern tea ritual, the iemoto are frequently blamed for chanoyu's perceived shortcomings. Japanese critics tend to worry about the iemoto's financial dealings, the appropriateness of their ascribed status, and what they interpret as failures in orthodoxy. Westerners are primarily concerned with the institutions' authoritarianism and their tradition of hereditary leadership. All are culturally specific manifestations of a deeper issue—the underlying rationale for the iemoto's predominance in chadō.

The most direct approach to analyzing the symbiotic relationship between the iemoto and the Way of Tea is to ask: (1) Is a central authority structure prerequisite to the perpetuation of *chadō?* And, (2) Must this authority be vested in a hereditary form of leadership? My research leads me to believe the answer to both questions is "Yes, if tea ritual as we know it is to survive."

First, Tea would not require a centralized system of authority if it were merely an artistic tradition or a casual form of social intercourse. These kinds of behaviors do not assume the existence of a strictly limiting or defining consensus among participants. But *chanoyu* is a highly focused form of religious practice. It is a *system* of symbolic thought and action directed toward achieving a *collectively* recognized soteriological goal. When people practice ritual, they participate in a special dialogue concerned with abstract, higher order concepts (such as time, space, and human values). A distinctive feature of this conversation is its quality of being "set aside" from everyday life. One reason the activity is meaningful is because it must be anticipated, planned, and sought after.

Ritual never occurs completely spontaneously. There is always some precedent to be considered. Moreover, its grammar differs from that of ordinary language or social interaction because it cannot be acquired in the normal course of everyday events. For these reasons, prospective practitioners must make a conscious effort to learn ritual. Often they need help: The more complex the ritual, the less frequently it is conducted; the broader its sphere of action, the more difficult it is to understand and the greater the need for expert assistance in learning and interpretation.

Because ritual practitioners speak in a second language, they need a shared informational resource that allows them to periodically reconfirm their common understanding of ritual grammar and vocabulary. If no coordinating mechanism is available, the dialogue degenerates over time and distance. The need for a human information resource (as opposed to textual references) becomes critical when some significant aspect of the ritual's social environment changes. If a ritual form is to survive the challenges of cultural evolution, someone (or some group) must be endowed with sufficient authority and knowledge of the ritual form to actively supervise the adaptation process. This is the job of social functionaries like elders, priests, and (o)*iemoto*.

What analysts unfamiliar with these principals and the *iemoto* system seldom realize is that the real power of an (*o*)*iemoto* emanates not from his ability to regulate tea school affiliation through the certificate system, but from his exclusive right to define and modify the structure of the tradition by maintaining or creating individual tea procedures (*temae*). There are no restrictions on inviting anyone to participate in any tea gathering (with the exception of "secret," orally-transmitted *temae*) regardless of tea school affiliation and/or certificate level. But, an individual who is totally ignorant of orthodox tea procedures cannot fully participate in Tea's ritual dialogue. He or she lacks the requisite grammar and vocabulary. In other words, the chances of conducting or experiencing effective tea ritual are negligible for aspiring practitioners who reject the orthodox *temae* structure. *Chanoyu* retains its coherence and ability to communicate because large groups of practitioners have agreed that certain individuals (their [*o*]*iemoto*) will establish the standards for their particular style of Tea.

But why should the right to define a ritual tradition be hereditary? The answer is that the custom is functionally expedient rather than structurally obligatory. For centuries, it has proved remarkably efficient to delegate the ultimate responsibility for preserving and promoting *chanoyu* to a few families who depend on identification with Tea for their self-esteem, self-cultivation, personal enrichment, social status, and economic well-being.

Moreover, culturally mandated and practical rationales for the sustained preeminence of the great tea lineages are mutually reinforcing. Remember that the Ashikaga established teaching Tea as a professional specialty when they added *dōbōshū* to their retinues. In doing so, they tacitly acknowledged that tea ritual had become so complicated, that it could only be mastered by specialists who could devote themselves to the activity full-time. Since lay practitioners (who had descendants to provide for as opposed to Buddhist priests who theoretically did not) began to dominate Tea during this era, the trend toward recruiting tea masters from families with experience in performing these kinds of services must have begun at this time.

By the beginning of the Momoyama period, changes in both *chanoyu* and Japan's leadership structure had created the potential for a Tea meritocracy. This initially meant enterprising merchants from Sakai were able to secure access to the elite and, hence, the upper echelons of Tea through individual skill and ingenuity. However, Toyotomi Hideyoshi and Tokugawa Ieyasu quickly put an end to this golden age of opportunity. Intent on minimizing the potential for social flux in Japanese society, they issued edicts, created social sanctions, and reorganized the economy in such a way that it was extremely difficult for most Japanese to follow anything but their fathers' profession. The descendants of recognized tea teachers had no more occupational mobility than anyone else in Tokugawa Japan, and, for most of the era, teaching Tea offered more prestige than economic opportunity.

I suspect there was little criticism of the hereditary character of *iemoto* during the period that practicing *chanoyu* remained the privilege of a small circle of nobles, feudal lords, and the professionals that served them. It was only when the Meiji oligarchy canceled the *samurai*'s stipends and simultaneously forced the *iemoto* to broaden their economic bases, that aspiring competitors began to question the major tea schools' exclusive character and their potentially lucrative control over an activity that showed signs of becoming a major leisure industry. By then, the size of the institutions and the depth of their traditions made internal changes in the custom of hereditary leadership unlikely and external challenges unsuccessful.

After all, the system works beautifully. At Urasenke, for example, an (o)*iemoto* customarily begins training an heir when the child is about six years old. The grand master's energy, his wife's, and his mother's (if she is living) plus that of selected *gyōtei* are all directed toward giving the prospective *waka sōshō* the best training possible.

By the time he reaches his majority, the young man's skills exceed those of his peers by virtue of the intensity and quality of his instruction and he has developed a loyal coterie of advisors. Furthermore, his professional status is unassailable because he has been taught advanced procedures known only to his father and, perhaps, one or two very senior *gyōtei*. Finally, having been literally raised in the tearoom, the candidate has thoroughly internalized important qualities of style, grace, and spirituality.

This combination of religious training, technical mastery, social experience, financial backing, and ascribed prestige inevitably endow him with authority. So, when the time comes for this carefully trained professional to assume his predecessor's responsibilities, challenges to his leadership (which could have disastrous potential for *chanoyu*, the *ie*, and the *iemoto*) never arise. The process is not particularly egalitarian but it is a wondrously effective mechanism for preserving the Way of Tea.

Chapter 8

Learning the Grammar of Tea Ritual

INTRODUCTION

*T*here are two inter-related bodies of knowledge to be acquired in the process of learning tea ritual. The first consists of learning to perform a selection of tea procedures (*temae*) specified by the *iemoto*. The student's progress through a set list of *temae* is periodically marked with the presentation of certificates (*kyōjō*) permitting advancement to new skill levels. It ideally culminates with conferral of a tea name (*chamei*), a title that attests to the student's status as a mature tea practitioner. The other body of knowledge pertains more directly to the actual performance of effective ritual. It involves developing a familiarity with manifestations of Japanese "high" culture other than Tea and accruing practical skills such as flower selection, cooking, ash formation, connoisseurship, and so forth.

The student's ultimate object in learning *temae* should be to integrate the skills thus obtained into actual tea rituals (as opposed to simply collecting a series of diplomas). There is enormous variety in the character and mood of such events. Different techniques of preparing tea are employed at occasions of contrasting atmosphere, purpose, degree of formality, and physical setting. Preparation methods and utensils (whose disparities dictate aspects of procedure) are selected according to the season and the availability of equipment. The taste and degree of expertise of the host and guests should also be considered.

In the following sections, I discuss the relationship between teacher (*sensei*) and student, and introduce some of the axes along which the character of tea rituals may vary. It is important to note that the descriptions included here do not exhaust the realm of possibilities. In other words, there is not one "tea ritual," but hundreds. Each gathering is a little different from any other and an infinite number of permutations on various themes are possible.

THE MASTER-DISCIPLE RELATIONSHIP

The student-teacher bond, which lies at the heart of *chadō*, reflects an amalgamation of Zen and Confucian ideals. It is an absolutely critical factor in every tea event. Attitudes created and modified during the learning process heavily influence subsequent interaction between tea practitioners, ultimately helping to determine whether the Tea experience will be one of form or substance.

To comprehend modern manifestations of the transformatory elements Rikyū and others incorporated into *chadō*, one must perceive the profound continuity between the practice of learning Tea and performing the ritual itself. It is important to understand that ritual is being conducted during tea lessons and individual practice, as well as at tea gatherings. Evan M. Zuesse provides a description of ritual that seems to perfectly express the experience of studying *temae:*

> The ritual participants must submit to those deeper realities. They must will their own bodies into identities and movements that stem from the ancestral past. They must be humble. (Zuesse 1987, 407)

It is in this personal struggle to stand outside of oneself that a student learns to reorder his or her perceptions, and perhaps, eventually, to transcend the self. The actual movements of practicing the *temae* facilitate this process. They cannot be memorized. There are no short cuts or ways to conceal failure. The body must learn through repetition. The result is almost hypnotic.

A student may approach a teacher either on an individual basis, usually through the introduction of a relative, another student or friend, or as a member of a tea club. Clubs are often formed in schools, businesses, hospitals, Buddhist temple ladies' groups, and even military units. Once established, the relationship becomes a lifelong attachment theoretically characterized by benevolence on the part of the teacher and respect on the part of the student.[1] In fact, the group with which one instructor is associated is called the teacher's *shachū*, a name originally used to designate the families who maintain and are protected by the deity of a neighborhood shrine.

Teaching techniques vary somewhat between individuals but, one fundamental premise is that communication is predominantly oral. While texts with photos (and even television programs) have recently been authorized, they are not intended as substitutes for personal instruction. They are inadequate to teach either spiritual values or complex techniques. Memorization of the sequence of procedures is usually firmly discouraged and notetaking in class is forbidden. Instead, emphasis is placed on "learning with the body" through repetition.[2]

First one learning sequence, then another is internalized. Eventually, the procedures develop into *temae*. The teacher seldom demonstrates a *temae* in class. (His or her pupils may occasionally have the opportunity to see their *sensei* make tea at actual *chaji* [full tea gatherings], culture classes, adult education classes, and so forth.) Students learn from watching others and from the suggestions the instructor makes as they move through the motions of the tea procedures. Thus, each student develops his or her own interpretation of any particular *temae*.

The lack of freedom to innovate inherent in this system often strikes the beginner as an emotionally and conceptually difficult situation. This is particularly true for young Japanese and foreigners who are extremely enthusiastic and anxious to strike out on their own artistically. Horst Hammitzsch best expresses the reasoning behind what initially appears to be a frustrating limitation on such freedom. He writes:

> In the pursuit of any given Way, the learner has to start by holding strictly to tradition. . . . The personal freedom of spontaneous activity is actually denied, as being not the true freedom that is to be striven for. Only when the learner has conquered his own willfulness and schooled himself—reexperienced the received tradition in its entirety—can he recognize what is of eternal worth for the Way in question. Only then, having attained maturity, can he "go on to such personal creations as now arise spontaneously from within him (Hammitzsch 1980, 8).

Sen Rikyū's own lifetime career in Tea, which is depicted in the literature as having been remarkably similar to that of Confucius, offers an ideal template for the learning process. This model career was described in the *Yamanoue Sōjiki*:

> From fifteen to thirty, leave everything up to the master; from
> thirty to forty, distinguish one's own tastes, following one's
> inclinations in preparation, instruction, and conversation, let-
> ting half of all one does be original; from forty to fifty, become
> as different from one's master as east is from west, creating a
> personal style and gaining a name for skill, for this is the
> means of revitalizing *chanoyu*; from fifty to sixty, transform
> tea as did one's master before one, pouring the water out of
> one vessel into another, and making one's performance as a
> master the standard in every respect. (From the *Yamanoue
> Sōjiki* as quoted by Allison Cort 1979, 25)

Of course, the *Yamanoue Sōjiki* was describing an exemplary
career for a tea master—not something every student has the
opportunity, talent, or dedication to achieve.

Sometimes, students, who start to study together, move as a
group through the various levels of proficiency. In other
instances, students progress according to their own individual
ability. There are no "stars" in Tea in accordance with Japanese
custom. Obvious attempts to excel are met with disapproval
from both teacher and peer group. Aspiring practitioners
advance at a rate determined by the instructor. These conform
with general guidelines recommended by the school.

It has already been mentioned that orally transmitted or
"secret" teachings play a significant role in *chanoyu*. Remember
that both Nobunaga and Hideyoshi tried to control Tea by limiting their tea masters' right to teach techniques relevant to the
use of the *daisu* (Sadler 1962, 103). The concept of cultural pro-
prietorship is broadly deployed throughout Japan's entire system of education in the arts. Rikyū apparently took a rather
iconoclastic view of the subject. He said:

> There are a hundred thousand rules and regulations govern-
> ing the daisu and the other aspects of tea. Men of the past left
> off with those and appear to have understood them to be the
> whole of *chanoyu*; they recorded and transmitted in secret writ-
> ings only that we should regard each rule form as important.
> (Rikyū from the *Nampō Roku* translated in Hirota 1980b, 43)

As one might expect of an institution that so enthusiastically stresses the vertical transmission of its techniques and values, there is a strict emphasis on hierarchy at all levels in Tea.
Moreover, status acquired in the Tea world is transferable to
other social spheres: Regardless of a teacher's age or standing

outside of Tea, students always respectfully refer to their teacher as *sensei* (the same term for "teacher" used for college professors, doctors, and Buddhist priests) in public. They also defer to him or her in every seating situation (a strong indicator of relative rank in Japanese social contexts). Tea teachers are regarded by their communities as people who are (or, at least, ought to be) particularly learned and socially adept—models of rectitude and high-class deportment.

This attitude is also manifest in the economic relationship between teacher and student, one which should never be regarded as a simple exchange of cash for knowledge. Every effort should be made to manage financial arrangements tactfully. For this reason, many teachers prefer that money never changes hands in the tearoom. Usually the student pays fees by mail on a monthly basis or places cash in a white envelope, which is deposited inconspicuously in the preparation area. If money must be transferred from hand to hand, the student kneels before the seated instructor, places the envelope on an open fan, turns the whole assemblage around so that it faces the instructor, and presents it with two hands. Bows are then exchanged. In typical Japanese fashion, unsolicited (but traditional) seasonal gifts of cash, (*o*)*rei*, also serve to partially compensate for the debt in which the student is placed through the generous transmission of expertise.

Contrary to popular opinion, it is not particularly expensive to study *chanoyu*.[3] At the time of this writing, teachers in Japan and the United States are charging the equivalent of about ten dollars (U.S.) a lesson with some variability for the rank of the teacher and the *temae*. Certificate costs begin around ten (U.S.) dollars and culminate at $320 for the *chamei* (tea name). Costs are higher in Japan (about ¥100,000 or $750 at the time of this writing) where the contrast between the statuses of instructors is more marked and the social formula for figuring remuneration is consequently more complex.

The teacher retains a small portion of the certificate fee sending the majority to the *iemoto*. (*O*)*rei* are usually presented to the teacher along with certificate fees. The amount varies with the locality but customarily should not usually exceed the cost of the certificate. The practice of giving (*o*)*rei* is quite justifiable considering the time and expenditure involved in the teacher's own on-going training, the cost of tea and sweets, the damage inflicted on practice utensils, and the time devoted to the instructional process.

TEMAE: SPECIFIC TEA PROCEDURES

Most of a teacher's effort is invested in familiarizing the student with the basic building blocks of *chanoyu*, the *temae*. This term can be translated "point in front" and it refers to actions that take place at a point in front of the host. The *temae* are specific procedures (usually with variations) related to the preparation of tea. They include techniques for making thick and thin tea, laying the fire, hanging scrolls, opening the tea jar, and arranging flowers. Skills required of both host and the guest must be learned. Most of the basic *temae* may be performed throughout the year. They order daily and seasonal variation in tea technique. This structure is fundamental to the integration of the tea school and to the daily practice of *chanoyu* because *temae* regularize all the activities of the *iemoto* from classes to demonstrations to the most sophisticated tea rituals.

When a student begins to study Tea, his or her teacher leads the individual through a set hierarchy of *temae*. The general order in which the student learns the skills related to these tea procedures is controlled by the *iemoto* through the certificate system. There is very little variation in the manner in which individual *temae* are performed. As previously noted, they have been created by (*o*)*iemoto* and cannot be altered by anyone else. Every hand movement and the placement of each utensil is strictly prescribed.

The student starts by learning individual action sequences such as bowing and purifying the tea container with a silk cloth (*fukusa*). He or she next combines these movements and others to perform a simple tea-making procedure in which all the utensils are carried into the room on a tray (*ryaku bon*). Then after a few months practice, the student will be introduced to the *hirademae*.

The *hirademae* are the two most fundamental ways of making tea. Thin and thick tea are made from different quantities and qualities of tea powder. The plants that supply the leaves are the same genus and variety (*camellia sinensis*), but thick tea powder is supposed to be made from the youngest leaves of the tea plantation's oldest shrubs. Thin tea comes from older leaves on younger plants and is consequently more bitter in flavor. The powders themselves are processed, packaged, and named separately. Thick tea powder can be used to make thin tea but thin tea powder should not be used to make thick tea. The two beverages also differ significantly in that thick tea is kneaded while thin tea is whipped with up to twice as much water.

Thin and thick tea procedures are varied to accommodate disparate heat sources during the primary subdivisions of the Tea year—the *ro* and *furo* seasons. The *ro*, a small firepit cut into the *tatami*, holds the charcoal used to heat the water in winter months. But it is replaced in summer by a *furo*, a brazier, which sits on top of the *tatami*. (The *furo* may, in fact, be used all year round.) Since a properly tended fire is critical to good tea preparation, a series of *temae*, which relate to handling charcoal (the *sumidemae*), have been developed.

Normally, a student practices the *hirademae* (and, perhaps, some simple *sumidemae*) for six months to a year before advancing to the study of the sixteen basic *konarai* ("lesser studies"). Learning these procedures cultivates a variety of skills used in handling utensils with special meaning or features. Such objects may be important because they are associated with certain statuses of people (such as nobles), because they have played a significant part in tea history, or because they are associated with solutions to logistical problems like serving thick tea to a large number of guests or inspecting a tea jar. Much emphasis is placed on learning respect for individuals like noble guests (*kinin*), figures in tea history (like Rikyū), donors of particular utensils, authors of scrolls, and so forth.

Once the student has been thoroughly exposed to the *konarai* (it will take many years to become really competent in them), the teacher may suggest he or she apply for permission to study the *shikaden* (literally "four transmissions," the first "orally transmitted" *temae* a student encounters). These procedures are never photographed or committed to writing and are taught only with the *iemoto*'s permission. Most are seldom employed at modern tea rituals but they are important.

Learning the *shikaden* cements the practitioner's bond to a particular school of tea and introduces him or her to some technical aspects of tea history. They also serve to acquaint the student with skills crucial to the performance of even more advanced *temae*. At this intermediate level, the student also learns a procedure (*wakindate*) created by Gengensai (the eleventh grand master of Urasenke) to feature material presented to him by the Emperor Kōkaku (1771-1840) and several *temae* for making tea using utensils carried in a box or basket (*chabakodate* and *shikishidate temae*).

The most advanced procedures (*okuden*) learned by the average practitioner focus on the use of the *daisu* and replicas of Chinese utensils. It is my understanding that there are at least ten additional *temae* (*jūdan temae*) that are taught only within Konnichian and only to the very highest ranking practitioners. Some are practiced exclusively by the (*o*)*iemoto* and his heir.

The total progress from beginning student to *chamei* takes a minimum of ten years unless one is a full-time student in Kyōto. Even graduation from the most advanced level does not ensure that one will receive the coveted tea name. It should be noted that during this period, students are learning a great deal that is not reflected in an abbreviated description of *temae* (see the "*Temae*" appendix for a more complete description). In addition to studying a series of group "drills" (the *shichiji shiki*), which sharpen timing and inculcate the need for cooperation, prospective practitioners are introduced to tea history, the history of the families of artisans involved in *chanoyu*, Japanese literature, tea architecture, the curatorship of utensils, and calligraphy. They also learn a great deal about Japanese historical, religious, and seasonal symbolism plus more practical subjects such as *kaiseki* cooking, *chabana* (selecting and displaying flowers for tea gatherings), gardening, and ash arrangement (*haigata*).[4]

Ideally, this lengthy period of practice and self-discipline promotes a type of personal growth that is ultimately reflected in the practitioner's tea style. *Chadō* is based on the Japanese concept of lifetime learning. The western idea of progressing from skill level to skill level with a finite goal in mind is theoretically rejected. The quality of an individual's tea performance is, from beginning to end, a reflection of their character.

THE MAIN CLASSES OF TEA GATHERINGS

There are several main classes of tea events and the disparities between them are critically important for later theoretical analysis. The term *kencha* is usually reserved for "tea ceremonies," which are conducted at *Shintō* shrines (or more recently at Christian churches). Similar presentations made at Buddhist temples are called "*kucha*." This variety of ritual is also associated with memorial services for certain focal Sen family ancestors. Examples are *Rikyūki* (for Rikyū), *Sōtanki* (for Sōtan), and *Seichū-Ennō-Mugenki* (for Gengensai, Ennōsai, and Tantansai). *Kencha* and *kucha* are most often performed in public by the current Grand master or the *waka sōshō* (his heir). However, private memorial services of a less formal character may be offered by any practitioner who wishes to honor the deceased. Such functions are annually conducted by Urasenke tea teachers and societies.   ·

The term *chaji* is reserved for occasions when thick tea, thin tea, and a meal are presented to the guest. Usually at least one charcoal *temae* is involved. *Chaji* are intended to be intimate and spiritually oriented. Tea practitioners, by and large, find it logistically awkward and emotionally exhausting to conduct full gatherings for more than five people. The more people involved, the more difficult it is to create a sense of communion.

Other gatherings have a more secular nature. They are commonly called "*chakai*" if only thin tea (*usucha*) and sweets are served. A light snack (*tenshin*) may also be offered. *Chakai* are usually held when the proposed number of guests is too large for a full gathering (*chaji*). Guests at *chakai* are sometimes seated at timed intervals called "*seki*."

Chakai are usually planned to require minimal participation on the part of the guests. This is the product of necessity. When a large number of people must be served, chances are increased a certain percentage of them will not be familiar enough with *chanoyu*'s highly particularized symbolic language to engage in a meaningful dialogue. To prevent awkward misunderstandings, the host chooses an experienced first guest and follows a format that minimizes the need to involve other guests. A large number of seasonal symbols are often employed because their visual similarity to the objects they represent make them comprehensible to the uninitiated.

SEVEN PRINCIPAL TYPES OF *CHAJI*

Urasenke recognizes seven main types of *chaji*: the *shōgo chaji*, the *yobanashi chaji*, the *akatsuki chaji*, the *asa chaji*, the *hango chaji*, the *atomi chaji*, and the *rinji chaji*. The standard type is the *shōgo chaji* (noon tea gathering). This tea will be described in detail later.

The *yobanashi chaji* (literally "evening chat") is a night gathering generally held in *ro* (winter, hearth) season. When skillfully conducted, this kind of event is particularly likely to generate a wonderful sense of warmth and friendship. Many factors contribute to the creation of such an atmosphere. For example, the *roji* (path to the tearoom) and the tearoom are illuminated with lanterns and candles. And, while they wait in the *machiai*, (waiting area) guests are frequently offered warm beverages such as *amazake* (sweet Japanese rice wine) rather than the usual hot water ([o]*sayu*).

At a night gathering, the host must be particularly careful to choose utensils that can be appreciated in poor light. For example, a scroll with particularly large graphic characters might be selected and very rough-textured ceramics utilized. Some authorities say flowers should not be displayed in the alcove (*tokonoma*) at night, for some blossoms close inauspiciously at nightfall. A fragrant plant, *sekishō* (*Acorus calamus*), is sometimes substituted. Others maintain that white flowers are appropriate as they can be seen best by lamplight.

The host welcomes the guests to his tearoom with *zencha*, a large, shared bowl of usucha. After the charcoal has been arranged (*shozumi*), a meal has been served (*kaiseki*), and sweets have been eaten; the guests withdraw to the garden for a break between the two major parts of the gathering (*nakadachi*). There they are likely be provided with hand warmers (*teaburi*) and a *hibachi* (a small charcoal-burning heater) in addition to the usual tobacco tray (*tabako bon*) and seat cushions (*enza*).[5]

When the guests return to the tearoom, *tsuzukiusucha* (the "usucha follows" procedure) is usually performed. For this *temae*, thin tea is served immediately after thick tea without an intervening charcoal preparation. During the thin tea segment of the gathering, guests are seated on cushions (*zabuton*) and provided with smoking equipment (*tabako bon*). (If the tearoom is particularly cold, they may also be provided with hand warmers.) A unique aspect of *yobanashi chaji* is *tomezumi*, charcoal added at the end of the gathering to encourage guests to linger and talk.

Another stunning type of *chaji* performed during *ro* season is the *akatsuki chaji* (dawn tea). *Akatsuki chaji* is performed only by experts as the host must be very skilled and confident to create an atmosphere that guests will enjoy at 4:00 A.M.! Lanterns and candles are used as they were at the night gathering but they are removed or allowed to burn out part way through the *chaji* so that the guests can appreciate the changing qualities of the dawn. If the tearoom has a skylight (*tsukiage mado*), an interesting feature of the gathering will be opening this aperture to let in the first light of day at a particularly dramatic point in the procedure.

Tsuzukiusucha is the preferred tea preparation technique for the dawn gathering but a shared bowl of thin tea (*zencha*) should first be served. A unique aspect of this event is the performance of a special charcoal *temae* during which embers from the previous evening are used to start a new fire. It is also notable that fresh fish and broiled foods are not included in the *kaiseki* meal because of the difficulty of obtaining and preparing them fresh at this early hour.

A more commonly presented *chaji* is the *asa chaji* (morning tea). Anyone who has suffered the heat and humidity of Kyōto from mid-June to mid-September will immediately appreciate the rationale for this gathering. For a morning gathering, the guests are invited to arrive by 5:45 A.M., before the heat of the day begins. After greetings, the first charcoal *temae* (*shozumi*) is performed. The guests ask to inspect the arrangement individually at this time (*furo chū no haiken*). They may notice that an unusually large amount of white ash (*fujibai*) has been sprinkled on the gray ash in the *furo*. This is meant to evoke the cooling image of snow-dusted mountains or a surf-flecked beach. The meal is customarily served next. Raw and broiled fish are once more omitted from the menu but, despite the early hour, *saké* (Japanese rice wine) is usually served. Again, *tsuzukiusucha* is the standard choice for tea preparation.

The three *chaji* just described are associated with particular seasons and times of day. The next three are related to specific social situations. *Hango chaji* (literally "after meal," also called "*tokihazure*" meaning "off time" or *kashi chaji* if the emphasis is on the sweets) may be presented after breakfast or the noon meal anytime of the year. It includes an abbreviated meal that takes busy schedules into account. *Hango chaji* are particularly popular around the New Year, an especially hectic period for tea practitioners.

The charcoal procedure for a *hango chaji* may be performed either before or after the host offers the guests a light snack (*tenshin*). *Suimono* (soup with delicacies) and a *hassun* (tray with mountain and ocean foods) are served accompanied by *saké*.

Sometimes, only sweets (*omogashi*) are provided. If sweets alone are served, guests return for tea plus a snack after the middle break. Once more, *tsuzukiusucha* is the preferred tea preparation.

Atomi chaji is the only tea event requested by the guests. The guests desiring an *atomi chaji*, having heard that a tea gathering is being held, respectfully ask to view the utensils afterwards. They remain in the waiting area until the first group of guests departs. While they are waiting, the host's assistant (*hantō*) frequently serves them *saké*, soup, and a tray of small delicacies (*hassun*). They may also eat their main sweets before entering the tearoom. When they do enter, they may find that the host has exercised his option to display the scroll and the flowers at the same time (*morokazari*). This gives the guests a chance to see these two important elements of the previous *chaji*. Thick tea is served and may be followed by a second charcoal *temae* (*gozumi*) and thin tea. Alternatively, *tsuzukiusucha* may be performed.

The final variant of the standard *chaji* is called "*rinji chaji*" or "*fuji chaji*" (spontaneous or "no time" tea gathering). This is a tea gathering given on impulse or short notice. There are no fixed rules for such events, although the *shōgo chaji* is always the point from which improvisation originates. A real Tea person (*chajin*) is always supposed to be prepared to serve tea at a moment's notice. Since at least some of the guests are likely to be fellow practitioners, they often volunteer to help the host. The guests may assist in the preparation area, in arranging flowers, setting the fire, and so forth. Dry sweets and some elements of the *kaiseki* meal can usually be improvised. Flowers come from the host's yard or some nearby place.[6]

THE YEARLY CYCLE OF TEA

The seven *chaji* formats just presented furnish only the basic outlines for one class of tea ritual. The accomplished practitioner is expected to enhance the spiritual and artistic potential of each event with carefully orchestrated imagery drawn in large part from Japan's massive repertoire of seasonal symbolism. Sensitivity to this imagery is a significant part of the national identity. As has been frequently noted, the Japanese consider themselves an agricultural people who dwell in a capricious environment. *Shintō* beliefs are generally cited as the source for the Japanese people's sublime regard for markers of temporal change. But the phenomenon is not so integral to the elusive "national essence" as some would have us believe. It is fundamentally learned behavior and the tearoom is one of the best places to learn it.

As noted in chapter 3, the Heian (794–1192) elite developed a life-style truly remarkable for its wealth, leisure, and dedication to beauty. Residents of the capital (Heiankyō, now known as Kyōto) were particularly enraptured with Chinese literature, art, and philosophy. Thus, while the nascent Buddhist priesthood poured over *sutras*, the less religiously inclined devoted themselves to generating their own versions of the elegant pursuits of the Sung (960–1279) intelligentsia. Tea competitions, incense-comparing, divination, music, painting, and calligraphy were prominent among their favorite pastimes. Poetry integrated all, possibly because it provided an excellent vehicle for rationalizing lives that were often not very productive, tragically brief, and incredibly circumscribed by etiquette.

So intense was the rivalry in verse competitions (*uta awase*), reputations were made and broken by the selection of a single metaphor. The fate of a love affair might even be determined by the sensitivity with which a *de rigueur* "next morning" poem was twisted around a carefully selected branch or flower. Not surprisingly, familiarity with seasonally appropriate natural images became a carefully cultivated social asset. Great masterpieces of the Heian literature like the magnificent *Tale of Genji* and the almost equally famous *Man'yō shū* (a collection of poetry written in the eighth century) ensured the phenomenon's constant regeneration in the years that followed.

Nowhere in Japan is the relationship between nature, the poetic imagery of ages past, and the slow progress of the seasons more regularly celebrated or assiduously preserved than in the tearoom. Moreover, there are few areas of *chanoyu* that reveal its culturally syncretic origins more blatantly than its calendar. To begin with, the actual dates of specific events usually vary from year to year due to discrepancies between the lunar and solar calendars.

The oldest set of elements contributing to the combination of calendars observed by tea practitioners is the "Ten Celestial Stems." These are symbols identified in pairs with the Taoist five elements (wood, fire, earth, metal, and water). They may have been employed by Chinese diviners as early as the Chou dynasty (1122?–256 B.C.). Probably at roughly the same time another system called "The Twelve Terrestrial Branches" was introduced, most likely by raiders from central Asia. The twelve branches were identified with zodiacal animals like the rat, ox, tiger, and so forth, and assigned to certain hours, days, and months. The Chinese combined the two systems to produce sixty-day and sixty-year cycles of units associated with both "stems" and "branches." These signs were thought to influence every aspect of human life.

When the Chinese calendar was introduced to Japan, the Japanese received it as a powerful revelation. Combined with both Sinitic and native systems of geomancy, it developed into an influential construct of complex directional and temporal auguries. The Heian elite consulted astrologers and geomancers about everything from building temples to washing their hair. The difficulty with the part of the system based on the lunar calendar was that it tended to fall rapidly out of synchronization with the natural seasons. This was a serious consideration to people who believed their rice would only flourish if the emperor planted the first shoots in a timely fashion.

The problem was resolved by adopting a Chinese solar calendar in addition to the lunar one. This calendar began with the winter solstice and was divided into twenty-four equal *sekki*, subdivisions identified by descriptive names such as "The End of Insect Hibernation" and "The Greater Heat." Unfortunately, since the system was fundamentally Chinese, the terminology was not always appropriate for Japan's climactic conditions. Farmers, nevertheless, found it more useful than the lunar calendar because it enabled them to determine appropriate times for planting and harvesting with some certainty. Lunar and solar calendars were coordinated by agreeing that the twelfth lunar month had to include the *sekki* called "Greater Cold."

The dates of holidays and rituals were calculated on the basis of both systems (taking ethnic derivation and date of origin into account) until the Gregorian calendar was introduced in 1873. Since then solar dates have been assigned to certain celebrations. Fortunately for tea practitioners, some modern calendars list *sekki* as well as Gregorian dates.

The symbolism associated with traditional Japanese holidays is central to the creation of each tea ritual's *toriawase*, the personally selected combinations of material objects, poetic images, and symbols that make each gathering unique. Most *toriawase* integrate a cross section of Taoist, Buddhist, *Shintō* Chinese and/or Japanese elements. For example, the *toriawase* of a gathering planned for July 7 (according to the Gregorian calendar) might include an incense container decorated with stars (evocative of the Star Festival held in China on the Seventh Day of the Seventh Lunar month), a moist, unlacquered well bucket (suggesting both coolness and the purity of *Shintō* ritual vessels), and a tea scoop named "Small Heat" ("*Shōsho*," the name of the relevant *sekki*).

Obviously, the association between *chanoyu*'s symbolic and calendrical systems is incredibly convoluted. Most tea practitioners do not immediately recognize every sign and symbol they encounter in the tearoom. But that is precisely why good *toriawase* are so delightful: Creating and interpreting these subtle compositions is like playing those clever and poetic guessing games beloved by the Heian elite.

Through seasonal *toriawase*, tea practitioners learn more about Japanese culture (with a capital C) and enhance their sensitivity to natural phenomena. Both ultimately help banish the suspicion "that life is absurd and the attempt to make moral, intellectual, or emotional sense out of experience is bootless" (Geertz 1973, 108). Indeed, *chadō*'s ritual calendar goes a long way toward defining an image of the kind of unified cosmos imagined by the Taoists.

Sen Rikyū. Early Edo period copy (by Kanei Sōtan, 1611–1672) of a portrait by Hasegawa Tōhaku (1539–1610). Property of Urasenke.

Toyotomi Hideyoshi. Portrait by Kanō Sanraku (1559–1535).
Property of the Itsuo Art Museum.

Sen Sōshitsu, the fifteenth generation Grand Master of Urasenke. Shown preparing thick tea during *ro* season. He is using a *daisu*.

Okumachiai ("inner waiting arbor"). One of two *koshikake machi-ai* at Urasenke. The round alcove is believed to have been constructed by Fukensai to enshrine the famous wooden statue of Rikyū during restoration of the Rikyūdo. The structure was converted to a waiting arbor by Gengensai.

Yohōbutsu no chōzubachi. A garden wash basin located near the Yūin teahouse at Urasenke. It is believed to have been owned by Rikyū and depicts buddhas of the four directions.

An exterior view of the Yūin ("Further Retreat") teahouse at Urasenke. It has been designated an "Important Cultural Property" by Japan. Note the *nijiriguchi* and the "moon-viewing" window cut into the thatched roof.

An interior view of Yūin shown during *ro* season. The characters written on the scroll in the alcove are *"Doku za dai yu hō"* ("I
am sitting on top of a tall mountain alone"). The phrase is
believed to have been used by Pai-chang to express his sense of
enlightenment.

Ōmizuya. The main preparation room at Urasenke. The characters on the vertical plaque to the left proclaim Ennosai's conviction that the *mizuya* is the true place for learning Tea. The horizontal inscription contains Gengensai's admonitions for proper conduct in the *mizuya* and tearoom. Note the *temmoku*-style tea bowl resting on a black lacquer stand on the second shelf. The bowl on the unlacquered stand (*dai*) is used for *kinindate*.

A *kaiseki* tray similar to the one described in chapter 12.

A charcoal basket (*sumitori*) prepared for the first charcoal arrangement (*shozumi*). The incense container in the upper right hand corner is a replica of Tantansai's Tamukeyama *kogo*.

An assortment of incense containers. The container at upper left is a replica of Gengensai's *"Ama obune"* ("Diver's boat"). It has a poem on its lid.

The brazier (*furo*) as it would appear after the first charcoal preparation. (The kettle has been removed for the photograph.)

The main sweet described at the model *chaji* ("Hagi no Tsuyu") in a *fuchidaka*. The pick in the foreground is a *kuromoji*.

An assortment of *mizusashi*. The box in the upper right hand corner is a *tsurube*, a copy of the well-bucket preferred by Rikyū.

Thick tea containers (*chaire*). The container on the left is a copy of a *karamono* (Chinese-style) tea container. The *chaire* in the center is representative of the Japanese "thrusting shoulders" style. The container on the right is a *"dai kai"* ("great ocean") *chaire*. The tea Eisai gave to Myōe was presented in this type of vessel.

Thick tea bowls. The bowls in front are Oribe and red *raku*. The rear bowl is *hagi*.

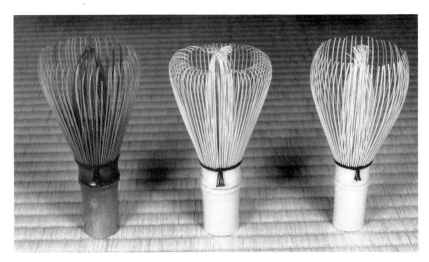

Tea whisks (*chasen*). The *chasen* on the left is fashioned in the *shin* style preferred at Urasenke. The *chasen* in the middle is a common variety often used for practice. The whisk on the right is a smoked bamboo *chasen* employed during the *kinin kiyotsugu* tea procedure.

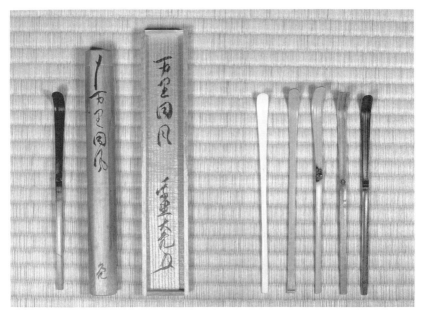

Tea scoops (*chashaku*). The scoop on the left is displayed with its container and box lid. It was made by Tachibana Daiki, the abbot of Nyoian, a sub-temple of Daitokuji. The light-colored *chashaku* near the middle of the photograph is an ivory tea scoop. The utensils to its right are shown in descending order of formality.

Waste containers (*kensui*). The bronze utensil at lower left is an *efugo kensui*. The container at lower right is a bentwood vessel of a type first used by Rikyū.

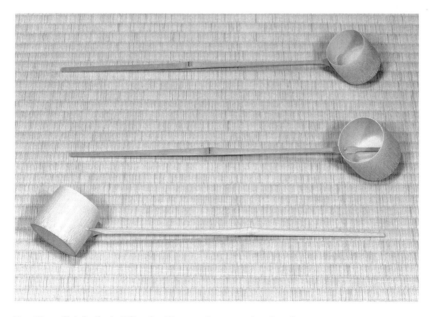

Ladles (*hishaku*). The ladle at the top is the form most commonly used. The ladle in the center is a *kazari hishaku*, a variant used with *daisu* and *nagaita* (a long board similar to the lower level of the *daisu*) tea preparations.

Lid rests (*futaoki*). The bamboo *futaoki* in the center of the back row bears the *kaō* (cipher) of a Zen monk. The lid rests in the front row replicate styles favored by Rikyū.

Some utensils for making thick tea. The *furo* is a bronze Dōan-buro. The kettle is made in the "crane's neck" style. The *mizusashi* is Seto with a lacquer lid. The bag (*shifuku*) covering the *chaire* is a fabric preferred by Rikyū.

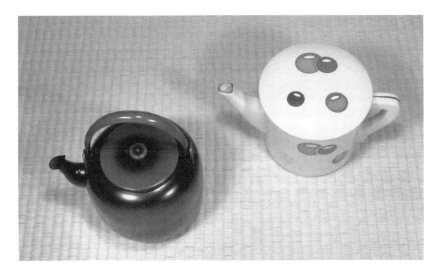

Two styles of water supplier (*mizutsugi*). The vessel at left is a modern replica of Rikyū's *koshiguro yakan*. (The original was naturally blackened with use.) The *mizutsugi* on the right bears of *tsubo tsubo* motif.

Dry sweets (*higashi*). Dry sweets such as these are described as being served at the model *shōgo chaji* depicted in part 3. They are called *"fukiyose"* ("wind gathered"). These particular sweets were made by Kameya Iori of Kyōto.

Thin tea bowls. The bowl on the left in the back row is *kyōyaki* (Kyōto-style pottery). The shallow bowl in the foreground is used mainly in the summer months.

Thin tea containers. The container at left rear is a Rikyū-style, medium sized *natsume*. The container at right front was "used" at the model *shōgo chaji* described in Part 3.

Part III

A Model Shōgo Chaji

Chapter 9

Behind the Scenes

EXAMINING A MODEL *CHAJI* FROM
THE STRUCTURALIST PERSPECTIVE

The program

I n order to realize their desired ends (be they confirmatory or transformatory), ritual practitioners must pursue a predetermined course of *action*. This involves establishing a believable relationship between the sensory perceptions of the participants and the symbolic message he or she plans to convey. As Zuesse so succinctly states:

> ...ritual is intentional bodily engagement in the paradigmatic forms and relationships of reality. As such, ritual brings not only the body but also that body's social and cultural identity to the encounter with the transcendental realm. (Zuesse 1987, 406)

There are three basic stages in conducting ritual. The officiant must: (1) substantiate his or her ability to perform the task, (2) explicate the cosmological model, and (3) create the illusion of effectively manipulating the relationship between the ritual constituency and the cosmological model. None of these aims can be credibly achieved in speech or writing because the mechanisms that link the knowable and the unknowable are inexpressible by definition. It is the feeling of physically participating in the interaction between higher and lower cognitive orders that makes ritual work. The actors need to sense that they (or their proxy) can interact with the universal order in a way that enhances their personal potential for transcendent satisfaction (salvation).

Defining roles   All rituals use symbolic devices to propose identification with extraordinary roles to the individuals involved. Active participants symbolize their ability to manipulate the cosmic model by dressing and/or moving in ways that suggest special access to the transcendent. Passive participants imply their receptivity to a changed perception of reality by dressing and/or moving in ways that suggest their liminal status. Since these symbols have to be mutually understood if the actors are to take part in a cooperative effort, they must be endowed with significance during the ritual or be suggestive of something mutually familiar to the actors. Ritual emblems of identity are usually culled from the memory of the culture at large. This allows the actors to identify with the cumulative experience of those who have played significant roles in their collective heritage. By "putting on the masks of their forbears" ritualists appropriate their experience and penetrate the temporal barriers generally assumed to exist between the timeless and the transitory.

Setting the stage   Once roles have been defined, the spatial and temporal dimensions of ritual action must be delimited. Once again, this task can be symbolically accomplished during the ritual itself (as, for example, when a sand painting is created in Navaho ritual). Alternatively, a preexisting environment (such as a temple, shrine, dance house, etc.), which structurally incorporates recognized symbolic boundaries, may be appropriated. When such a edifice is employed, the actors almost always perform some action (such a purification) that redefines the spatial model for the present ritual constituency. Ritual is most effective when every individual present has the opportunity to experience the sensory illusion of being lifted to or centered in another reality.

Making ritual work   With the participants agreed on their roles and the stage set, ritual action is ready to commence. As Zuesse pointed out there are two possibilities—the actors may confirm their relationship to the transcendent by assuming prescribed positions in the existing symbolic matrix or they may alter the dynamic of the paradigm by effecting changes in either their roles or the supporting structure. This gives practitioners the opportunity to either verify the effectiveness of their present strategy for integrating all levels of existence or to try a new approach at minimal risk. Ritual is effective to the extent that the participants are able to associate the possibilities mapped out through ritual action with their everyday life.

The amount and character of the symbolic interaction that takes place at tea gatherings varies quite dramatically from one type of event to another. For the most part, practitioners do not expect the onlookers at *kucha* and *kencha* to understand the symbolic import of all their actions. Under these circumstances, communication is supposed to flow between the officiant and the spiritual entity being propitiated or memorialized.

The practitioner establishes his authority and defines the ritual precincts as usual. But rather than involving other actors, he functions as proxy for the assembled multitude. His authority is heightened by mystery so the general populace's complete understanding of the proceedings is both unnecessary and undesirable. The symbols employed at such events usually refer to Japanese tea ritual's Chinese antecedents.

The symbolic repertoire

The nature of symbols   If the ritual world were unambiguously separated from mundane reality, it would be impossible to draw parallels between the two spheres. Fortunately, their integration is facilitated by the multivocal quality of symbols. In essence, the grammar of ritual and daily discourse may vary but the vocabulary is the same: A cup of tea consumed in the ritual setting may be endowed with a host of philosophical implications but, by some criteria, it can be assigned to the same set of behaviors as a cup of tea shared with a neighbor in the kitchen. As Nancy Munn has pointed out, symbols have the ability to "channel and reintegrate" meaning at different levels of logical synthesis (Munn 1973, 590).

Victor Turner wrote that the symbols he saw in a ritual context were "objects, activities, relationships, events, gestures, and spatial units..." (Turner 1967, 19). And, Nancy Munn observed the ritual message system included "symbols, action sequences, and the rules governing these; the categories of participants and their modes of participation, etc." (Munn 1973, 580).

Symbols clearly do their work in a variety of ways. Some evoke other objects or ideas by partial reference, and others suggest subsequent action. Some signs are emblematic of certain statuses, individuals, or roles, while others display a sensory likeness to absent elements.

The most complex group of symbols are those that elicit series of associations. These often bear no resemblance to the phenomena they represent but, they do communicate multiple layers of meaning. Because their lack of specificity allows more room for personal interpretation, such entities are often capable of eliciting unusually powerful responses. (See Firth 1973, 74–75 for a more detailed explanation of symbol types).

Toriawase   All these diverse components must be carefully orchestrated to make a ritual effective. In Tea, the general structure of the individual gathering is determined by the school through the standardization of *temae* and *chaji* sequence. The practitioner, however, is left with a great deal of responsibility for integrating symbolic themes. The sum of his or her optional choices is called the *"toriawase"* of the event—the part of ritual's symbolic message that is intended to be unique to one particular gathering. (See the *Toriawase* appendix for complete examples.)

A host or hostess uses the *toriawase* to share something that cannot be fully expressed in words. Creating *toriawase* is an art form like poetry. The combination of symbols, literary, and historical allusions is calculated to conjure up an atmosphere in the same way a few well chosen words might be used to sketch a natural scene or emotion.

For example, a gathering where plum branches are displayed in the alcove, young bamboo shoots are served with the meal and the tea scoop is named for an early spring bird evokes more than blossoms, new shoots, and birds. The guest is simultaneously encouraged to think of warming weather, clear skies, new life, and so forth, and to relate these ideas with a constellation of associated utensils, poems, foods, personal memories, and historical anecdotes.

Just as an aspiring poet acquires a knowledge of language through the study of literature, *toriawase* is learned by study and imitation. As Horst Hammitzsch writes in *Zen and the Art of the Tea Ceremony*:

> In Japan the learning of any one of the many arts is an almost wordless process. The Master supplies the model, the pupil copies. The process is repeated again and again, month after month, year after year. (Hammitzsch 1980, 22)

This process is used to learn physical technique, aesthetic taste, and modes of symbolic communication. Because symbolic language and aesthetics are being taught as well as actual procedure, Tea teachers often progress to new *temae* before the student has become competent in the previous one. The seasonal nature of *temae* and *toriawase* make this practice imperative.

There are a few recognized conventions that regulate the creation of *toriawase*. One is the principle of non-duplication. The host should not name the sweet *"Hagi no Tsuyu"* ("Dew of the Bush Clover," *Lespedeza thunbergii*), if *hagi* appears in the flower arrangement. Similarly, one should not call the *chashaku* (tea scoop) "Bamboo Shoot" as it is already made of bamboo. (Bamboo is, nevertheless, inevitably duplicated in the tearoom because of its prevalence as a construction material. A bamboo flower container often appears at the same time as a bamboo tea scoop. But unless the main guest is a specialist in breeding bamboo, it is better not to have a bamboo motif on the lid rest as well as the water jar.)

Other important principles of *toriawase* relate to conventional Japanese aesthetic preferences. Asymmetry is preferred to symmetry. Empty space is used in a positive sense and clutter is avoided. Color is used sparingly. Textures are chosen to subtly contrast with each other. Horizontal line characteristically takes precedence over vertical line and the scale of utensils must be considered in relation to the individual tearoom.

Toriawase always include seasonal elements. Flowers, foods, and artistic motifs are generally not employed at times of the year when they would not occur in nature. (Displaying abnormally late blooming flowers in October to symbolize a lingering regret for the past season is a typical violation of this principle and a classic example of the "proper" way to deviate.)

The host also tries to match the relative degree of formality of the utensils to the *temae* and the tearoom. A famous example of this is given in a anecdote that describes an incident that occurred when Sōtan made tea informally for the imperial regent, Konoe Nobuhiro: His surprised guest asked when it was proper to serve tea using a *temmoku* tea bowl on a stand in the formal manner. Sōtan politely explained that it was proper to do so for guests of high rank but, as his august visitor had purposely come to visit the tea master in his humble tearoom, he thought it more considerate to offer tea in an informal manner. Sōtan later formally served his guest thin tea in an adjoining room using the etiquette and utensils commonly considered appropriate to his guest's noble status (Sadler 1962, 55).

Other principles of *toriawase* relate to the quality and degree of elaboration in the utensils. For example, when the officiant uses the very formal black lacquer *daisu* (tea stand) in an advanced *temae* featuring a Sung dynasty thick tea container (*chaire*), it is customary to use other utensils of correspondingly high quality (such as a *temmoku* tea bowl with its stand). Advanced tea students also learn to coordinate characteristic products of specific generations of well-known, utensil-making families. Thus, if a *chashaku* (tea scoop) identified with a particular tea master is used, its historical provenance must correspond within a generation to era of the potter who made the bowl. (Scoops associated with Rikyū constitute an exception to this rule.) For this reason, students must learn to recognize copies of famous bowls in each generation and to know which *chashaku* to use with them.

Precedent also regulates the combination of native and foreign utensils. One does not usually see a plethora of foreign articles (such as southeast Asian ceramics or Portuguese cut glass) at a single gathering unless the country of a guest's origin is specifically being emphasized. (The exception to this is Chinese utensils that are used abundantly in a more formal *temae*.)

Further, the degree of gorgeousness of the utensils should be matched to the character of the occasion and the personalities of the guests. At the New Year, items with gold and silver decorations are frequently employed because they reflect the festive nature of the occasion. They would be less appropriate in October, the *wabi* month. Similarly, the lively and decorative utensils, which might be suitable for very young guests, would probably be incongruous at a gathering of monks.

Finally, a sense of the historic provenance of the specific symbols or utensils chosen (or that of the items from which they have been copied) must be considered. Certain utensils recall incidents in Japanese history and the personalities of the individuals related to them. For example, the *konomi* of tea masters evoke thoughts of their achievements at memorial gatherings. And, wild ginger (*aoi, Asarum caudatum or caulescens*) or ox carts recall the festival associated with Kyōto's salvation from terrible storms in the sixth century. The foregoing are but a few of many possible principles of *toriawase*. The majority cannot be expressed in concrete terms because they rely on subtle discriminatory senses cultivated through experience. Just as an Eskimo would have trouble describing his method of distinguishing between forty kinds of snow to a citizen of Ecuador, so a tea master cannot explain precisely what is right or wrong about a particular combination of utensils.

The paradigmatic chaji

I have chosen to describe a *chaji* in detail (rather than *kencha*, *kucha*, or the *chakai*) because I feel this class of tea gathering best reveals the interplay of social, religious, and artistic elements in *chanoyu*. Religious ceremonies provide no opportunity to analyze the interaction of host and guests and *chakai* tend to emphasize sociability to the exclusion of intimacy and religious meaning. Only at *chaji* do host and guests become fully engaged in a symbolic dialogue.

The most stimulating communication in the tea world takes place at *chaji*. While non-practitioners are occasionally invited to attend such events, they are necessarily relegated to secondary positions because of their unfamiliarity with the structural conventions of the ritual. A more experienced practitioner is charged with the responsibility for holding up the guests' end of the symbolic conversation.

It is only in the unique environment of the *chaji* that tea practitioners can truly express themselves as ritualists. But, with an attitude that appears paradoxical to Westerners, they make their statements in a very restrained way. This has a great deal to do with the Japanese sense of group membership. One reveals what is truly important only to selected intimates. It also partakes of the ancient Japanese tradition of playing highly refined guessing games. In such an atmosphere, much can be left unsaid.

There are several reasons I have elected not to describe an actual tea gathering. The first is that the symbolic structure of ethnographic events is frequently obscured by a lack of material assets (such as tearooms, utensils, etc.). With today's stratospheric real estate prices, very few tea practitioners can afford to invest in a freestanding teahouse and garden. Gatherings must often be held in physical surroundings (such as an ordinary living room or restaurant), which compromise important principles of spatial symbolism, aesthetics, and so forth.

The second reason I prefer to describe a "fictive" gathering is that "first time" guests (such as the reader) might be confused by the manner in which real hosts compromise carefully selected aspects of the tradition to communicate personal messages: There is a great deal of consensus among tea practitioners on the way that things "ought to be." The *iemoto* sets the standards and students uniformly recognize deviations from the norm. Doing something different makes a statement.

This is not to say that guests react to originality in a critical manner. (Though—human nature being what it is—some do.) Most tea people appreciate a little variety. But, the truth is experienced tea people have internalized Tea's symbolic structure: they cannot avoid employing the cognitive system with which they have been so thoroughly inculcated, and they are most comfortable with variations that fit into familiar patterns.

In fact, when an important symbolic element is lacking, practitioners often intuitively correct for their absence—supplying missing features though their imaginations with the subliminal intent of creating a coherent illusion. Learning which elements are inviolate, which may be manipulated, and which have to be supplied by the imagination is an important aspect of practicing Tea. But, these are skills acquired over time—not material for a basic paradigm.

I cannot emphasize strongly enough that my decision to present a model *chaji* rather describe an actual gathering is founded on the belief that the model is paramount in the minds of tea practitioners when they attend an actual *chaji*. They are constantly relating their immediate experience to the standards of the tea school.

In order to eliminate personal idiosyncrasy from this account and communicate the symbolic structure of Tea as simply as possible, I have also decided to depict a very conventional gathering. The *chaji* recounted here did not take place, but if the host had access to the items described, it could have.

As I narrate, the emotive and symbolic significance of each segment of the *chaji* will be discussed in detail. If any interpretations are not orthodox (that is, not from official publications of the Urasenke school or learned in class from my teachers), I will register them as such. As stated in the introduction to this book, my exegesis is fundamentally that of a practitioner.[1]

PRELIMINARY PREPARATIONS FOR *CHAJI*

As previously mentioned, the *shōgo chaji* (noon tea) is the basic model for all formal tea gatherings. The preparation techniques, which I am about to describe, are almost uniformly the most fundamental in their classes. I have chosen early October as the period during which the model *chaji* takes place.

Planning for a *chaji* ideally starts months in advance. The host or hostess (*teishu*) first decides who the main guest will be and the approximate date the gathering will be held. Once it has been determined that the date will be convenient for the main guest the *teishu* will either visit the main guest (*shōkyaku*) personally to issue the invitation or write. Thought is also given to inviting other guests who will be pleasant companions for the person being honored. Often, the main guest is asked to suggest the names of friends whose company he might particularly enjoy. Once invited, all the guests are expected to respond to their invitations promptly in writing (or by telephone these days).

The host then begins making more definite plans. If he does not have a tearoom, arrangements must be made for access to a fitting location. Often teahouses, which belong to clubs, can be used. Temples also frequently have tearooms or teahouses that can be used in exchange for a donation. Today, even some hotels or restaurants have *tatami* rooms for rent. An alternative may be to hold a tea gathering outside (*nodate*) or in a western-style room. Once the guest list and location for the gathering are secure, the host can turn his thoughts to creating a specific character for the *chaji*. This involves deciding on the theme that will be symbolically and aesthetically expressed through the *toriawase*. Major consideration is given to the season and to the preferences and interests of the *shōkyaku*. If, for example, the main guest is a fan of the *Nō* drama, certain themes from his favorite drama may be suggested by the decorations on the utensils or by their poetic names. Or, if some happy event such as a birthday or recent wedding suggests congratulations are in order, the host might employ symbols of felicity and longevity such as the turtle, the crane, and the pine.

Symbolic themes often suggest the use of specific utensils. These, in turn, determine the particular *temae* to be used. Everything from the flowers to the menu for the *kaiseki* will be carefully coordinated to create the desired atmosphere and convey the messages that the host wants to send. In the interests of spontaneity, some decisions will be left to the last minute. The availability of particular food ingredients or flowers cannot be totally predicted.

A day or so before the actual gathering, the guests recon-firm their understanding of the date and location along with their intention to attend (*zenrei*). In traditional times this was always done with a visit to the home of the host. The guest came with the excuse of bringing some small gift (a food item, for example). Today, this is sometimes done by telephone. (Even so, as houses are unnumbered and streets are winding in Japanese neighborhoods, it is a good idea to go in person to make sure one knows the location of the *chaji* if it is held in an unfamiliar location).

About this same time, the host who is having the gathering at home, does the heavy cleaning, gardening, unpacking of utensils (which are usually kept in boxes), ash preparation (*haigata*), some shopping and some preliminary food prepara-tion. The morning of the event, he or she does last minute shop-ping (buying fish for example), final cleaning, fetching water, *kaiseki* cooking, preparing the flowers and flower container for *chabana* and arranging the utensils in the tearoom and prepara-tion area (*mizuya*). (It should be becoming obvious why it takes so much training to learn to hold a successful *chaji*). The host is usually aided by one or more assistants.

Just before the guests are due to arrive (which is at least fif-teen minutes before the *chaji* starts), the host once more sweeps the path leading from the main house gate to the foyer (*yoritsu-ki*) and sprinkles it with water (*uchimizu*).[2] Sprinkling water on the path is a *Shintō* act of ritual purification. Because it helps define sacred precincts (contributing to the construction of a cosmic model), evokes ancient tradition, and is considered uniquely Japanese, sprinkling water may be considered a con-firmatory act. Sweeping, on the other hand, is associated with Buddhist injunctions to cast off the dust or impurities of earthly life. It anticipates a transition to life on a higher plane and is, therefore, a transformatory symbol.

If the guests were to arrive and discover that the main gate was still closed and the path was not sprinkled, they would know the host was not prepared for their arrival. Performing this simple act and opening the main gate shows everything is in readiness. Thus, *uchimizu*, which also conveys a feeling of cleanliness and coolness, and an open gate have come to symbolize welcome.

Chapter 10

The Event Begins

THE GUESTS ARRIVE

*T*he tea gathering begins with the arrival of the guests at the host's main gate. This is where ritual behavior becomes the rule and the guests assume learned and "extraordinary" attitudes toward each other and the host. Symbolic communication also starts at the main gate as does the host's responsibility for the guest's comfort and emotional well-being.

The host does not greet the guests at the door: They simply walk through the open gate and proceed to the area (*yoritsuki*) where they will remove their coats and leave any packages or umbrellas they are carrying. In traditional times, samurai would divest themselves of their long swords in the *yoritsuki* and some retainers would wait there. (Others might continue to the *machiai* or tearoom depending on their rank).

Today the *yoritsuki* is simply a small room used for straightening kimono and putting on fresh *tabi* (traditional split-toe Japanese socks). Male guests may put on *juttoku* (a short black jacket worn in the tearoom by qualified individuals) or *hakama* (formal divided trousers for wear over kimono). Correctly attired, the guests arrange the articles necessary for use in the tearoom in their *kimono* breasts and sleeves and set street wear neatly to one side. It is also customary to leave an envelope with a small contribution from each guest in the *yoritsuki*. The money is supposed to help defray the kitchen expenses (*mizuya mimai*). The behavior among the guests even in the *yoritsuki* is particularly refined. Matters of precedence, polite speech, and

141

mutual consideration are treated in a manner that is different from that of ordinary daily life.

SYMBOLISM IN TRADITIONAL CLOTHING AND ACCESSORIES FOR TEA

Here it is appropriate to digress a little and talk about the symbolism connected with traditional Japanese clothing and objects carried into the tearoom. This discussion is intended to help the reader understand the symbolic communication that takes place between individuals attending tea events even before greetings are exchanged. Details of traditional dress can always be counted on to reveal the wearer's identity and confirm his or her status within Japanese society in general and the Tea world in particular.

Men's *kimono* are usually brown, blue, gray, or black. Certain weaves in the *obi* (belt) are suggestive of particular occupational groups such as monks. Inner *kimono* are of a dark color. Zen clergy (including monks and the [o]iemoto in his capacity as an abbot) are the only men who wear white collar lining. White *tabi* are always worn for tea. Preferred men's *kimono* materials are hemp or lightweight silk for summer and heavyweight silk for winter. The material of inner *kimono* and the use of lining also vary seasonally. *Kimono* cost about as much as western business suits (with the same range in price and quality). Cheaper polyester and wool or cotton blends are often worn for practice.

Kimono are worn in the tearoom because they are more comfortable for sitting in Japanese fashion and because they encourage correct posture and style of movement. (In a bit of symbolism which is not unique to Tea, *kimono* are always wrapped with the left side over the right in front, except when worn by a corpse or someone about to commit *seppuku*. The symbolic implications of wrapping one's *kimono* incorrectly should be obvious.)

As mentioned previously, *juttoku* or *hakama* are frequently worn in more formal tearoom situations. The *juttoku* should not be worn by men who do not have their *chamei* (tea name). (When the [o]iemoto awards a tea name, he often grants men the separate privilege of wearing *juttoku*.) There are two exceptions to this rule: (1) the *juttoku* worn by Buddhist nuns as part of their habit, and (2) those of some very senior female instructors (*gyōtei*).

Monks and nuns usually participate in Tea in the habits of their orders. The colors of their outer robes indicate their rank. (Purple is the highest.) Some men in the Tea world take holy orders and also maintain their status in other capacities within the Tea world (male members of the Sen family, for instance). If they have not totally retired to the monastic life, they do not wear emblems of holy orders unless performing *kencha* or *kucha.*

Women's *kimono* for tea are ideally more subdued in color and design than those worn for festivals or parties. *Kimono* of unassuming character are chosen so that attention remains focused on the event rather than on the appearance of the participants. A tea *kimono* differs from a dance or formal *kimono* in that the sleeves are shorter and the front panel is wider. Shorter sleeves are more practical for making tea and the wide panel helps the *kimono* to stay wrapped when getting up and down from one's knees frequently.[1] Like those of men, women's *kimono* vary in material from season to season as do linings, inner *kimono*, and *kimono* motifs.

Particular types of *obi* material and style are also specific to the season and degree of formality. While there are various ways of tying *obi*, the only proper *obi* knot for wear in the tearoom is the *taiko* (the drum knot that usually signifies the status of married women). This applies to both married and unmarried women. The elaborate knots commonly worn by unmarried women are felt to fall into the same category as brilliantly colored *kimono:* They draw attention away from the character of the gathering to the individual. Exceptions to these general principles are sometimes made for particularly festive occasions such as those of flower-viewing and the New Year. At these times, festive *kimono* enhance the gorgeousness of the event.

Different colors and patterns of dress are appropriate for each age group (specific to about ten year increments). Very young girls wear the gayest *kimono* usually in pink cr peach tones. However, they should not wear the gaudy patterns that are appropriate to their age group for parties and festivals that take place outside the tearoom. Nor should they ordinarily wear the "butterfly" or other fancy *obi* knots characteristic of young Japanese girls. Flashy hair ornaments or flowers are considered inappropriate for similar reasons. Girls can show more *obiage* (a cloth that peeps out of the top of the *obi*) and more nape of the neck (a sensuous line in Japanese aesthetics) than older women. They can also wear the *obijime* (a belt which goes over the *obi*) higher. On the whole, however, this subdued dress is symbolic of the seriousness of a young lady's approach to Tea.[2] *Kimono* are supposed to be unobtrusive. Tea teachers teach students to focus on the guests, not on themselves.

Older female tea students and instructors wear increasingly quiet patterns and colors according to their age. Certain types of black *kimono*, however, are worn only for funerals or memorial services and for weddings. The two kinds of black *kimono* for formal occasions such as weddings and funerals are distinct (as are their accessories). Married women's most formal *kimono* are black with a colored band of pattern at the hem. The *obi* that go with them are white with gold or silver details. Mourning *kimono* are plain black with white stitching and a black *obi*. The manner in which the loose ends of the *obijime* are tucked under the rest of the belt are also significant. Two ends tucked under the *obijime* from the bottom indicate mourning and two ends tucked in from the top are for particularly happy occasions. For ordinary events and tea, one side is worn up and the other is worn down.

At the Tea world's most formal events, Tea instructors and students usually wear *montsuki* (kimono with their family crest). Typical occasions for wearing *montsuki* would be a visit to Konnichian (the headquarters of the *iemoto*), (*go*)*aisatsu* (formal greetings to the (*o*)*iemoto* usually performed at the first of each month), observing *kencha* or *kucha*, or making tea formally using the *daisu*. (They may also be worn to *chakai* and *chaji*.)

The *mon* is a family crest signifying the family (or originally, clan) to which one belongs. Today, various schools and occupational groups (such as *kyōgen* players) have *mon*. Most Japanese wear the *mon* of their own family at Urasenke headquarters. Women may wear the mon of their natal family until they are married or an unexplicit "women's *mon*." They usually wear their husband's family *mon* after marriage symbolizing their new affiliation.

There are four *mon* that symbolize certain statuses within the Sen family and the Urasenke organization. The *koma mon* is worn by male members of the Sen family (with slight variations among the three branches). It is a good example of a multivocal symbol because while it is now said to stand for the "flaming jewel of enlightenment" (a familiar image in Buddhist iconography), it was originally inspired by a *kōgō* (incense container) in the shape of a traditional top. Its name is written with characters that mean "solitary pleasure." Hideyoshi gave Rikyū permission to use this *mon*, the emblem of the Kinoshita family (a name among the many used by Hideyoshi at various times of his life). Since Sen males who are not in the direct hereditary line of the *iemoto* (i.e. not the head, retired head, or heir to the leadership of any of the three schools) are adopted out or take another name, the practical use of this *mon* is limited to a few individuals.

The *uzumaki mon* is worn by women of the Sen family. It represents the motion of spinning or the whirling of a top. It also symbolizes wind or water in motion. The inspiration may be linked to the domestic activities of women as they relate to spinning and sewing.

The *tsubo tsubo mon* was devised by Sen Sōtan at the time he divided the family property among his sons. They consist of three circles with a line indicating a lid on each. They represent *denbo*, balls of earth from the Inari Mountain which were tossed into the rice fields to please the gods. Later, *Shintō* offering vessels were made from this same earth to contain sacred water. They were round containers with pointed lids. Still found in Japanese *Shintō* shrines today, they are called *hōju* (treasure jewels). This *mon* represents the Urasenke *ie:* When the (o)*iemoto* presents a *chamei*, he usually confers permission to wear this crest.

The last *mon* with specific symbolism for the Sen family is the *ichō mon* or ginkgo leaf emblem. This *mon* is used more as a design motif than a family crest. Legend has it that Sen Sōtan planted a ginkgo tree near Konnichian and it became his favorite tree. According to legend, when a fire occurred in the neighborhood, the heat melted snow on the ginkgo. The water then dropped onto the roof of a famous teahouse and saved it from burning.[3] Subsequently, (o)*iemoto* began to use the ginkgo leaf as a theme on their *konomi*. It was considered a felicitous choice because of its resemblance to a fan (ever expanding good fortune) and the crane (felicity). When the *Tankōkai* (professional teaching organization of Urasenke) was formed, two ginkgo leaves became their insignia. Clearly, much information about a tea practitioner's status is symbolically communicated by his or her clothing. Orthodoxy in dress itself conveys a message of good training and respectability. There is, however, no point in discussing the question of expense and quality. *Kimono* are expensive and, no doubt, some judge social status through a quick assessment of the price of a *kimono*. Let us, instead, consider the objects the guests will take into the tearoom.

The most important accessory carried by the guest is his or her fan (*sensu*). Short swords used to be placed between *samurai* and their lords or allies during formal greetings. This indicated their readiness to defend their principles, families, lords, or allies. When Rikyū forbade the presence of swords in the tearoom (it was unlikely that the merchants ever greeted each other this way as they were not generally entitled to wear swords), an etiquette problem was created. The fan was substituted for the sword and greetings could continue smoothly.

The fan may also be interpreted as a *kekkai* or ritual divider of space. It defines the space of each individual as the area behind or in front of the fan. Fans are always placed in front of the guest when entering the tearoom or making formal bows (either to the host or to the scroll). They are never used for cooling oneself in the tearoom. To open the fan is considered aggressive and rude, like brandishing a sword. (Some martial arts forms use both ordinary and steel reinforced fans as weapons.) It is also impolite to let too much of the top of the fan show when it is put away in the top of the *obi* (for women): *Samurai* women carried their daggers in their sashes where female tea practitioners now carry their fans.

Tea fans are small (compared to dance fans, for example). They may be lacquered black or plain. Men's fans are slightly larger than women's. Designs are often inspirational such as "The One Hundred Maxims of Rikyū," designs of appropriate tea flowers for each month, or the *kaō* (artistic signature) of various (*o*)*iemoto*. When it becomes necessary to pass money to someone (as when one has forgotten to put a fee in a shared envelope, for example), it is wrapped in *kaishi* (special paper) and presented on an open fan.[4]

The next most important accessory is the *fukusa*. *Fukusa* are square silk cloths used by hosts at a tea gatherings to purify utensils. They are the emblem of the host just as the fan is the mark of the guest. However, the guest always carries a folded *fukusa* in his or her *kimono* breast to indicate a symbolic willingness to make tea at any time. One never knows if the host (particularly if he is an instructor) may have planned a tea ritual that requires the participation of guests such as *shichiji shiki*.

The color of the *fukusa* may also indicate the school affiliation of the guest. Women of the Urasenke school may use patterned or unpatterned *fukusa* of any color, although many teachers at Urasenke headquarters consider patterns in poor taste. They prefer unpatterned *fukusa* in red, orange, or pink tones. Purple may be employed for some of the higher *temae*. Men use purple *fukusa* most often. For special occasions, the foreign students at Urasenke (members of the Midorikai program) wear green *fukusa* at the request of the present (o)*iemoto*. The Omotesenke school prefers unpatterned orange *fukusa* for women. Heavy-weight, purple *fukusa* are also customarily used as backgrounds for displaying utensils in the *tokonoma* during tea gatherings.

Another smaller square of material is also kept folded in the breast of the *kimono*. It is called the "*kobukusa*." *Kobukusa* come in many patterns of woven silk. Some have floral patterns and others have stripes or checks. Some of these materials are the *konomi* of famous tea masters. Most have famous historical antecedents such as one that is modeled on the material that backs an ancient mirror in the Imperial Repository in Nara. Today, new designs are also being invented.[5] It is important to know the name of the pattern and its history as *kobukusa* are sometimes used by the host to convey particularly important (or hot) tea utensils. The guests may consequently ask the name of the material (*kireji*). Needless to say, the *kobukusa* selected by the host to convey a precious utensil to a guest is likely to be a planned part of his or her *toriawase*. The guest carries a *kobukusa* in order to be prepared to handle fine utensils with it.

The guest completes his or her set of tearoom accessories with items needed to eat sweets and wipe eating utensils. *Kaishi*, a pack of special soft, disposable papers, are used as a plate for sweets and to clean the *kaiseki* dishes at the end of the meal.[6] In addition, an individual spicewood, ivory, or silver pick (sometimes with a symbolic motif decorating the end) is taken in a case. It will be used if the host does not provide picks with the sweets. Finally, a moist *chakin* (linen wiping cloth) is carried in a moistureproof envelope in order to be prepared to wipe thick tea from the lip of the bowl after drinking.

Today, people also put plastic bags in one *kimono* sleeve (the right one for clean things) to dispose of any leftover bits of food or garnish. (This should not be necessary as all food should be eaten and nothing served should be inedible.) A handkerchief for wiping one's fingers dry after using the *tsukubai* (washing area in the *roji*) is also handy. If wearing western dress, the guests carry these items into the tearoom in a special purse-like bag (*fukusabasami*).

MACHIAI, KOSHIKAKE MACHIAI, AND OUTER ROJI

After preparing their dress and accessories for the gathering, the guests proceed to the machiai or waiting area. Many hosts prefer to use a room with *tatami* (Japanese-style straw mats) as a *machiai*, but a western-style room will do as well. Guests enter Japanese-style rooms on their knees, placing their fans in front of them. If the room contains a *tokonoma*, they go to inspect the scroll (*kakemono*, "hanging thing" or *jiku*, "words and phrases") they find there. The *kakemono* is usually something of a light character that suggests the theme of the *chaji*. A picture or delicate poem of a seasonal nature is appropriate. Perhaps, something like a *Nō* mask or a classical Japanese instrument will also be displayed nearby.

If the guests' order of precedence has already been established, they will sit in an arrangement that reflects their eventual entry into the tearoom. The relaxed atmosphere of the *machiai* will probably be enhanced by coverings spread to soften the *tatami:* In the winter, guests are usually seated on cushions. Heavy felt matting (*mōsen*) serves the same purpose during other parts of the year. For this imaginary *chaji*, let us suppose that the guests sit on *mōsen*. And, as the crisp fall weather has just begun, a small *hibachi* (charcoal heater) warms the room. The host also provides a tray containing traditional Japanese smoking materials (*tabako bon*) for his guest's enjoyment.

If the seating order has not been specified in advance (which sometimes happens when the individuals invited are peers), the guests must decide on the roles they will assume in the tearoom. The position of "first guest" is particularly critical since he or she represents the others in the symbolic dialogue. Consideration must also be given to the qualifications of the (o)*tsume* (last guest). This role is significant because it entails special responsibilities best dispatched by someone familiar with Tea etiquette. A good friend or relative of the host is often selected as (o)*tsume*.

The seating positions of the guests are usually determined on the basis of criteria other than experience in *chanoyu*—except when one guest is a tea instructor and the others are students. Sex (men are typically seated first at tea gatherings) and age are primary criteria. When guests are not familiar with each other and relative status cannot be determined on the basis of other information (such a job prestige, civic position, etc.), it is customary for the host or hostess to assign roles by asking the guests to sign a guest book in which his or her preferences have been indicated. This eliminates a potentially awkward situation.

Once the question of precedence has been settled, the attention of the guests may be directed to pleasant small talk, often inspired by the decorations in the tokonoma. (At this model autumn *chaji*, a painting of geese flying would be appropriate). The last guest has the responsibility of audibly closing the door to indicate that everyone is present.

Whatever the arrangement of the room, a tray with cups of plain [o]*sayu* ("white hot water") or a flavored beverage will be served. In summer, the drink may be ice water and, in spring, cherry-blossom "tea" is especially popular. Flavored *saké*, plum wine, or herbal Japanese drinks serve as possible "cold weather" alternatives. Plain hot water is always an appropriate drink because it gives the guests the opportunity to taste the water used to make tea. At this fictional *chaji*, a light chrysanthemum tea is served. Such beverages are usually presented in cups called "*kumidashi*." These modest vessels frequently bear a seasonal motif and, consequently, form part of the host's *toriawase*. In the case of the proposed gathering, the cups might be decorated with the *aki no semi*, an autumn cicada. The refreshments are taken to the door of the *machiai* by the *hantō*. The last guest serves the others. In winter time, a kettle and brazier are sometimes provided so that (o)*tsume* can serve hot water to his or her companions.

When their (o)*sayu* has been consumed, the guests proceed to the *koshikake machiai* (garden waiting bench).[7] Special soft sandals made from the sheathing of bamboo stalks are often provided for their use (*roji zōri*).[8] If it is raining, the well-equipped host might also supply *roji geta* (Japanese wooden clogs) and *roji gasa* (a type of straw umbrella without a handle that resembles a big hat).

The area of the *machiai* and the *koshikake machiai* is called the "*soto roji*" (outer *roji*). It is usually landscaped with trees, bushes, and stepping stones. It should never have a contrived or flashy appearance. Often the ground covering is sand with a few patches of moss. Particularly gorgeous visual effects (such as lavish flower beds, flowering cherries, or brilliant maples) are considered in poor taste. Moreover, while the outer *roji* should look well-tended and freshly swept, it is considered obsessive to pick up every fallen leaf. For an October gathering such as this one, a few fallen leaves are admired as a part of the event's atmosphere. As with the path to the *machiai*, the stepping stones are sprinkled with water to suggest purity (and coolness, if it is hot).

The *koshikake machiai* is an arbor that contains a bench. A privy (*setchin*) is often located nearby. If the privy is intended to be purely decorative (as some are), it is traditionally constructed of fresh wood with a floor of rocks and clean white sand. Since some *setchin* are of historic interest (such as the one in the waiting arbor at the Katsura Imperial Villa), the guests may want to inspect it. In this situation, it would be inconsiderate to foul the premises with practical use. A functional privy will be located nearby.

Prefacing a tea gathering with a tour of an ornamental privy often strikes westerners as peculiar. But, the custom was a regular feature of gatherings that took place in the early eras of Japanese tea ritual. At that time, there were both practical and symbolic reasons for viewing the *setchin*. In his classic work, *Chanoyu; The Japanese Tea Ceremony*, A. L. Sadler includes an account of an assassin found lurking in the *setchin*, and his tastefully quiet dispatch (Sadler 1962, 33). The impeccable cleanliness of both ornamental and functional privies is considered emblematic of the host's consideration for purity and for the comfort of his or her guests. Cleaning the privy also recalls Zen monastic routine. In monastic communities, performing such tasks is believed to promote humility.

The bench area of the *koshikake machiai* is supposed to be supplied with a second *tabako bon* and round straw cushions (*enza*). Usually, a fresh palm leaf broom hangs to one side of the structure. It symbolizes purity and the need to brush away worldly concerns. If the weather is very cold, "hand warmers" (*teaburi*, small braziers) and a small *hibachi* may be provided. A lantern (*roji andon*) lights the area during night and dawn *chaji*.

The main guest properly arrives at the bench first and arranges the *tabako bon* next to his seat. Out of consideration for other guests and humbleness, he also distributes cushions along the bench for the other guests. Characteristic of the customary Japanese combination of humility and deference, the main guest's seat may be a little higher or of finer material than the other guests. The stone on which he rests his feet may also be slightly elevated.

Now the guests sit quietly and attempt to compose their thoughts for the journey through the *roji*. They mentally prepare themselves to move from the liminal spiritual state of the *machiai* and outer *roji* to the state of suspended (or concentrated, depending on one's philosophical approach) reality of the inner *roji* and the tearoom.

Chapter 11

Physical Aspects of the Ritual Environment

THE INNER *ROJI*

*W*hen the host hears that the guests have arrived in the *koshikake machiai,* he leaves the tearoom through the *nijiriguchi.* Carrying a wooden bucket (*teoke*) of water which he has previously placed in an inconspicuous spot nearby, he moves slowly toward the water basin in the inner *roji.* This is the first time the guests see their host. The fact that he appears to them initially within the "inner" ritual precincts helps define his special role. Furthermore, his role as an intermediary between the transcendent and the mundane is confirmed through the act of providing a medium of purification to the other ritual participants.

The water that the host carries has ideally been drawn at dawn (preferably from a sacred or famous well or spring). Dawn water is called the "flower of the well" and is used to make offerings as well as medicine. Water drawn at night was traditionally considered poisonous (i.e. powerfully *yin*). The basin (*tsukubai* or *chōzubachi*) into which the bucket is emptied is usually made of stone but, a large clay bowl is sometimes substituted.[1] The size and height of the outside of the basin is dictated by the character of the *roji.* The basin should contain a volume of water that is slightly less than that carried in the wooden bucket. Some basins are made of carved stone decorated with archaic Chinese characters or the Guardians of the four directions. Others are simple stones with holes in the top.

153

A contained environment (ideally in half-shade) made up of special stones and a stone lantern (*tōro*) surrounds the washing area. The guest squats on a single large stone while using the basin. Located on either side of the basin are stones for the main guest's candlestick and for a hot water bucket (used by elderly guests in very cold weather). A fourth stone is sometimes located in front of the *tōro*. The host stands on it when lighting the lantern.[2] Its glow is called "the flower of the lamp," an auspicious sign of congratulations or celebration. Among the stones in front of the basin, a few pieces of broken roof tile may be found. These are reminders of the impermanence of material things (not a contrivance considering the fire and earthquake history of Japan). A special cedar ladle rests across the basin (*tsukubaibishaku*).

The host stands on the stone in front of the basin and places the bucket to his left. He crouches down (if the basin is the common low-type innovated by Rikyū), picks up the dipper, and sprinkles some water from the basin around the area. The act of crouching is called "*tsukubau*." It gives the area of the basin and its surroundings its name, "*tsukubai*." The host then dips more water to rinse both hands and mouth. This act is identical to the act of symbolic purification performed outside *Shintō* shrines. The host purifies his mind and spirit in this manner. Afterwards, he empties the rest of the bucket of water into the basin. Some water should overflow and wet the outside of the receptacle.

The guests, hearing the splashing water, sense both purity and coolness. They are also alerted to prepare to greet their host. When he has completed his ablutions, the host opens the middle gate (*chū mon*), which divides the inner and outer *roji*. Immediately, the main guest, followed by the others, rises to greet the host silently with a formal bow. This greeting signals the beginning of a new stage in the ritual. Most previous events (with the exception of filling the water basin and sprinkling *uchimizu*) related to conventional social intercourse. In opening the gate, the host symbolically clears the way to spiritual communion and potential enlightenment: A more intensely spiritual phase of the ritual now begins.

After greeting the host, the guests return to their sitting positions on the bench. The main guest apologizes to the second guest for going first and proceeds through the middle gate into the inner *roji* (*uchi roji*). The guests will pace themselves so that they move at a measured distance along the path. This spacing prevents them from piling up in a group at the entrance to the teahouse, creating an awkward moment that might spoil the atmosphere. Isolation also helps the ritual participants shift from their conventional social roles to that of their ritual personae.

The guests do not speak, but absorb the beauty of the *roji* and its meaning. The word "*roji*" has been the object of considerable discussion among tea historians. Apparently, the original characters for "*roji*" meant simply "road or alley." After the publication of the *Nampō Roku*, characters from the Lotus Sutra, which mean "exposed or dewy ground," were substituted. This indicates the word was first applied to the path to the tearoom by Rikyū. *Roji* comes from a verse in the Lotus Sutra that may be translated: "Escaping from the fire-stricken habitations of the Three Phenomenal Worlds they take their seats on the dewy ground" (Sadler 1962, 19). The phrase is found in a parable describing the flight of noble children from a burning house (of earthly passion) to an open spot (enlightenment) (Tanikawa 1981b, 34). Adherents of Tendai translate *roji* "land of heavenly purity" on the basis of this reading (Ishikawa 1970, 58).

Before it became a part of the specialized vernacular of *chanoyu*, *roji* was applied to particular areas with the precincts of Buddhist temples. Using it for the path to the tearoom was quite likely part of Rikyū's campaign to revitalize the transformatory aspects of *chadō*. A homonym for this ideograph also means *arawasu* or "reveal." *Roji* is sometimes translated "to reveal oneself naked" or "reveal one's true being" (*Urasenke Newsletter* [Spring 1976]) and, to complicate matters further, the Chinese character for "open" may also be read as "dewy" in Japanese. To the Japanese, the idea of a "dewy" path evokes a feeling of purity derived from the *Shintō* tradition of sprinkling *uchimizu*. For this reason, the inner *roji* is always dampened before a tea gathering.

The inner *roji* is supposed to look different from the outer *roji*. The way this atmosphere is created has been a matter of much aesthetic debate in *chanoyu* but the general consensus is that it should be very cool, mossy, and natural. For all its simplicity, a *roji* can be loaded (even overloaded) with symbolism: Pines represent longevity, and, bamboo means strength and resiliency. A group of three stones may imply the presence of three Buddhas or a vertical arrangement of rocks—a waterfall. On the whole, however, the symbolism in a tea garden is supposed to be restrained. Too many special stones, dry waterfalls, lanterns, and ponds make the garden fussy. As with the outer *roji*, spectacular shows of nature are out of place.

There are, nevertheless, a few symbolic elements present in nearly every Tea garden. First, the *roji* is angled, both to indicate that the path to enlightenment is not straight and to make it difficult for demons to follow. Second, a small pit containing a pair of green bamboo chopsticks and a few dry leaves can frequently be seen. This is the *chiriana* (dust pit). When cleaning the garden, the host usually places a few broken twigs and some leaves in this hole with the chopsticks (which are used to remove extraneous matter from the carefully tended moss before the arrival of the guests). The *chiriana* functions as a symbolic receptacle for the dust of temporal existence.

A final item of interest almost invariably found in the tea garden is the *sekimori ishi*, a heart-sized stone tied with black string. If a guest finds such a stone at the beginning of one of two intersecting paths, he knows that he should not follow the route blocked by the *sekimori ishi*. Its presence symbolizes the consideration a host shows for his guests and their deep spiritual relationship: By keeping a guest from taking a wrong path, the host shows his willingness to assist the former along the path to enlightenment.

Whatever their personal interpretations of the meaning of a walk through the *roji*, the guests continue their short stroll. As mentioned earlier, not every symbol is actively brought to mind by each individual in the course of a *chaji*. It depends on the personality and experience of the guest. What is clear is that the walk through the *roji* facilitates the transition from the mundane to the ritual personae. While the experience should be as natural as a stroll down a mountain path, it transcends time and space.

TEAHOUSE ARCHITECTURE

The atmosphere changes dramatically inside the middle gate. After purifying themselves at the *tsukubai*, the guests proceed to the door of the teahouse. If it is raining and the guest entrance is unprotected by eaves, they will hold *roji gasa* over each other as they enter.

Coming upon a teahouse toward the end of a *roji* is supposed to be like discovering a charcoal burner's hut at the end of a mountain path. Not all buildings for Tea are so humble. The type of building described as part of the environment of this model *chaji* is a classic, freestanding teahouse or "*sōan.*" This was the style preferred by *wabi* Tea men such as Jōō and Rikyū. It should be noted, however, that many tearooms are attached to buildings. Some have guest entrances that one approaches from the garden. These are considered informal (*sō*). Others can be entered from a standing position (although one does not usually do so) and are characteristic of the *shoin* style.

At this fictive *chaji*, the teahouse, which the guests at this ideal *chaji* approach, features a *nijiriguchi*, the crawling in entrance favored by Rikyū. A *katanakake* or sword rack is sometimes found near this type of entrance. Rikyū is believed to have designed this interesting object to encourage the *samurai* to leave their swords (and belligerent attitudes) outside the tearoom. Later tea masters added yet another architectural element evocative of the strict social hierarchy of the Momoyama and Edo periods. This is the *kiniguchi*, a full sized door created for the convenience of visiting nobles. It precludes the necessity entering the tearoom in a kneeling position.

The awkwardness involved in entering the teahouse through the *nijiriguchi* is intentional. The first guest stands on a large flat stone in front of the door and slides it open. (The door is freshly wiped with water to convey a feeling of purity.) He then places his fan on the *tatami* and slides in a few inches. The guest next removes the sandals (*roji zōri*) from his feet and turns slightly to stand them against the outside of the house. *Zōri* properly disposed of, the guest reverses direction to face the *tokonoma*. Then, he picks up his fan and stands (except in a very small room).

The dominant impression one has in entering a *chashitsu* is one of restful and very subdued light. The teahouse stands in contrast to ordinary Japanese household architecture in its lack of openness, a feeling ordinarily achieved by using *shōji* (sliding, full-length window panels). In teahouses, window openings are small and carefully placed to put light exactly where it will be most effective. Depending on the season, time of day, and the type of opening, the windows may be hung with moist *sudare* (reed blinds) and/or *shōji* panels. In the summer, *shōji* are sometimes replaced with special *sudare*-like reed panels. The ideal directional orientation of a teahouse is said to situate the *nijiriguchi* in the south wall and the *tokonoma* on the north wall.[3]

This particular October *chaji* will be held in a four-and-one-half mat tearoom. Its main features the *nijiriguchi*, a *tokonoma*, and the *sadōguchi* (full-length host's entrance). Since it is *furo* season, the hearth cut in the floor (*ro*) is covered by *tatami*. The brazier (*furo*) sits in the northwest corner of the room. The guests do not see the preparation area (*mizuya*). This is a room or part of a room that contains shelves for utensils in current use, a place to store charcoal, and a source of fresh water (either a jar alone or a jar under a faucet). The water jar rests on a drain area covered with a bamboo grid. The floor adjacent to the bamboo grid is wood. When the guests are in the process of being seated in the room, the host is in the *mizuya* making his final preparations for the ritual.

Once the guest is inside the tearoom in a standing position, he goes immediately to kneel in front of the *tokonoma*. He observes the scroll and any other objects that might be displayed there carefully. Then he makes a formal bow, stands, and walks to the area where tea is to be made. He also inspects the tea utensils he finds assembled there.

VIEWING THE *TOKONOMA* AND UTENSIL AREA

According to the *Teijōzakki* written by Ise Teijō (1715–1784), the origin of the *tokonoma* is to be found in an area called the "*oshiita*," an architectural feature of a Kamakura era Zen temple. It was quickly copied by the *samurai* and aristocracy as part of the *shoin* style. The *tokonoma* is usually a raised alcove of variable size. (It may also be a section of the wall that rises above a simple wooden board.) This area is the highest ranking part of a Japanese style room. For this reason, the main guest sits closest to the *tokonoma*. If a noble person (*kinin*) is present, he may sit directly in front of the alcove with his back to it.

When the guests for this *chaji* approach the *tokonoma*, they see a vertically hanging scroll. The words "*Jikishin kore dōjō*" (The direct mind is the training ground) are written on it in very dark ink with a strong, formal calligraphic style. The reader should imagine the *kakemono* (literally "hanging thing") was written by an old friend of the host who has taken holy orders as a Zen monk. The fictional host has chosen the hanging because it evokes the relationship of a novice to his chosen discipline. One might imagine that the message on this particular *kakemono* is relevant to the occasion because the main guest is a former tea student of the host. The mounting is done in simple, plain materials and the colors are subdued.

The scroll is the highest ranking object in the tearoom. Its symbolism encompasses far more than the calligraphy (*kakeji sho*) or painting (*kaki e*) it physically represents. Equally important is the character of the author. Practitioners bow to scrolls because such works symbolize the presence of the author, his values, teachings, and often, his contribution to *chadō*. Even simple "thank you" notes from great figures in tea history are considered inspiring.

Scrolls are ranked *shin*, *gyō*, and *sō*. The original system for ranking such hangings was established by the *dōbōshū* during the Ashikaga period. The most formal *kakemono* were labeled *shin*; semiformal were called "*gyō*"; and informal were called "*sō*." Today, ranking takes into consideration the age of the scroll, its subject matter, its authorship, and its historical associations.[4]

The nature of the brush strokes, the style of mounting, intensity of ink, and the choice of background papers all form part of the message the writer wishes to convey.[5] Calligraphy is particularly suited to Tea because of its transience. Once the ink is applied to paper, there can be no changes. There is only one moment and one chance (*ichi go, ichi e*) to produce an effective painting or a good specimen of calligraphy. Tea practitioners are taught to regard each tea ritual as the same type of unique opportunity.

Various items besides the *kakemono* are frequently displayed in the *tokonoma* during tea ritual. They always have some symbolic import. Sometimes a *kōgō* (incense container) is presented on a folded pack of special paper. This signifies that the host will abbreviate the gathering by eliminating the charcoal ceremony (a common omission when an electric heater is used for a *chakai*). The *kōgō* is included despite the fact that incense will not be added to the fire in front of the guests because the container remains a significant part of the host's *toriawase*. If the gathering celebrates the presentation of a new tea certificate, the relevant document may also be displayed in the alcove. Sometimes special arrangements are created for memorial teas, New Year's celebrations, or to featuring specific tea utensils (*kazari mono*).

After viewing the *tokonoma* the guests cross the tearoom diagonally and view the area where tea will be made. First, the guests examine the brazier, the kettle, and the ash. If a *tana* (tea stand) is used, they will also inspect it and the utensils it holds. Sometimes a screen is placed between the tearoom wall and tea equipment. If so, the guests also have the opportunity to examine this accessory. For the sake of simplicity, let us assume that only a brazier (*furo*) on a lacquered board and a kettle (*kama*) are displayed. The *kama* can be visualized as an iron kettle of the "crane's neck" type. The brazier for this particular gathering might be a black ceramic *furo* called the "*Dōanburo*" (a style favored by Dōan, Rikyū's eldest son).[6] Such *furo* are properly presented on ridged black lacquer boards called "*arame ita.*" The host at this imaginary *chaji* has arranged the ash in the *nimonji* (meaning "character two") style. There are many ways of arranging ash. The style used is determined by the type of *furo* employed, its size, the season, and the formality of the event. For *nimonji*, two parallel mountain ridges are represented at the front and back of the ash in the kettle. A little white ash has been sprinkled on the "mountains" to suggest coolness. A three pronged, iron tripod (*gotoku*, "five virtues") rises from the ash to support the kettle.

Under the three pieces of burning charcoal (*shitabi*) initially placed in the brazier, the trigram for water from the *I Ching* has been written in the ash. Since metal (the kettle and trivet), wood (the charcoal), earth (the clay brazier), fire, and water are all present; the Taoist material universe is portrayed in microcosm. Also embedded in the ash are some pieces of sandalwood incense (*byakudan, Santalum album*). They lightly scent the air.[7] The main guest views the ash with his hands in the position of a semiformal bow, but does not actually bow. After viewing the utensil area, the *shōkyaku* takes a temporary seat while all the other guests inspect the *tokonoma* and utensils. The last guest makes sure the sandals are stacked neatly and closes the door loudly (a sign to the host that all are present). When they have all viewed the *tokonoma* and utensil area, the guests assume their designated positions in the room.

THE TEAROOM AS COGNITIVE MODEL

Tearoom design physically manifests the tension between the "confirmatory" and "transformatory" elements in *chanoyu*.

Shukō, Jōō, and Rikyū clearly identified their transformatory approach to Tea with the small or *wabi* tearoom. *Wabi* teahouses contain four-and-one-half mats or less. They often have thatched roofs, clay walls, and are constructed of inexpensive (as contrasted to rare and costly) materials such as cedar, bamboo, paulownia, and pine. Such teahouses evoke the classic abode of the Buddhist recluse. They are also called *"sukiya"* ("abode of fancy," "abode of the asymmetrical," and "abode of the void") (Young 1970, 37).

While the size of tearooms (*chashitsu*) can vary from one-and-three-quarter mats up (although not more than eight are commonly used), the classic standard for a *wabi* room is a four-and-one-half area called the *("yojōhan)."* This is said to be the same size as the dwelling of Vimalakīrti, (Yuima in Japanese) a Buddhist Saint. According to legend, Vimalakīrti's hut accommodated the Four Deva Kings seated on their sacred mountains and thousands of *bodhisattva* when they came to hear him preach the *dharma.* Okakura Kakuzō identifies this as "an allegory based on the theory of non-existence of space to the truly enlightened." (Okakura 1956, 60). Thus, the *yojōhan* may be regarded as a model of the Buddhist cosmos.

Considering the Chinese origin of tea ritual, the Taoist elements in Zen, and the fascination with directional divination current during the early years of Japanese tea practice, it is not surprising to discover that the *yojōhan* also serves as a cognitive model of the Taoist universe. As indicated in Figure 11.1, a four-and-one-half mat room can be divided into nine equal segments. Each of the eight peripheral segments is then assigned one of the trigrams originally suggested by Chinese tortoise shell divination. The middle square is the abode of the Tao. Each of the eight trigrams is further associated with a direction, an attribute such as wind, water, fire, and so forth, and a virtue such as strength, pleasure, and so forth (Williams 1974, 149).

The relationship between the virtues associated with the eight peripheral segments of the *yojōhan* and the tea activities that take place on them is suggestive. Guests enter from the direction associated with flexibility or penetration. The main guest sits on the mat segment linked with resting. The host makes his entrance from the direction of submission and sits on the segment related to pleasure. Tea is prepared in the area of the room connected with strength and power and the complet-

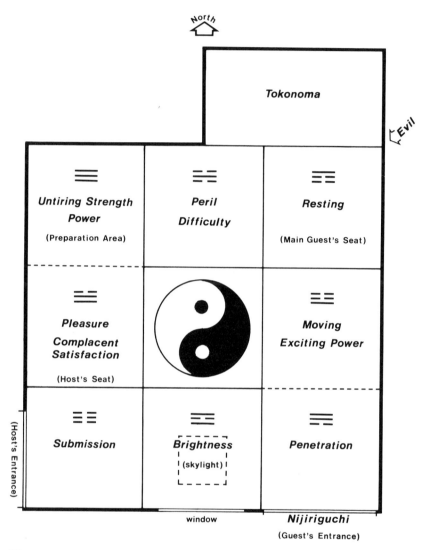

North

Evil

Tokonoma

☰	☵	☶
Untiring Strength Power	Peril Difficulty	Resting
(Preparation Area)		(Main Guest's Seat)

☱		☳
Pleasure Complacent Satisfaction		Moving Exciting Power
(Host's Seat)		

| ☷ | ☴ | ☲ |
| Submission | Brightness (skylight) | Penetration |

(Host's Entrance)

window   Nijiriguchi
              (Guest's Entrance)

Figure 11–1

ed bowl of tea is placed on the middle half mat assigned to the
Tao. The segment of peril or difficulty is normally left unused
in such a room.[8]

Possibly influenced by the memory of his grandfather's
regard for the Taoist cosmic model, Sōtan built a famous *yojōhan*
(Yūin, "Further Retreat") with both a window and a skylight
(*tsukiage mado*) near the mat segment devoted to brightness.

Sōtan also appears to have followed Japanese geomantic convention in leaving no opening in the northeast quarter of the room: (The northeast quarter was considered the source of malevolence by the Japanese, see Beardsley, et al. 1959, 78 for an extended discussion of Japanese geomancy.) Since Yūin is thought to have been built with careful regard for Rikyū's preferences, it seems quite possible that the master himself intended to synthesize spatial elements of Buddhist, Taoist, and native Japanese cosmic models within tea ritual's physical environment.[9]

Yūin is also exceptional in that it includes features subtly indicative of the fundamental equality of the assembled participants: In some other tearooms, the main guests' position is located under a section of the ceiling that is higher and of finer materials than other parts of the room while, the host sits under the lowest and most rustic area. Because of the interesting aesthetic effect achieved, ranked ceiling sections were sometimes incorporated into the tearoom designs of otherwise egalitarian tea masters. In Yūin, however, host and guest sit under a ceiling which is uniform in height and material. This, both literally and figuratively, adds a vertical dimension to the horizontal geomantic paradigm represented in the four-and-one-half mat room. Obviously a monumental amount of information about both the spiritual and social dimensions of the Transcendent are condensed in this nine foot square ritual space.

Chapter 12

Shoiri—*The First Half of the* Chaji

EXCHANGING GREETINGS

*W*hen the guests have taken their places, the host, who is seated, slides open the door of the preparation area and enters the tearoom on his knees. The eyes of the host and the main guest meet and every one makes a formal bow. The bow is a mirror of their respect for each other. The bow should be performed slowly and well to reflect their attitudes. The host then thanks the guests for coming and, one by one, they express their gratitude for being invited. At this point it is proper for the main guest to inquire about the scroll found in the *machiai*, both tobacco trays, and the cups in which the beverage was served. He also thanks the host for the beverage served in the waiting area. The host answers the main guests questions and then announces that he will bring the guests a light meal and closes the door.

THE *KAISEKI* MEAL

The food associated with tea gatherings is the flower of the Japanese cuisine. *Kaiseki* cooking has its foundations in *shōjin ryōri*, the cooking of the Buddhist temples. The two characters in *shōjin* mean "to progress spiritually" (Yoneda 1982, 33). The term was applied to temple vegetarian cooking because the patriarchs of Zen Buddhism believed the lessons, which led to enlightenment, could be learned in the course of performing even the most mundane tasks. The preparation of the simple meals, which fortified monks for long hours of meditation, was considered an ideal opportunity to learn self-discipline, thoroughness, and humility.

Tea masters who practiced Zen, such as Rikyū, could not fail to be influenced by the approach to food preparation taken in the Buddhist monasteries. The light meals served in these institutions were called *"yakuseki"* ("medicinal stones") because they served the same function as the hot stones placed inside monks' robes to fend off hunger during long hours of meditation.

The term *kaiseki* was originally written with characters meaning "sit together." These characters were later replaced with others pronounced in the same way but read *"breast stones,"* an allusion to the *yakuseki* of the temples. The Zen influence on tea cuisine survives in *chanoyu*'s emphasis on the frugal and aesthetic presentation of food (Sen, in Tsuji 1972, 12–13). The meal served during tea ritual need not be vegetarian although it is traditional to prepare such a repast at *Obon*.

Rikyū felt that the *kaiseki* should consist only of a bowl of soup, three dishes of vegetables, and some sweets.[1] According to extant menus, however, more dishes were commonly served even at Rikyū's own gatherings. One such menu (detailed in the *Nampō Roku*) tells of a meal served on October 1 to Hideyoshi in a two-and-one-half mat room. It consisted of miscanthus (pampas grass) soup, boiled salmon, trumpet seaweed, roast chestnuts, and mushrooms (all appropriately seasonal items) (Sadler 1962, 235).

General principles of the *kaiseki* require that all ingredients be of good quality and seasonal. They should not be especially expensive nor should they be exotic (because the guests may not like unfamiliar items). Foods should be attractively arranged and suit the dishes on which they are served. The cook should avoid excessive ornamentation such as elaborately carved vegetables and inedible decorations. Since etiquette requires the guests to wipe the empty dishes clean with the papers they carry in their *kimono*, anything uneaten (such as bones or garnishes) must be taken home in their sleeves, a potential inconvenience that may be avoided.

The *kaiseki*'s emphasis on frugality also theoretically precludes the presentation of lavish amounts of food as well as relying on caterers (unless there is no practical alternative). The components of the *kaiseki* should be balanced between vegetables and fish except at vegetarian meals. An attempt should also be made to incorporate all the usable parts of each food-stuff into the meal. For example if a plant is purchased with both edible leaves and roots, both should be used. This is symbolic of respect for living things and the determination not to waste anything. If the tastes of the main guest are known they should be considered.

Kaiseki meals of the most standard type are characteristically served on square black trays with matching sets of covered, lacquered bowls. These nesting bowls were probably originally suggested by those used in temples. If the meal is vegetarian, the trays and bowls supplied are often covered with a vermilion lacquer similar to the kind used at temples.[2] Utensil sets used for tea ritual can be distinguished from those of the monks by the black lacquer usually applied inside the top of the lid and the bottoms of the bowls. Some artistic touches such as a sprinkling of gold flecks on the plain black lacquer have become the *konomi* of individual *(o)iemoto*. Various other items of ceramic, wood, and glass contrast with the lacquer eating utensils and carry out seasonal themes.

When the host at this fictional October *chaji* is ready to serve the meal, he places a *shiki* (food tray) in front of him and opens the door to the tearoom. On the front of the tray are two covered bowls of slightly different sizes. In the one on the left, as it faces the guest, is a scoop of soft white rice in the shape of the character for "one" (*ichi mon ji*). This symbolizes that among foods, rice is first and holds the place of honor.[3] The other bowl is filled with *miso shiru*, a soup of soy paste and a stock (*dashi*) made from seaweed and bonito shavings. The cook has chosen to place a small grilled eggplant garnished with a dab of Japanese mustard and a bit of green vegetable in the soup. The eggplant is symbolic of the richness of the autumn harvest. Diminutive portions are served, emblematic of the hypothetically spartan nature of the meal.

On the back of the tray rests a third bowl (the *mukōzuke* or "opposite side dish") made of ceramic (an old Seto dish formed in the shape of a chrysanthemum might be used). In it, the guests see a mound of raw fish, cut in slivers and garnished with Japanese horseradish. It has been sauced with *yuzu* (a Japanese citrus) juice, soy, and *dashi*. A scattering of edible chrysanthemum petals and tiny pile of chrysanthemum greens (lightly cooked in *dashi*) add visual interest. Special cedar chopsticks originally designed by Rikyū rest on the tray in front of the bowls. They are only used once. Such chopsticks are always dampened. The clean, fresh wood suggests purity.

The host seats himself in front of the main guest and the *shōkyaku* slides slightly forward to receive the tray. He lifts it slightly and inclines his head to show appreciation. As he places the tray in front of himself, he apologizes to the next guest for preceding him. After everyone has a tray, the host kneels in the doorway and bows. He invites all to enjoy their meal. The guests bow and the main guest announces their intention to begin. When the host has closed the door, the guests take the lids off their rice and soup bowls and place them to one side. Symbolic of its importance, the rice is eaten first, then the soup. The seafood dish (*mukōzuke*) remains untouched.

After the guests have eaten a little rice and soup, the host reenters the tearoom carrying a black stand (*haidai*), which supports shallow, red *saké* saucers (*hikihai*). He also carries a small iron pot (*kannabe*) full of warm *saké*. The host sets the *haidai* in front of the main guest who takes the bottom cup and passes the rest down the line. The host then pours *saké* for each guest. The guests do not eat their raw fish until after they taste the *saké*.

The host leaves the room with the *saké* server and returns with a container of rice on top of which rests a shallow tray and a rice scoop. He offers to serve the main guest more rice, but he declines, saying that the guests will serve themselves. The host places the scoop in the rice and picks up the tray that was on top of the rice container. He then offers the main guest more soup. If the reply is in the affirmative he will take the bowl to the kitchen to be refilled. While he is out, the main guest takes the lid off the rice container and passes it to the others. The guests help themselves to additional rice and the host brings more soup.

The next course is the "star of the show." It is called "*wanmori*" ("piled up in the bowl") and it falls in the class of boiled foods (*nimono*). The bowls in which wanmori are served (*nimono wan*) are often quite beautiful. The ones used for this September *chaji* might be made of clear lacquer over dark, natural wood. The insides of such bowls are frequently lined with red or black lacquer. When the lids of these particular *wanmori* are removed and inverted, the guests will see red lacquer with a pattern of gold waves lining the top of the lid.

The smell of the *nimono* is as important as the taste. For a gathering such as this, it would be appropriate if the host were to arrange a shrimp ball, a little piece of green *yuzu* citron, a leaf of spinach, and a *shiitake* mushroom in a clear stock of the best quality *dashi*. The ingredients are carefully arranged with an eye to proportion and color.

The main guest is served his *wanmori* individually on a round tray. The other bowls are brought in a group on a long tray (said to be a timesaving convenience, not an example of status differentiation). The host returns to the door of the preparation area, sits, and advises the guests to eat while the dish is still hot. They bow to thank him and remove the lids of the bowls. While they are eating, the host refills their *saké* saucers.

Yakimono, broiled foods, are served as the next course. The course may include grilled meats but fish is the more common choice. For this gathering the reader might imagine that squares of barracuda (*kamasu*) are served. The fish is at its best in the fall. It has been marinated with soy and *saké*, skewered, and cooked on a *hibachi* over oak charcoal. The skewers have been removed and the fish arranged on a flat dish with a handle. The gold and muted green colors of the Oribe-style glaze suggest the transition from summer to autumn. Grilled foods are always served with fresh green chopsticks made in a special shape that indicates that they were made exclusively for *yakimono*.

The guests serve themselves, placing the grilled food in their empty *mukōzuke*. More rice and soup are offered but it is not customary to accept a third bowl of soup. (An additional bowl of food called the *"azukebachi,"* "entrusted dish" is sometimes served after the broiled food. It is supposed to use cooking ingredients leftover from the preparation of the other elements of the *kaiseki*.)

The host then announces that he will eat his meal in the preparation area and the main guest invites him to join the group. The host almost always refuses. He is there exclusively to serve his guests. He will eat in the tearoom only if there is a solitary guest. The commensal aspect of tea ritual will be manifested later when a *saké* cup is passed back and forth between host and guests. Westerners tend to find the absence of a shared repast surprising as commensal meals are central to our ethic of hospitality. Such is not the case in Japan.

After about fifteen minutes, if everyone is finished, the

guests wipe the inside of their *wanmori* bowls with the soft papers they carry in the breasts of their *kimono* (*kaishi*). The last guest then takes the rice container and other serving dishes to the door of the preparation area. Hearing this, the host opens the door and removes the dishes. Bowing, he says that his meal is finished and he hopes that they have enjoyed their food.

The course that follows is called "*hashiarai*," a name that means "chopsticks wash." It consists of a light broth (*kosuimono*) served in tall, lidded cups (*kosuimono wan*). A motif of red pine needles on a black lacquer background might be found on such utensils. (Since the pine is always green, these can be used in any season.) The broth is lightly flavored for this gathering with dried Japanese apricots (*umeboshi, Prunus mume*) and giant kelp (*konbu*). Some seasonal flavoring ingredient is usually added. This time, little balls of tapioca have been selected. The broth is used to wash the ends of the chopsticks and purify them for the next course. It also cleans the palate of the guest. As the *kosuimono wan* are served, the *nimono wan* are removed.

The next course is highly symbolic. It is called "*hassun*," from the size of the tray on which it is served. The *hassun* is an unlacquered tray of fresh cedar eight *sun* (23.5 centimeters) square. Such trays are used to make offerings to *Shintō* spirits (*kami*). Sen Rikyū is believed to have been the first to have used this serving piece for tea ritual. It is always moistened with water to suggest purity and is used but once in accordance with *Shintō* practice. Its dimensions are probably significant: There are sixty-four trigrams in the Taoist *I Ching* and sixty-four square *sun* in the tray.

On the tray, bits of food from the mountains and the sea are arranged. (They should be small enough to fit in the lid of the *kosuimono wan*.) Such morsels are heaped and stacked in very specific positions on the tray. The precise methods by which they are cut and piled are classified *shin, gyō*, and *sō* (formal, semiformal, and informal). The heap in front is supposed to be higher than that in the back so that seen in perspective, there appears to be equal amounts of each food.

One pile is customarily very casually arranged (*gyō* or *sō*), while the other is more structured. Needless to say color, texture, and shape are carefully considered. For this October meal the mountain delicacy is grilled chestnuts and the specialty from the sea is the meat from crab legs poached in *dashi*. These foods are always consumed with *saké*, a practice recalling the *Shintō naorai* ritual. At *naorai*, celebrants consume food and *saké* previously offered to deities in order to share their divinity. *Saké* is considered the essence of rice and the food of the gods.

Proffering the *hassun*, the host serves *saké* again to everyone. Then he returns to the spot in front of the first guest—as if to pour another round of *saké*. The *shōkyaku* instead offers to serve *saké* to the host. The host demurs saying that he has no saucer so the main guest offers to let the host use the one from which he has been drinking. When the host accepts, the *shōkyaku* wipes his saucer with his *kaishi* and places it on the *haidai*. While he is doing this, the host turns the *hassun* around and places it to his own left. The spout of the *saké* pourer (*kannabe*) is reversed and placed so the second guest can conveniently pour *saké* for the host. While the second guest pours, the main guest takes some of each food from the *hassun* and puts them on several folded sheets of *kaishi*. Then he replaces the papers on the *tatami*. The host usually does not eat these delicacies, but they are made available in the belief that this food must always accompany *saké*.

After the host drinks his rice wine (lifting the cup slightly and inclining his head to show his appreciation to the main guest), the second guest asks to share the same cup. The host asks the main guest if he (the host) can borrow the cup for awhile. The main guest consents and the host goes down the line of guests alternating drinking and pouring *saké* for everyone. While he does so, he distributes the mountain delicacy. This is called *"chidori no sakazuki"* because the zigzag motion recalls the motions of the plover as it runs over the sands.

Finished drinking with the last guest, the host returns the saucer to the main guest (after wiping it), refills it, and thanks him for its long use. The principle guest then pours one more cup for the host, saying that he would now like to have some hot water. The host places the *saké* saucer back on the stand, arranges the uneaten food in the middle of the *hassun* and places the *kaishi* with his uneaten tidbits on the tray. The host then exits with the tray and the *kannabe*.

The host returns with the final course of the *kaiseki* meal. This custom recalls the routine of the Buddhist temples. It consists of *yutō* (a broth of browned rice and salt water) and *kōnomono* (pickles). According to temple ethics, no food should ever be wasted. Since rice cooked over wood fires usually leaves a little brown crust in the bottom of the pot, this is scraped out, seasoned, and eaten as a variety of soup called "*yutō*." It is served in a utensil that resembles a lacquer coffee pot with a flat lid. The browned rice is removed with a matching ladle. *Yutō* freshens the mouth and can also be used to clean the last bits of food out of the remaining lacquer bowls. Impeccably clean dishes indicate respect for those who produced and prepared their contents.

A bowl of pickles accompanies the *yutō*—no Japanese meal would be complete without them. Since they are such a humble foodstuff, it is appropriate to serve them in rough native ceramics of a *wabi* character. The host for this gathering might select a gray bowl from the Karatsu area. It would be likely to contain several kinds of pickles such as those made from cucumbers, eggplant and giant icicle radish (*daikon*). *Daikon* pickles are always included. This kind is called "*Takuan*" after the monk purported to have invented them (Takuan, 1573–1645). *Takuan* are cut in a rectangular shape so that they can be used to clean the bottoms of the dishes.

When the host brings the *yutō* into the room, he removes the *kosuimono wan*. After the guests have eaten the *yutō* and pickles, they clean their empty dishes. When the last guest has taken the *yutō* tray and pickle bowl to the host's door and returned to his seat, the guests drop their chopsticks loudly on their trays in unison. This sound tells the host he may return to the room and collect the trays. The guests individually thank the host for the meal as he removes their trays. With the last tray in front of his knees, the host sits in the entry to the preparation area and closes the door to the tearoom.

SHOZUMI—THE FIRST CHARCOAL PREPARATION

When the host opens the door a few minutes later, the guests notice he has placed a basket containing implements used to repair the charcoal fire to one side. The charcoal container (*sumitori*) and ash dish (*haiki*) have been prepared in advance for the *temae* (*sumidemae*) that follows.[4] The *sumitori* contains eight pieces of charcoal made from oak (*kunugi*) and three pieces of white "branch" charcoal (*edazumi*). *Edazumi* is made from azalea twigs covered with a plaster-like substance. Each piece of charcoal has a name, specified dimensions, and a predetermined position in both the charcoal basket and the fire. The black charcoal has been washed so it is clean to handle. In addition to the charcoal, the *sumitori* holds a pair of metal chopsticks (*hibashi*), metal rings with which to move the kettle (*kan*), a feather brush (*haboki*), and an incense container (*kogo*).

Let us imagine that the host for this model *chaji* has selected a *sumitori* made from a Chinese-style vegetable basket (Rikyu's *konomi*). It has been lined with paper lacquered black so that the charcoal dust will not sift through. A feather has been laid across its rim. In October, it would be appropriate to choose the feather of a wild goose, evocative of autumn.[5] The host has suspended the metal rings (*kan*) from the chopsticks (*hibashi*) so that they hang over the edge of the basket. These are sometimes decorated with incised designs. One popular style of *hibashi* resembles the large needles used for sewing *tatami*.

The incense container rests on the largest diameter of charcoal (*kodai*) in the basket. The *kogo* selected for this particular gathering is round and lacquered black on the outside with a design of scarlet maple leaves. The inside is lacquered red. It is called a "*Tamukeyama kogo*" because it is evocative of a mountain outside of Nara famous for its brilliant autumn cover of maples. This style of *kogo* was prized by Tantansai. Three pieces of sandalwood incense have been placed inside.[6]

The incense used in *furo* season consists of small pieces of fragrant wood. Such incense is considered the original Chinese form of *ko* (incense). It is properly used with the *furo* because the brazier is considered Chinese also. In contrast, the *ro* is thought to be native. Thus, Japanese kneaded incense (*neriko*) is used in the fire pit.[7]

The host will also need a *haiki*, a shallow bowl about nine inches in diameter filled with a mound of white wisteria ash (*fujibai*). The ash dish for this particular gathering has a green glaze with gold slash marks in it. A special bronze ash spoon (*haisaji*) with a handle wrapped in bamboo leaf will be placed on its edge in the ash. The spoon is made in a size and style appropriate only for *furo* season. The host will carry the *haiki* and a thick pack of folded paper (*kami kamashiki*) into the room after he brings in the charcoal basket.

With the charcoal container at his side, the host announces that he will lay the fire and bows. (The brazier initially contains three pieces of burning charcoal, so he is repairing rather than starting the fire.) The guests make a formal bow at the same time. This marks the beginning of the first charcoal preparation (*shozumi*, "first charcoal"). Salutations accomplished, the host rises and enters the room carrying the charcoal basket. He places it to the right of the *furo* and returns to the preparation area to pick up the ash dish and kettle rest pad. He tucks the papers (*kami kamashiki*) into his *kimono* breast and reenters the room with the *haiki*. When he has been seated, he puts the ash dish next to the wall, slightly to his rear.

The host begins the *temae* by removing the utensils from the basket and arranging them on the *tatami*. Then he adjusts the lid of the kettle so it is completely closed. (It is usually left slightly ajar to allow steam to escape.) Women handle the lid using their *fukusa* as their fingers are felt to be more sensitive to heat than those of men.

Picking up the metal rings (*kan*), the host places them in the lugs of the kettle. He subsequently withdraws the kettle rest pad from his *kimono* and places it on the *tatami*. Grasping the *kan*, the host sets the kettle on the pad and slides the kettle with the papers underneath to his right. Replacing the *kan* on the mat, the host turns back to face the brazier. He then dusts the rim of the *furo* with the feather. The pattern of these purificatory strokes differs with the type of brazier used.

Once the *furo* has been dusted, the host uses the metal chopsticks to slightly rearrange the original three pieces of burning charcoal. He is then ready to add charcoal from the basket to the fire with the chopsticks. Another purifying sweep of the brazier follows. Finally, the ash spoon is used to remove a small scoop of ash from the front of the arrangement. This indicates that the ash formation (*haigata*) is to be used only once and symbolizes the imperfectibility of human efforts.

After giving the brazier a final dusting with the goose feather and replacing it on the *sumitori*, the host takes two pieces of incense from the *kōgō* and places one in the ash and another on one of the pieces of charcoal. The incense is considered a gift to the guests. The smell itself is believed to purify the room, a custom that probably came to Japan with Buddhism. The fragrance is supposed to be that of Buddha's paradise.

As the host replaces the lid on the incense container, the main guest asks to see it more closely (*haiken*). The host places the container on the *tatami* in a spot where the main guest can easily retrieve it. He then puts the kettle back on the *furo* and the *kan* in the basket. With the feather, he draws the *katakana* "*a*" (a type of Japanese syllabary character) on the lid of the kettle. The action is purifying and symbolic of "openness." He concludes the sequence by placing the feather on the basket.

After the host has returned the ash dish to the preparation area, the main guest comes forward to pick up the incense container and return to his seat with it. Then the host dusts the mat where the charcoal preparation took place with a large swan feather duster (*zabōki*). After he has left the room and closed the door to the preparation area, the guests examine the *kōgō*. When they have finished, the main guest returns the incense container. (The main guest is responsible to the host for the utensils that the guests are permitted to handle.)

The host subsequently enters the room and seats himself in front of the *furo*. He folds his *fukusa* and wipes the sides of the brazier and the lid of the kettle with it. When he completes this final gesture of purification, he opens the lid of the kettle and returns his *fukusa* to his belt. Then he turns to answer the main guest's inquiries about the shape and maker of the incense container.

Both parties sit facing each other in a respectful attitude with fingers on the mats as if performing an informal bow. At the end of the conversation, the host and main guest bow to each other and the host leaves the room with the *kōgō*. Once inside the host's door, he turns and seats himself with the incense container at his side. The host then announces that he will offer the guests some sweets.

OMOGASHI—THE MAIN SWEETS

Japanese sweets are called "(*o*)*kashi*" and sweets appropriate for tea ritual are called "*chagashi*." Originally, fruits and nuts were served before drinking tea, a practice that was thought to prepare the palate for what is sometimes described as a "bitter beverage." When refined sugar was introduced to Japan by the Portuguese, a whole new class of foods sweetened with sugar developed. Since both sugar and tea were high status imports, it is not surprising that they were served together. Sweets are served twice at a *chaji*. The main sweets (*omogashi*) that are offered before thick tea and dry sweets (*higashi*) accompany thin tea. (This discussion will be confined to moist sweets as dry sweets will be described later.)

There is a great deal of variety in the type of sweets served before drinking thick tea. Some *omogashi* have an interior of red or white beans mashed with sugar and an exterior of steamed or baked dough made from the flour of various plants. (The use of sweet rice flour, *mochi*, is particularly popular.) Other types of moist sweets are made completely from one or two kinds of bean paste or *mochi* formed in a multitude of shapes.

Most (*o*)*kashi*-makers are very artistic. Seasonal flavorings, shapes, colors, and ingredients are used to great advantage enabling some shops to stay in business making particular kinds of (*o*)*kashi* for hundreds of years. (*O*)*kashi* have specific poetic names and the guests may inquire about these and the maker during the tea gathering. If the host has made the sweets himself (a particularly thoughtful and somewhat uncommon gesture), he may assign a poetic name to his creation. The preparation and selection of sweets is part of the host's *tori-awase*. A sweet must have a name that evokes a particular seasonal or historic theme to be of value in Tea. Some instructors feel that the (*o*)*kashi* shapes should not be overly realistic as nothing is left to the guests' imagination.

There are three different types of utensils used to serve *omogashi*. The most formal type is a tier of lacquered boxes called "*fuchidaka*." These are usually covered with plain black lacquer, but great variety of finishes and design motifs provide additional interest. They are often the *konomi* of various (*o*)*iemoto*. A second type of container used for moist sweets only at *chakai* is the cake bowl (*kashibachi*). *Kashibachi*, too, are decorated with various seasonal motifs and come with many different glazes. Finally, individual plates or trays (*meimeizara*) in various shapes are sometimes used.[8]

To serve sweets, the host slides open the door to the preparation area. He then stands and conveys the container to a spot in front of the first guest. After placing the sweet container on the mat, he leaves the room. Seating himself briefly in the doorway, the host invites the guests to eat the sweets. Afterwards, he suggests, they may stretch their legs in the garden. The host then bows and closes the door.

If the *fuchidaka* is used, one sweet will be found in each tier (if there are five guests or less). The lid of the top box is usually sprinkled in summer with water to suggest coolness and purity. The sweet picks (*kuromoji*), resting on the lid, are always moistened. The picks are meant for one time use and may be kept by the guests as souvenirs of the gathering.

The main guest lifts the whole *fuchidaka* to show appreciation and turns the top boxes diagonally on top of the bottom box. This enables the first guest to slip a *kuromoji* into the bottom box. He then passes the top boxes to the next guest who repeats the action. Each guest uses a pick to place a sweet on top of their *kaishi*. (They place their packs of folded papers on the *tatami* in front of their knees just prior to removing the sweets from the box). The guests eat their sweets simultaneously.

The host for this October gathering has chosen to serve a sweet called *"Hagi no Tsuyu"* ("Dew of the Bush Clover"). These sweets called *"kinton"* are made of a type of bean paste. The bean paste is easily tinted and for this event the outside layer (rubbed through a sieve and applied in short strings with bamboo chopsticks for textural interest) has been colored green. The inside has been made pink. Crystals on top suggest the dew on *hagi* (a bush clover with pink blossoms that blooms in the fall). The sweets have been made by the host.

After the *omogashi* are finished, the guests will examine the alcove, brazier, and kettle. They then leave the room through the *nijiriguchi*. (The main guest leads as usual.) The last guest returns the cake box to the door of the preparation area and closes the *nijiriguchi* with an audible sound. This alerts the host to return to the room for further preparations.

Chapter 13

The Break and the Return to the Tearoom

REFLECTING ON *SHOIRI*,
THE FIRST HALF OF THE TEA RITUAL

*T*hus far, most of the ritual participants' behavior has been associated with the model building or confirmatory element of the event: First, the guests arrived at the host's home dressed in *kimono*. Certain aspects of their clothing indicated their status as tea practitioners and as members of Japanese society at large. Second, when the guests passed through the front gate, they found the path freshly dampened. But, neither wearing *kimono* nor sprinkling *uchimizu* is unique to tea ritual. *Kimono* are worn in many Japanese social arenas and *uchimizu* can even be seen on the sidewalks outside some stores. These behaviors serve primarily to establish the ethnicity of the event that follows.

In contrast, the acts that occurred in the changing room (*yoritsuki*) were almost purely utilitarian. The guests removed their street clothing and changed to clean *tabi*. Only the fact that they inserted *fukusa, kobukusa,* and *kaishi* in their *kimono* breasts indicated something out of the ordinary was about to happen. Later, in the waiting area (*machiai*), the ritual practitioners accepted and began to function in their assigned roles. The last guest, for example, served chrysanthemum tea to the others.

The transition from everyday to ritual behavior intensified with the stroll through the outer *roji*. Rikyū envisioned this as a transformatory act and tea practitioners are generally aware of its special significance. After allowing the guests a brief respite in the waiting arbor (*koshikake machiai*), the host confirmed his role as ritual officiant by filling the *tsukubai* with water. His ablutions and those of his guests were their first active gestures of involvement with the religious aspect of tea ritual.

Passing through the inner *roji* and *nijiriguchi*, the guests were symbolically purified and transformed into their ritual personae. Subsequently, every gesture and word contributed to the collective ritual effort. Previous training made all the participants aware that they were operating on a "ritual plane" and within sanctified boundaries. Comprehension and interpretation of the origin, meaning, and importance of specific symbols, nevertheless, varied.

The greetings that preceded the meal (*kaiseki*) served a confirmatory function. By exchanging a few words with each ritual participant, the host, as officiant, symbolically verified their mutual intent to engage in ritual behavior. Serving and eating the *kaiseki* meal involved all the participants in a collective act of ritual world maintenance. This behavior closely resembles that associated with "first fruits" and "commensal" food rituals conducted throughout the world. But, because it emphasized the central role of rice, included raw fish, and was eaten with chopsticks, this particular meal reinforced the ethnic identification of the Japanese that shared it. The strongly native character of the cuisine and the presence of *saké* created a sense of communion with the spirit of the land characteristic of the *Shintō naorai*. The only aspects of the *kaiseki* associated with the transformatory character of the *chaji* pertained to the culinary philosophy of the Zen monasteries. Rikyū also tried to incorporate the ideals inherent in his concept of *wabi* Tea into the *kaiseki* by recommending it be restricted to a spartan "one soup and three dishes."

The main function of the charcoal *temae* (*shozumi*) was to heat water for making tea. The procedure did, however, contain symbolic elements that advanced both the confirmatory and transformatory goals of the *chaji:* For example, the presence of the "five elements" in the brazier and associated materials suggested the Taoist cosmic paradigm while burning incense ("the scent of Buddha's paradise") evoked transformatory aspects of Buddhist philosophy.

In sum, during the first half of the *chaji*, a great deal of time and energy were invested in collective model-building. An image of an ideal society (with defined ethnic boundaries) was carefully constructed. Much less attention was devoted to the transformatory aspects of tea ritual. Nevertheless, with the actors' roles assigned and the stage set, we may anticipate observing more dynamic efforts to modify the cognitive structure during the second half of the ritual.

NAKADACHI—THE MIDDLE BREAK

Returning to the fictive *chaji*, we find the guests have passed through the inner *roji* and assembled at the waiting bench (*koshikake machiai*). The guests may now go to use the toilet or smoke. While they are gone, the host, with the help of his assistant, prepares the tearoom for the second half of the gathering, which is called "*goza*" or "*goiri*." Their activities include closing the lid of the kettle to raise the water temperature and eliminate some of the precipitation from the bottom of the lid, adding incense to the fire, removing the scroll from the *tokonoma*, and sweeping the room.

Toward the end of the break, the host arranges flowers in the *tokonoma* and opens the kettle. Finally, he strikes a gong (*dora*) to summon the guests from the *koshikake machiai* (five times for five guests or less and seven for more). (If the gathering had been held at night, a clapperless bell, *kanshō*, would have been used.)[1] Hearing this sound, the guests squat with hands at their sides in the waiting arbor to show their respect, a physical attitude assumed by monks when called to a spiritual interview with their Zen master. The guests then repeat their journey through the *roji*, stopping to purify themselves at the basin (*tsukubai*) as before. They enter the tearoom in the previously established order of precedence.

TEA FLOWERS AND THEIR CONTAINERS

After negotiating the *nijiriguchi*, the guests will once again examine the *tokonoma*. This time it contains a flower arrangement instead of a scroll. Placing flowers in a place of honor such as the alcove of a tearoom reflects the *Shintō* belief that all living things contain a divine spirit. It is thought, however, that the actual custom of arranging flowers as an offering to the gods came to Japan with Buddhism in the sixth century.

Early techniques of flower composition (the *rikka*-style) were quite structured. After all, the flowers placed on altars were offerings to the deities, not casual decorations. Large arrangements were felt most suitable for the paired vases, which flanked holy images. The symbolism of the three main floral design components was standardized at this time. The tallest group of flowers was said to represent heaven, the middle stood for man (and/or Buddha), while the lowest symbolized earth.

By the Muromachi period the Japanese love of asymmetry had asserted itself once again. *Shoin* decorations often included only one candle, one incense brazier, and one flower arrangement. This configuration was described by observers of the tea-tasting competitions. Another method of flower arranging, the *nageire* or "thrown in" style, was also developing at this time. It offered a casual alternative to the more rigid *rikka* structure.

Influenced by *wabi* tea masters such as Jōō and Rikyū, *nageire* technique was further refined. The elegant and strictly ordered approach favored by the nobility for *shoin* decoration was called "*seika.*" The more modest style of flower arrangement preferred for tea ritual became known as "*chabana.*" (Mittwer 1974, 32).

As part of his effort to make Tea more spontaneous, Rikyū (inspired by Jōō and others) transformed the art of arranging flowers for the tearoom. His basic tenet was that flowers should be presented as they grow in the fields. Flower arrangements with artificial structural supports and exotic flowers were deemed too demanding for *wabi* tea. Rikyū stressed a more natural approach. He often displayed wild flowers in "found" objects such as baskets, gourds, and sections of bamboo.[2] He also favored hanging containers as an alternative to more rigid standing arrangements of the *shoin.*

Today's *chabana* stresses composition techniques that are less contrived than those of most flower-arranging schools. Pronged, metal supports for flower stems and wires are not used in the tearoom. Flowers found growing wild or grown at home are preferred. To arrange them, the host picks flowers considered seasonally appropriate and holds them in an attitude that reflects their relative heights and natural disposition (grass flowers are placed below tree flowers, for example). When satisfied with the proposed design, the practitioner places the flowers in a container where they may be slightly rearranged.

The number of flowers in a vase should be odd (if more than two blossoms are used), stems should not be crowded, and leaves should not rest on the edge of the vase. Lavish displays of five to seven elements are reserved for the end of summer and beginning of autumn when flora grows in profusion. In winter or spring, a single blossom is considered adequate.

Of course, there is more to *chabana* than meets the eye. Flowers, flower containers and the boards on which they rest (in a *tokonoma* with a *tatami* mat floor) are all ranked in formality (*shin, gyō,* and *sō*). The type of flower, the style of arrangement, and the character of the vase must be selected with care. If flowers are to be displayed in the *tokonoma* with a scroll (as at *atomi chaji* or a lesson), the formality of the arrangement should be coordinated with the status of the hanging and the architectural environment.

The most formal types (*shin*) of flower containers are those of bronze, which include *sutra* containers, Chinese ceramics, and certain old Korean wares. Japanese copies of the originals are classified with the wares they imitate. These containers are placed on highly polished, black lacquer (*shin nuri*) boards with notched edges (*yahazu ita* or "arrow notch board"). Glazed Japanese ceramics are considered *gyō* (semiformal) and displayed on black lacquer boards with edges like those of clamshells (*hamaguriba ita*). Most other containers (unglazed Japanese ceramics, bamboo, gourds, and some vases of southeast Asian manufacture) should be set on moist, unlacquered cedar boards (*kiji hamaguriba ita*).

If the status of the *hanaire* has not been firmly established (*raku*, cut glass, and most western vases remain unclassified) a round, black lacquer board with a clamshell edge is used (*maru kōdai*). Baskets are never placed on boards as they enclose waterproof bamboo containers. In this instance, the baskets themselves function as boards. Bamboo vases, gourds, and unglazed ceramics are always sprinkled or soaked in water to convey a feeling of coolness and purity.

Some flowers are ranked like *hanaire* and boards. The camellia (probably because of its botanical relationship to tea), some varieties of chrysanthemum (the emperor's symbol), the peony (quintessentially Chinese), and the lotus (Buddha's flower) are all high-class floral specimens. They are generally displayed in the most formal (*shin*) containers. In contrast, grasses and many wild flowers are considered lower in status and used mainly in informal (*sō*) arrangements.

A few kinds of flowers are generally avoided in *chabana*. The pot marigold is eschewed because it is reminiscent of Buddhist memorial altars. Rape (*Brassica napus*) is not used except for *Rikyūki* due to its association with Rikyū's last tea. Cherry blossoms lack subtlety and are often made superfluous by the riot of bloom seen outdoors. In addition, odoriferous flowers such as daphne are avoided because their smell overpowers the incense used in the tearoom. Other flowers, rejected because their names elicit thoughts that threaten tea ritual's spiritual ambiance. For example, *"kōbone"* includes the word for "bones" and *"kinsenka"* brings "money" to mind. (Hirota 1980b, 45.)

When the guests examine the *tokonoma* for the second time at this model September *chaji,* they see an arrangement of five autumn flowers—Japanese pampas grass (*susuki, Miscanthus sinensis*), burnet (*karaito sō, Sanguisorba officinalis*), smartweed (*mizuhiki sō, Polygonum filiforme*), pigeonberry (*yōshu yamagobō, Phytolacca americana*), and pink (*kawara nadeshiko, Dianthus superbus*).

Pampas grass and the pink are often celebrated in Japanese poetry. Pampas grass is associated with the autumn full moon and the pink with the fragile beauty of young Japanese girls. They are two of the famous "seven grasses of autumn," which also includes *hagi*, arrowroot (*kuzu, Pueraria lobata*), patrinia (*ominaeshi, Patrinia scabiosasaefolia*), hemp agrimony (*fujibakama, Eupatorium fortunei*), and the balloon flower (*kikyō, Platycodon grandiflorum*).[3] The host has placed the flowers in a moist basket which is a copy of one preferred by Sensō (fourth generation grand master of Urasenke). The original was made by Hisada Sōzen (1647–1707). As the container is a basket, no board is needed.

VIEWING UTENSILS USED FOR *KOICHA*

After viewing the flowers in the *tokonoma*, the guests individually approach the area where tea will be prepared. For the first time, the guests also see the cold water jar (*mizusashi*) and thick tea container (*chaire*) that will be used in the coming ritual. These utensils have been placed to the right of the brazier.

The characters for *mizusashi* mean "to indicate water." Because the vessel holds water and is concave, the *mizusashi* is considered a *yin* or "female" utensil in Tea's Taoist symbolic paradigm.[4] There are many styles of water containers in use today. The most formal (*shin*) *mizusashi* are those originally included in the nested sets of bronze tea implements brought from China (*kaigu*). Celadon and Chinese blue-white wares are also regarded as quite formal.

The class of semiformal (*gyō*) water containers encompasses many glazed ceramics from Japanese kilns. *Mizusashi* of western and southeast Asian origin are also popular, particularly those of cut glass. They usually fall into the informal (*sō*) category along with unglazed Japanese pottery, a special wooden bucket (*tsurube*) historically associated with Rikyū, and bentwood, lidded containers of unlacquered cedar.[5]

Mizusashi play a critical role in the host's *toriawase*. They can be used to express symbolic and/or seasonal themes. Or, they may be selected simply on the basis of shape, color, or texture. Let us suppose that our host has elected to use a brown, unglazed water jar from the Iga area. Like many fine *mizusashi*, this particular water container has a black, lacquer cover. The lid's round handle forms a perfect circle as it is reflected in the glossy surface, another *yin* symbol.

A thick tea container (*chaire*) has been placed on the mat in front of the water jar. Its presence indicates that the thick tea part of the gathering is about to begin. Today's *chaire* are copies of the medicine bottles that originally conveyed tea from China to Japan. They usually have ivory lids, which are lined on the bottom with gold leaf (originally believed to turn color on contact with poison). The host for this gathering has chosen to use a *chaire* of the most common *katatsuki* ("thrusting shoulders") shape. It is typical of those from Seto kilns in that it has a shiny, brown glaze.

Chaire are displayed in woven silk storage bags (*shifuku*). A famous *chaire* may have many bags. Bag fabrics generally fall into three categories: *donsu*, *kinran*, and *kantō*. *Donsu* is a satin weave that integrates various patterns. It is considered *wabi*, formal, and quietly elegant. *Kinran* is made with a satin weave and gold threads. It is considered Chinese, very elegant and is semiformal in character. *Kantō* is woven in stripes with either a plain or satin weave. It is more modern and informal than the other two types of fabric. A bag can be constructed of virtually any cloth.

The bag enclosing the Seto *chaire* previously mentioned might be made of multicolored damask (*donsu*) woven in a checkered pattern designed by Enshū. Such material is usually colored blue, green, gold, ivory, and white. Each square holds a flower or treasure motif. This particular fabric is considered very sophisticated. It can be used for all seasons. Imagine that the bag the guests see has acquired a tone of subdued elegance (*shibui*) through repeated use. The host has chosen this *chaire* for its aesthetic qualities.

The last things the guests examine before returning to their seats are the kettle and brazier. (The other necessary utensils will be carried into the room by the host.) The fire has changed the character of the ash formation and the charcoal arrangement. This means the host's skill in these art forms can be enjoyed in a new state of development.

Chapter 14

Thick Tea Preparation

KOICHA BEGINS

*T*he sound of the (*o*)*tsume* closing the *nijiriguchi* indicates that all the guests are present. *Koicha* (thick tea), the most important part of this tea ritual, will be the next segment of the *chaji*. When all the guests are seated, the host slides the door to the preparation area open and enters, carrying the tea bowl. It contains the whisk (*chasen*), tea scoop (*chashaku*), and a linen cloth used for wiping the bowl (*chakin*). The host sits in front of the water jar and sets the bowl temporarily on the mat next to the wall. He then moves the *chaire* slightly to the right so that both utensils can be centered in front of the *mizusashi*.

The tea bowl, which this fictional host has chosen to use, is called "*Kimamori.*" It is named for a persimmon that is left on the tree as its guardian when all the other fruit has been plucked. The bowl used at this *chaji* is a copy of a famous red, *raku* bowl made by the first generation master of Raku family Chōjirō (1516–1588). It was one of seven bowls known to have been particularly prized by Rikyū. (The original was destroyed in the great Kantō earthquake in 1923.) This bowl is well-suited to thick tea prepared in the *wabi* style. The clay feels warm in the hands and the shape is full and sensuous.

A *raku* tea bowl of thick green tea is considered the preeminent symbol of *chanoyu*. ("*Raku*" with a lower case "r" indicates the firing technique not the maker.) It represents intimacy as it touches the lips. It also symbolizes communication because the bowl is shared among the participants. Tea practi-

187

188 JAPANESE TEA RITUAL

tioners love *raku* bowls for their historical associations with Sen Rikyū and because they are frequently used for the type of tea ritual that binds people together. These *wabi* vessels stand in contrast to the less intimate, *temmoku*-style *raku* bowls used for *kencha* and *kucha*, tea events focused on the suprahuman dimension.

Bamboo tea whisks (*chasen*) are more plebeian utensils than tea bowls but they are indispensable to tea ritual. Modern whisks are made by cutting one end of a section of bamboo so that one hundred sixty to two hundred tines are formed. A black thread then is wrapped around the base of the tines at the node of the bamboo.[1] Proportions, size, thread color, and the color of the bamboo vary with the whisk's ritual function and the tea school identification of the practitioner.[2]

Chasen have been used since ancient times. An Edo period document, *Chasen no Ikken* (A Short Commentary on Tea), describes a Chinese T'ang dynasty whisk that was constructed from bamboo slivers bound to a metal handle and wrapped with thread. Beasts such as dragons, turtles, and phoenixes were etched on its handle. Such whisks must have come to Japan with powdered tea but historians can find no verifiable references that predate one on a fifteenth century picture scroll, (the *Fukutomi Zōshi*).

Early in Japanese tea history, *chasen* appears to have been identified with a shaved willow stick called the "*kezurikake*." *Kezurikake* are thought to have been used in early versions of *kencha* and *kucha*. (They look too fragile to have been used to whip tea, however.) The noted tea historian Kumakura Isao speculates that these objects were related to the paper-decorated willow wands used in *Shintō* ritual (Kumakura 1984, 48). The fact that they were made of willow and used but once supports this theory. At any rate by Murata Shukō's time, the *Shintō* association was apparently so strong that tea masters recommended discarding *chasen* after one use, a custom observed at today's tea rituals.

With their characteristic propensity for philosophical synthesis, tea masters later combined aspects of *Shintō* rite with a Confucian regard for social status. This resulted in the creation of the *kinindate* and *kinin kiyotsugu temae*, tea rituals performed for nobles and their retainers. Since a significant portion of Japanese court etiquette is directed by *Shintō* priests, tea masters felt it appropriate to incorporate *Shintō* symbolism into the tea services they created for nobles. As the result, nobles drink from individual bowls that are used once and discarded.[3] The bowls are presented on new, unlacquered wood stands and the tea made in them is whipped with white bamboo *chasen*. To further elevate the noble's status, accompanying retainers are served from ordinary bowls and their tea is whipped with smoked bamboo whisks.

While not quite as essential as the *chasen*, the *chashaku* (the tea scoop) is a higher-ranking and more versatile symbolic vehicle than the whisk. An individual tea scoop's name expresses the theme of a tea gathering. Central to its importance is the fact that it is ideally made by a tea practitioner rather than a faceless professional (as is the *chasen*).

The first *chashaku* were ivory measuring spoons for medicine brought from China. These are the most formal (*shin*) scoops. They are used during formal and semiformal tea rituals with genuine Chinese utensils or imitations of them. Shukō decided to copy these Chinese scoops in bamboo. These are also *shin chashaku*. Jōō took the evolutionary process one step further, innovating a scoop with the node at the base of the handle.[4] This created a semiformal (*gyō*) class of *chashaku*.

Rikyū ultimately decided to put the node in the middle of the *chashaku*, making this natural feature of the bamboo central to the scoop's character. His scoops are *sō*, or informal, as are scoops made from anything other than bamboo such as other wood, silver, tortoise-shell, or lacquer. Various methods of carving the tips of the tea scoops have become the *konomi* of individual tea masters. More than any other utensil, the tea scoop communicates the personality of its maker. This is because it alone can be created at home with a piece of bamboo and an ordinary knife. Most tea utensils require the more specialized equipment and skills of professional artisans.

Examination of the tea scoops made by important figures in tea history reveals much about their personalities. They are considered symbols of the virtues of their creators as well as inspirations to those that follow in their traditions. Special tea scoops such as these are kept in individual bamboo tubes, which are usually signed by their makers or subsequent owners. Such *chashaku* are given names that are meaningful in terms of their history or their aesthetic character.[5]

The ideal *chashaku* for thick tea is not purchased but inherited or received as a gift. A *chashaku* made by the host may be used for *usucha* as suggests humility (i.e. the host is not "above" taking the time to make a simple bamboo tool for use in serving his guests). Such scoops are often made with a particular tea gathering in mind. Sometimes homemade *chashaku* are given to the main guest as a souvenir of the gathering. The recipient may then properly use the scoop for *koicha*. It would be presumptuous, however, for the maker to use his own creation for thick tea. It would imply that he felt his artistry compared favorably to that manifest in the other utensils selected.

The imaginary tea scoop used by the host at this gathering is informal in style (the node is in the middle). It was made by the priest of a Zen temple where he studied in his youth and given to him as a gift. The host has chosen this *chashaku* because it has a name (to be revealed later) that contributes to the general theme and mood of the gathering. The last remaining item in the bowl carried into the tearoom by the host is the *chakin*.[6] Chakin also manifest characteristics important to *Shintō* symbolism in that they are white and used only once.

After these utensils are brought into the tearoom, the host returns to the preparation area to collect the waste water container (*kensui*), bamboo water scoop (*hishaku*), and lid rest (*futaoki*). The most common *kensui* are modeled on Chinese originals included in the nesting sets of bronze utensils previously mentioned. They can be constructed of a variety of materials.

The most popular style of *kensui* is a bronze vessel with a flaring lip. It is called an "*efugo*" after a similar container used to feed hawks by falconers. The *efugo*'s shape makes it particularly convenient to handle. Another common type of *kensui*, the *mage kensui* (bent wood waste water container) is made of bent cedar. As its unvarnished wood might suggest, this utensil has *Shintō* antecedents. It is moistened before use and theoretically used for a single tea gathering. Rikyū is said to have been the first to use such a container in the tearoom.

Inside the *kensui* rests the *futaoki* (lid rest). The most commonly used *futaoki* are sections of bamboo about 5.45 centimeters in height. (Rikyū designated this height, expressed in Japanese as "*issun hachibu*," one *sun* and eight *bu*.) The bamboo section is usually cut just above the *fushi* so that the septum of the bamboo forms a top for the hollow cylinder.[7] Unadorned cylinders are considered the best for *wabi temae* but bamboo lid rests may also be incised or painted with motifs like the ginkgo leaf or *tsubo tsubo* mon. Most are left plain.[8]

The original *futaoki* were included as one of the four cylindrical units of the *kaigu* (matched sets of Chinese utensils). Lid rests in particular seem to have inspired the creative instincts of tea masters through the ages because these simple objects now come in an unlimited number of styles and materials.[9] As with other utensils, the *futaoki* chosen must suit the host's *toriawase*. Let us imagine that the host for this October *chaji* has chosen to use a simple bamboo *futaoki* with a design of ginkgo leaves for this autumn gathering. (It is customary to use a bamboo lid rest for *temae* performed without *tana* or *daisu*.)

The final utensil, which the host carries into the room resting on the lip of the *kensui*, is the bamboo water ladle. There are several styles of ladle used in different seasons. Some are slightly more formal than others. *Hishaku* are chiefly distinguished by the angle at which the end of the handle has been cut and the manner in which the handle is attached to the cup.[10]A fresh ladle should be used for each gathering. On rare occasions, *hishaku* decorated with painted or incised designs are used.

PREPARING AND DRINKING THICK TEA

As soon as the host enters the room carrying the waste water container and associated articles, he turns and sits facing the door to the preparation area. Then he places the tea utensils in front of his knees and slides the door closed. The door to the *mizuya* is always closed during the thick tea portion of the *chaji*. This gesture symbolically defines the perimeters of the ritual environment.

After the door has been closed, the host rises and walks to the center of the mat on which tea will be made.[11]He sits and places the waste container to his left side, picking up the ladle with the left hand. The gesture he performs is called *"kagamibishaku"* or "mirror-handling." The ladle is held as if it were a mirror into which the host could reflect his thoughts. Here the ritual practitioner pauses to calm his mind. The symbolism is *Shintō*, based on an ancient belief in magical mirrors that faithfully reflect the true nature of all things.

The host's next move is to extract the *futaoki* from the *kensui* and place it on the mat at the base of the wall to the left of the brazier. Since the lid rest is bamboo, the ladle is knocked on the *futaoki* with a sound that suggests that which is made by the wood chopper working in the forest. No such sound is made when a ceramic or bronze *futaoki* is used because of possible damage to fragile utensils. At this point, everyone makes a full formal (*shin*) bow. This is considered the beginning of the thick tea segment of the *chaji*.

The host begins the tea procedure by picking up the tea bowl and the utensils within it with his right hand. He respectfully manipulates the bowl, handling it three times before placing it on the mat in front of him.[12]The thick tea container (*chaire*) is positioned between the bowl and the host's knees. With very specific gestures the bag is removed from the *chaire* and placed between (and to the rear of) the brazier and water container. The host subsequently removes the silk wiping cloth (*fukusa*) from his belt. He will examine it in a way that is particular to *koicha* preparations called "*yohō sabaki*."

Yohō sabaki ("four-direction examining") is a particularly solemn portion of *koicha*; it is always conducted in silence. The host examines all four sides of the *fukusa* while meditating on entities relevant to tea philosophy. Typical of Tea's syncretic philosophy, the act combines *Shintō*, Buddhist, and Confucian symbols. Ritually purifying an already clean vessel probably has *Shintō* precedents. Examining the four sides of the cloth, however, relates to Taoist, Buddhist, and Confucian thought.

Pure Land Buddhists are supposed to repeat the "*nembutsu*" while examining the *fukusa*. This recitation of faith in Amida Buddha is believed to guarantee salvation to all who pronounce the formula with conviction. Buddhists of other persuasions say they are worshipping the *shi tennō*, the four Deva kings who protect specific quarters of the universe. This symbolism has Tantric origins and may also owe something to Taoist or native Japanese geomancy. Since meditation is involved, Sōtō and Rinzai Zen also contribute to the significance of the act.

There is also a Confucian rationale for four-cornered examining. Tea teachers explain *yohō sabaki* as a gesture of respect to "the nation, one's parents, one's teachers, and one's friends." (Previous to the American Occupation of Japan, "emperor" was substituted for "nation" in this formula.) This symbolic exegesis was probably inspired by the Confucian concept of "five key relationships."[13]

While the host is folding the *fukusa* and wiping the tea container, the guests listen to the sound of the kettle. It is traditionally said to make the noise of the wind in the pines. After purifying the *chaire*, the host places the container on the mat in front of the cold water jar (*mizusashi*) and repeats (in an abbreviated fashion called "*fukusa sabaki*") his previous manipulations of the silk cloth. He then purifies the *chashaku* by wiping it with the *fukusa*, subsequently balancing the scoop on the lid of the *chaire*. If the *mizusashi* has a lacquer lid, the host will also wipe it with the silk cloth.

In the next few action sequences, the host places the linen cloth (*chakin*) on the lid to the water jar, handles the ladle, and removes the kettle lid to the lid rest (women protect their fingers with the folded *fukusa*). He then puts a dipper half full of hot water into the tea bowl and places the whisk in it. The act of purifying and inspecting the whisk called "*chasentōshi.*" The *chasen* is carefully examined to make sure that no tines are missing or loose. The whisk is then swished in the water to clean and moisten it. An invisible *hiragana* "*no*" (a Japanese syllabary character) is written in the bowl with the *chasen* before removing it to its place on the mat. "*No*" is said to signify "continuance."

After *chasentōshi* the water in the bowl is discarded into the *kensui* and the remaining moisture is wiped off with the *chakin*. The bowl is then replaced in front of the host and the *chakin* is relocated to the lid of the kettle. Lifting the tea scoop with the right hand (this is supposed to be done as if the scoop was a sword with a heavy blade), the host picks up the tea container with the left hand. The lid of the *chaire* is removed and set on the mat. The amount of tea correct for the size of gathering has been placed in the container in advance.

Only three portions of tea powder are extracted from the tea container with the tea scoop (about 1 gram each). The remaining powder is poured directly from the mouth of the *chaire* as it is rotated over the bowl. After the lip of the tea container has been cleaned with the fingers (to prevent tea from soiling the gold foil lining the lid), the cover is put on the *chaire* and it is returned to its former position on the mat.[14] The host then evenly distributes the tea in the bottom of the bowl with the *chashaku* (a step calculated to aid the uniform incorporation of tea powder and water). The tea scoop goes back on top of the *chaire*.

By *furo* season, tea powder has theoretically become weak with age (the tea is supposed to have been harvested in the spring of the previous year). For this reason the lid of the water jar is removed, enabling the host to add a dipper full of cold water to the kettle. Doing so lowers the water temperature, which in turn, protects the delicate flavor of the tea. Only two or three tablespoons of hot water are added to the tea bowl for every three grams of tea powder. The beverage is supposed to be very thick and viscous.

Excess water from the dipper is returned to the kettle. Then the ladle is rested on rim of the open *kama* with a gesture called "*kiribishaku*." This involves balancing the cup on the edge of the kettle and lowering the handle with a flat hand. The motion is believed to imitate that of archers knocking their arrows, a legacy from the *samurai* who followed "the way of archery" as well as "the Way of tea."

The tea powder and water are combined with the whisk. A respectful silence prevails while the host kneads the tea. Additional water is added to correct the final consistency. When the host is satisfied with the texture of the tea, a second invisible *hiragana* "*no*" is written with the *chasen*. The whisk is subsequently returned to the mat and the bowl picked up. It is rotated on the palm two times so that the front of the bowl faces the guest when it is offered to him.

After the host places the bowl on the *tatami* to his right, the main guest comes forward (walking or sliding on the knees depending on the size of the room). He picks up the bowl and takes it back to his seat. There he places the bowl to his left and all the guests make a formal bow. This indicates that they accept and will share the tea. The main guest raises the bowl in appreciation and turns it clockwise twice so that he does not drink from the front (a gesture of respect). He takes one sip. This is the dramatic climax of the gathering. If the ritual is effective, host and main guest will share a sense of profound satisfaction and intense tranquillity at this point.

The host breaks the spell by inquiring about the texture of the tea. The main guest replies that the texture of the tea is just fine. Then, he takes a second sip. As he is doing so, the host turns to face the guests. Meanwhile, the second guest excuses himself to the third guest for preceding him in drinking.

When the main guest finishes his share of the tea (about

three-and-one-half sips), he wipes the edge of the bowl with a moist *chakin,* which he has brought with him in a waterproof envelope. (Some hosts supply these amenities.) He then carefully passes the bowl to the next guest, who shows appreciation and drinks in the same fashion. While the second guest is drinking, the first guest compliments the host on the tea and asks its name and grower.

For this fictional gathering let us imagine that the tea is called *"Kiun"* ("Joyous Cloud"), and it comes from Koyama En, a tea plantation in Uji. The main guest also compliments the host on the sweet previously served and asks its name and maker. The host says that is it named *"Hagi no Tsuyu"* ("Dew of the Bush Clover") and he has made it himself. The guest continues the conversation, asking about the flowers and the vase. To the novice, tearoom conversation may seem formulaic. In reality, skillful practitioners make such exchanges sound light and casual. The guests are always genuinely interested in the answers to these questions.

When all the guests have consumed their tea (the last guest politely finishes it), the host turns to face the brazier and adds a scoop of cold water. This replenishes the hot water and indicates no more thick tea will be made. The gesture used in returning the ladle to the top of the kettle is called *"hikibishaku."* It emulates an archer drawing his bow. The host also returns his *fukusa* to his belt at this time.

While the host is attending to these details, the main guest asks to examine the bowl and the last guest returns it to him. The *shōkyaku* carefully observes the texture of the tea remaining in the bowl and then the bowl itself. He notices the potter's mark and the way in which the foot is formed. He also appreciates the ceramic's shape, glaze, and texture. When he has completed his examination, he passes it to the second guest (who has excused himself once more for preceding the third guest). When everyone has seen the bowl, the last guest returns it to the first guest. The *shōkyaku* then takes the tea bowl back to the host. Before putting the bowl on the mat where he originally received it, the main guest rotates it so that the front faces the host and returns to his seat.

The host picks up the bowl and places it in front of his knees. Everyone makes a formal bow indicating their appreciation for the shared experience. After this the host draws some hot water to rinse the bowl and discards it in the waste water container. At this time, the first guest asks about the tea bowl, its maker, and its poetic name. The host answers and then announces that he will finish the tea procedure.

To clean the bowl, the host pours a dipper of cold water into the tea bowl and returns the ladle to the top of the kettle with the *hikibishaku* gesture. Then, the whisk is cleaned in the cold water and reexamined. The clean *chasen* is put back on the mat and the water in the tea bowl is discarded. Lastly, the *chakin* and whisk are rearranged in the tea bowl.

Preparatory to completing the procedure, the host moves the waste water container back and closer to the wall. He cleans the *chashaku* with the silk cloth and places the scoop across top of the tea bowl. Excess tea is dusted into the *kensui* from the silk cloth which is subsequently replaced in the host's belt. Then, the tea container and bowl are restored to their original positions in front of the cold water container. After this, the host adds a scoop of "finishing" water to the kettle and manipulates the ladle, putting the lid on the *kama* at the same time. He leaves it slightly ajar to let steam escape. When the lid has been removed from its rest, the host quietly places the ladle on the *futaoki*. Finally, the cover is put back on the cold water container.

THE GUESTS ASK TO SEE THE UTENSILS

Now the main guest asks to examine the tea container, the tea scoop, and the bag. The host picks up the ladle, and places it on top of the *kensui*. The lid rest is repositioned under the handle of the ladle. The host also moves the tea bowl to a spot near the wall and to the left of the brazier. Then, he picks up the *chaire* and turns to face the guest.

Once the host is facing the guests, he removes the silk cloth from his belt, folds it as before (*fukusa sabaki*), and purifies the thick tea container once more. After rotating the *chaire* so that the front is away from himself, the host places it on the mat where the tea bowl was set out for the guests. The host then moves back to the location where tea was made. There he picks up the tea scoop and turns again in the guest's direction. He puts the *chashaku* down to the right of the *chaire*. This indicates that the scoop is a lower ranking utensil than the tea container. Approximately the same action sequence is repeated for the bag (*shifuku*).

After preparing the utensils for examination (*haiken*), the host picks up the ladle, lid rest, and waste container and turns toward the wall. This is the only time he turns his back to the guests. It is done because the *kensui* is full of impure water and is considered an unsightly object. The host shields it from sight with his body. He then goes to the door of the room, kneels to open it and exits. A few seconds later, he returns and picks up the tea bowl, which he also takes to the preparation area. The last object to be removed is the cold water container. The host sits in the door to the preparation area with this object in front of him and slides the door closed.

The main guest comes forward as he did for the tea bowl. He returns to his seat with the utensils, which will be examined, and apologizes to the second guest for preceding him. Each utensil is inspected in order of rank and passed to the next guest. Care is taken to look at the foil underneath the lid of the *chaire.*

After all the guests have seen the tea implements, these objects are returned to the spot where the host left them. The host then opens the door, enters the room, and sits facing the guests. The main guest compliments the host on his choice of utensils and asks about the shape of the *chaire* and its kiln. He also inquires about the maker of the tea scoop, its poetic name, the bag's fabric and its maker.

In the case of this fictional gathering, the host announces that the *chashaku* was made by his mentor in Zen studies and that it is called "*Sottaku Dōji.*" He notes that the tea scoop's name was inspired by a phrase in the *Hekigan Roku,* a famous Rinzai Zen text. It refers to a mother bird's intuition: Hearing that her chick is about to hatch, the mother pecks at the shell just when her chick is about to break through. "*Sotsu*" means "noise," "*taku*" is the word for pecking, and "*dō ji*" means "at the same time." It describes the ideal relationship between a teacher and a student. The host has chosen this name because the main guest is a former student with whom he has experienced spontaneous mutual understanding. Such a thought-provoking name is appropriate for a *chashaku* used at the thick tea segment of a *chaji.*

After hearing the name of the material from which the bag was constructed and learning about its maker, the main guest thanks the host on behalf of everyone present. All bow. Then the host removes the utensils from the room. Stopping in the doorway, he exchanges one more obeisance with all the guests and declares that he would like to make them a little thin tea. In order to do so, he says he must replenish the charcoal. The main guest assents, everyone bows, and the door is closed. *Koicha* is ended.

Chapter 15

The Preparation of Thin Tea

GOZUMI—THE SECOND CHARCOAL *TEMAE*

G *ozumi*, the second arranging of the charcoal, is a utilitarian event that traditionally takes place between the thick and thin tea segments of a *chaji*. During a long tea gathering, the fire often burns too low to heat the water for thin tea. The host must then perform a second charcoal *temae*. This procedure may be omitted if a sufficient quantity of charcoal remains unconsumed. Under such circumstances, *tsuzuki-usucha* is frequently substituted for separate charcoal and thin tea preparations. In any case, I include a brief explanation of the second charcoal *temae* for the sake of describing an unabbreviated tea gathering.

As he did for *shozumi* (the first charcoal procedure), the host slides the door to the preparation area open with a *sumitori* and related utensils to one side. He makes a formal bow and announces that he will repair the charcoal. The utensil basket is arranged differently than it was for *shozumi:* It now includes a woven reed kettle rest (*kumi kamashiki*) and a very large piece of charcoal called a *"wadō."*

Once more, the host enters the room and deposits the basket next to the brazier. He returns to the preparation area for the ash dish (*haiki*) and spoon (*haisaji*). Seating himself in the center of the *temae tatami* (the area where tea is made) and placing the ash dish next to the wall, the host takes the feather and incense container from the basket. He puts them on the mat and closes the top of the kettle. Next, the *kan* (metal rings) are removed from the basket and inserted in the kettle lugs. After laying the *kumi kamashiki* on the mat to his right, the host puts the kettle on top of it and slides the whole assemblage to one side. He then dusts the *furo* with the feather, replenishes the charcoal using the metal chopsticks (*hibashi*), and dusts the brazier a second time.

In an interesting variation on the first charcoal procedure, the host now uses the ash spoon to insert *fujibai* (white ash) into the incision previously made in the gray ash (*furobai*). After one more dusting, incense is added to the fire and the kettle is moved back to the place where it was originally set on the *kumi kamashiki*. Carefully, the host removes the *kan* from the lugs and places them to the right of the kettle. At this point the main guest asks to examine the brazier and associated utensils. The host bows in assent and subsequently leaves the room with the ash dish and spoon.

The guests come forward one by one to examine the charcoal basket, kettle, metal rings, feather, and so forth. They also appreciate the way in which the character of the fire and ash have changed. After they have returned to their seats, the host reenters with a water supplier (*mizutsugi*), a bamboo lid rest, and a very damp, folded *chakin* (linen cloth).

The type of *mizutsugi* the host has elected to use for this particular *chaji* is called a "*koshiguro*" or "*Rikyū yakan*." It looks very much like a standard western tea kettle. Rikyū found this pot and used it to boil water when he was on the battlefield with Hideyoshi. Because it was heated on an open fire, the kettle became black with soot. *Koshiguro* means "black-waisted." This discolored utensil suited Rikyū's *wabi* taste so he had a replica made in copper by the first of the famous Nakagawa family of metal workers, Jōeki (1559–1622). Similar kettles have become standard equipment for tea ritual. Today, most are artificially blackened.

Seating himself once more on the *temae tatami*, the host removes the bamboo lid rest from the spout of the water supplier and places the lid of the *kama* on it. Then he adds water to the kettle from the *koshiguro*, holding the linen cloth (*chakin*) under the spout to catch any drips. He also wipes the lid and the body of the hot kettle with the moist *chakin*. The guests admire the way the steam rises as he does so. (Steam is believed to purify like incense.)

After the kettle has been wiped, the host takes the *koshiguro* and lid rest back to the preparation area. Reentering the tearoom, he inserts the metal rings into the lugs of the kettle. Then the *kama* is replaced on the brazier. Finally, the *kumi kamashiki* is returned to the basket, the *kama* is straightened over the fire, and the kettle lid is opened. When the metal rings have been put away, the host carries the *sumitori* to the preparation area. There he turns and sits in the doorway with the charcoal basket to one side. The second charcoal preparation (*gozumi*) is completed when everyone bows.

USUCHA—THE THIN TEA PORTION OF THE *CHAJI*

The final part of the *chaji*, the preparation of thin tea, is meant to be relaxed and cordial. It may be compared to the "Downward Training" necessary for Zen adepts who have attained enlightenment. Shibayama Zenkei says this is a period of training dedicated to returning the enlightened to their "original" humbleness, something which helps them live an ordinary life without displaying undesirable spiritual pretentiousness (Shibayama 1970, 136).

The host brings a *tabako bon* and cushions into the room, exchanging a bow with the main guest as these things are accepted by him. The host then returns to the preparation area and reappears with a tray of dry sweets (*higashi*). *Higashi* are often made from a simple mixture of *kanbaiko* (flour made from sweet rice), sugar, water, and food coloring. They are also created from pure sugar and water like western "hard candy." Molded and colored, these sweets can take any shape the maker's fancy leads him to produce—the variety is endless.

Like so many other things associated with tea ritual, *higashi* are ranked *shin*, *gyō*, and *sō* and presented accordingly. Pressed sweets are *shin* (formal). They are stacked in an orderly fashion in the upper right hand corner of the tray. *Gyō* and *sō* sweets are gathered irregularly in the lower left hand area. Such refreshments are always provided in uneven numbers and in quantity. Guests may have one or more of each kind. An exception to the general rule of orderly presentation occurs when special scattered *higashi* are offered. These sweets imitate natural objects dispersed by the wind: In the spring, masses of cherry petals may be represented. Or in the summer, a drift of flowers, leaves, and butterflies might be depicted.

There are also many kinds of sweet trays. Sometimes these utensils are flat and made of wood. Interesting baskets may also be used. The shape and seasonal character of both sweets and their containers are part of the host's *toriawase*. They convey a symbolic message, usually something about the beauty of the season. Let us imagine that the host for this gathering offers scattered sweets recalling fall leaves, pine cones, and ginkgo nuts strew about by a gust of wind. He presents his selection in the type of basket used to separate rice from chaff at the harvest.

After bowing to the main guest and returning to the preparation area, the host seats himself in the doorway with the cold water jar to one side. Once again he bows, announcing that he will offer thin tea to his guests. The host then enters the room and places the *mizusashi* to the right of the brazier. Afterwards, he returns to preparation area for the tea bowl and *natsume*.

Bowls used for thin tea usually differ from those in which thick tea is made. The host for this imaginary October *chaji* has planned to use a copy of a *kyōyaki* ("ceramic from the capital") bowl made by Nonomura Ninsei (active seventeenth century, dates unknown), a gorgeous ceramic patterned with fall leaves. The piece captures the autumnal brilliance of courtly Kyōto. The host may serve everyone from this bowl (cleaning it between uses), or carry a second bowl into the room with the waste container. For this small gathering, the host has elected to use a single bowl.

The *chakin*, *chasen*, and *chashaku* are arranged in the bowl as they were for thick tea. The tea scoop is different from the one previously used. This one is made in a style identified with Tantansai. It has a distinctively pointed scoop end (called *"kensaki,"* sword point).[1]

In his right hand, the host carries a *natsume*. The creation of this class of thin tea containers (*usuki*) is said to have been suggested by the turned wooden boxes that once encased *chaire* made in Japan. One of Rikyū's favorite *usuki* shapes was similar to that of a Chinese date. It was called a *"natsume"* in Japanese. Like many of Rikyū's *konomi*, thin tea containers in this shape soon became extremely popular. The most formal objects in this class are covered with plain black lacquer but many other possibilities exist. Let us imagine that the host for this gathering has chosen a medium-sized, black-lacquered container with a gold design of mother and baby quails.

The host enters the room carrying the bowl and *natsume* and places them in front of the cold water jar. He then returns to the preparation area for the waste container, lid rest, and ladle. The same utensils used for thick tea are used again with the exception of the bowl, whisk, tea scoop, and tea container. Note that the door to the preparation area is not closed. This *temae* does not define a closed ritual environment as did the thick tea segment of the gathering.[2]

The *kensui* is placed on the mat at the host's side. The ladle is then mirror-handled as before and rested with a knock on the lid rest. After pausing to collect his thoughts and straighten his kimono, the host moves the *kensui* slightly forward. He puts the tea bowl in front of himself and the *natsume* between the bowl and his knees. The silk cloth (*fukusa*) is then removed from the belt and folded *fukusa sabaki*-style. This is done so that *natsume* can be ritually purified as the *chaire* was for thick tea.

Placing *natsume* in the tea bowl's former position in front of the water jar, the host picks up the tea scoop and refolds the silk cloth to wipe it. The *chashaku* is then gently rested on top on the *natsume* and the host returns his *fukusa* to his belt (if the practitioner is female or the kettle knob is made of very conductive material, the silk cloth remains in the left hand).

The whisk is next withdrawn from the bowl and placed to the right of the tea container. The host then moves the bowl closer to his knees. After picking up the ladle, he puts the kettle lid on the *futaoki*, (putting the *fukusa* in back of the *kensui*, if it has not already been returned to the *obi*) and rests the linen cloth on top of it. Now the tea bowl is empty, so the host can fill it with hot water using the ladle (*hishaku*). When this has been accomplished, the *hishaku* is returned to the top of the kettle and the whisk is inspected (*chasentōshi*) as it was for thick tea. The clean *chasen* is replaced in front of the water jar and the hot water in the bowl discarded. Finally, the bowl is wiped dry with linen cloth and restored to its position in front of the knees.

Picking up the tea scoop in his right hand, the host invites the first guest to sample the dry sweets with a one-handed, semiformal bow. The main guest accepts with a full formal (*shin*) bow and excuses himself to the second guest for taking sweets before him.[3] All the guests will place their sweets on the papers they carry (kaishi) after lifting the tray in a gesture of thanks. They do not take their sweets until the host raises the tea scoop preparatory to making their individual bowls of tea. The main guest may inquire about the sweets and their container at this time.

Still holding the tea scoop in one hand, the host responds, grasps the *natsume* and brings it to the edge of the bowl where the lid is removed. The powdered green tea used for *usucha* is piled in a rounded, mountain-shape inside the tea container. Carefully scooping from one side of the mountain so as not to disturb it, the host puts one-and-one-half to two scoops of tea in the bowl (1.5–2 grams). He then replaces the lid and puts the *natsume* in its former position. The tea scoop is tapped lightly on the edge of the bowl to remove excess tea and replaced on the *natsume*'s lid.

At this time the host takes the cover off the cold water jar (*mizusashi*) and leans it against the side of the container. This is a precautionary measure. The temperature of the water in the kettle must occasionally be lowered with an infusion of cold water. In this case, however, hot water is simply drawn out with the ladle and poured into the bowl. Thin tea requires more water in proportion to tea powder that thick tea. The quantity used depends on the guest's preference. The excess water in the dipper is returned to the kettle and the *hishaku* is lowered to the rim of the *kama* with the *kiribishaku* gesture.

The motion used to make *usucha* is rapid whipping, unlike the kneading of thick tea. The ratio of water to tea need not be adjusted as it was for *koicha*. So, the whisk is simply removed from the bowl (after the "*no*" pattern is written) and replaced in its former position. Turning the bowl twice, the host places it facing the guest on the mat to his own right. The main guest comes forward and takes the bowl back to his seat. He puts the bowl to his left and excuses himself to the second guest for drinking first. He then lifts the bowl in appreciation, turns it to avoid the front, and drinks the tea.

The *shōkyaku* may now ask the name and origin of the tea. The host replies that the name of the tea is "*Wako*" ("Light of Harmony") and it comes from Koyama En. The main guest then wipes the edge of the bowl where his lips touched with his fingertips, and places the bowl in front of himself on the mat.

Since only one bowl is used, the main guest returns it to the host immediately. The main guest may ask about the bowl at this time. A second bowl of tea is made in much the same way as the first (starting with a warm rinse and a wipe with the *chakin*). The sequence continues until all guests have had tea. They are customarily offered a second bowl of tea and it is not impolite to accept.

When everyone has had enough tea, the main guest asks the host to finish. He does this immediately after the host discards warm water into the *kensui*. The host acknowledges the request with a one-handed informal bow. He then places the bowl in front of his knees, makes a semiformal bow and announces that he will finish the *temae*.

Cold water is drawn from the *mizusashi* and placed in the bowl for cleaning and examining the whisk. The ladle is returned to the kettle rim in the *hikibishaku* gesture. Once *chasentōshi* has been performed, this water is also discarded and the linen cloth is placed in the bottom of the bowl. The bowl then goes back on the mat and the whisk is placed on top of the *chakin*. The host next picks up the tea scoop with his right hand and moves the waste container toward the wall with his left. Removing the *fukusa* from his belt, the host folds the cloth in the familiar *fukusa sabaki* fashion and wipes the tea scoop with it.

Now the bowl and *natsume* are returned to the positions they occupied at the beginning of the *temae*. While the host is cleaning the utensils, the main guest asks about any interesting utensils as yet undiscussed. The conversation is light and casual. After a dipper full of cold water has been added to the *kama* to restore the water level, the ladle is put quietly put on the *futaoki* and the lid returned to the *mizusashi*.

Putting the lid on the water jar signals the main guest to ask to see the *natsume* and the *chashaku*. If the host responds that the tea scoop is the same as the one used for *koicha*, the guest will ask to see it a second time. The host accepts with a bow and places the ladle across the top of the waste water container. The lid rest is moved behind the *kensui* under the handle of the *hishaku*. Finally, the tea bowl is relocated to a position next to the wall.

At this point, the host picks up the *natsume*, turns toward the guests, and puts the tea container down on the mat in front of his knees. After folding the *fukusa* in the usual fashion, he purifies the *natsume* with it. This purification differs from the first one in the *temae* because the lid of the container is removed (the host glances inside to see if the design or *kaō* (tea master's or Zen monk's cipher), if any, is facing in the right direction and that there is no tea on the inside of the lid. The lip of the *natsume* is also wiped.

After replacing the lid and rotating the whole object to face the guests, the host puts the tea container on the mat where the tea was offered to the guests. Then he turns back in the direction of the brazier and picks up the tea scoop. He places it next to the tea container on the side away from the *tokonoma* (because the *chashaku* is a lower-ranking utensil than the *natsume*). This accomplished, the host picks up the ladle, lid rest, and waste container. Turning to the wall as he did during *koicha*, the host leaves the room. He reenters to remove the tea bowl and cold water jar.

As soon as the host has taken the *kensui* back to the mizuya, the main guest comes forward to pick up the *natsume* and the tea scoop. He returns to his seat with them. The etiquette of the *haiken* (examination of tea utensils) is the same as that for *koicha* except when the guests remove the lid of the tea container. Then they check to see if there is any decoration or *kaō* on the inside. They also observe the shape of the remaining mound of tea, an indication of the skill with which the tea was scooped.

When they have finished, the host comes back into the room to answer any questions the main guest may have about the utensils. He asks the host about the shape of the *natsume* and the lacquer used. (It is a medium-sized container with *makie* lacquer.) He will also ask the name of the lacquer artisan. In this case, the *natsume* was decorated by the present scion of the Nakamura family. The main guest also inquires about the tea scoop. He is told that it was made by Tantansai and that its poetic name is "*Akatonbo,*" a type of red dragon fly seen all over Japan in the fall.

The main guest thanks the host for selecting such enjoyable utensils and they both bow. After this, the host will return these implements to the *mizuya*, stopping once more in the doorway to apologize for any offense he might have given. This is a customary demonstration of humility. It is often said that neither host nor guests can make errors at a real *chaji*. Ideal and reality frequently diverge, of course.

After putting the *natsume* and *chashaku* away, the host reenters the room for final greetings. Everyone thanks the host for a lovely time and the main guest comments that it is not necessary for the host to see them out. The host thanks everyone for coming and leaves the room, closing the door to the preparation area behind him. The guests inspect the *tokonoma* and utensils once more. Then, they leave through the *nijiriguchi* in the order in which they entered. The last guest takes the *tabako bon,* cushions, and the sweet tray to the door of the *mizuya*. He also closes the *nijiriguchi* with a slight noise. When the host hears this sound he will open the door to the preparation area and remove the utensils. Then he will go to the guest entrance and slide it open. The guests give him one last formal bow and turn to leave. The host bows in return and watches his guests until they are out of sight—it is now his time to pause and think about the *chaji*.

Chapter 16

Interpreting Tea Ritual

THE OBJECTIVES OF TEA RITUAL

Confirmatory ends

*A*s noted in chapter 14, the preparation of thick tea is the apex of a *chaji.* The instant a practitioner enters the tea-room to prepare *koicha,* he or she confronts a unique opportunity to achieve that "condition of original wholeness, health, or holiness" that is the objective of all religious behavior (Girardot 1983, 7). Whether the officiant elects to sustain the confirmatory focus of the ritual by reinforcing the extant cognitive model or to modify it depends in large part on his or her training and personal philosophy.

Under most circumstances, the personalities and expectations of the participants mandate the choice of the confirmatory alternative. Since the host controls only one-half of the spiritual dialogue, he cannot unilaterally determine the character of the conversation.

Practicing confirmatory tea has always been the norm, probably because it satisfies the religious needs of the majority without running the risk of generating a confrontational atmosphere: Social overtures of this nature clearly have the potential to be more frustrating than enlightening. Most ritualists, no matter how pure their motive and intense their desire, do not have the confidence, skill, and requisite spiritual maturity to challenge others' inherent conceptual biases—though many are positively influenced by the aspiration.

Thick tea preparation is deeply infused with a confirmatory

bias evident in its symbolic repertoire. When the host shuts the tearoom door at the beginning of the *koicha* procedure, he defines a select ritual constituency. Then he briefly recalls the Taoist cosmic paradigm by symbolically arranging, blending, and balancing "the five elements" (fire, water, wood, metal, and earth). When his companions share the tea he makes, they physically internalize the product of this very specialized environment. Tea nourishes in a universal sense. It is food, drink, and medicine all at once.[1]

The closed atmosphere of the tearoom is particularly meaningful to Japanese because of their high regard for definitively circumscribed group membership. Japanese are socially conditioned to cherish a sense of being "inside" (*uchi*) both formal and informal groups. These differ in size and structure but their members invariably share some binding interest and/or obligation. Identification with the group is frequently so intense that challenges to the structure of the group are perceived as personal attacks by individuals.

Like most people, tea practitioners generally prefer to function in an atmosphere free from structural ambivalence. They devote a great deal of energy to safeguarding the perimeters of their ritual territory and defining individual spheres of action. If these vital tasks are successfully performed, the participants are briefly rewarded with the pleasurable sensation of functioning in a totally supportive atmosphere—one characterized by the absence of outsiders (i.e. people who are dangerous because they might not play by the rules) and potentially chaotic behavior. In this manner, the teahouse has come to represent a safe and gentle haven in a volatile and occasionally hostile social milieu—a special plane of existence where the individual is fully integrated with the cosmic model and participants' sense that everything and everyone is in their proper place.

Transformatory goals

The transformatory elements in Tea are manifest much more infrequently. Remember Rikyū himself remarked that he had experienced *chanoyu* true to his ideal only once or twice in his lifetime. This was not an admission of failure but a realistic assessment of the difficulty of the task: Most people seek salvation in the familiar.

Religiously motivated individuals willing to sacrifice all (to

"Die while alive and be completely dead" in Zen parlance) for an instant of transcendent understanding were undoubtedly as scarce in the sixteenth century as they are today.[2] The chance of two such individuals meeting—in the tearoom—and sharing the essence of their most profound realizations is even more remote.

Rikyū's vision must be interpreted in the context of Zen—a "way" dedicated to inducing revolutionary changes in the personalities and perceptions of its devotees. As a Zen adept, he was trained to seek salvation within himself, not in the confirmation of an external cognitive structure. Shibayama Zenkei calls training in Zen "a desperate inner struggle to smash ordinary dualistic consciousness" (Shibayama 1970, 106). Rikyū was firmly committed to following this course of action. As he said:

> In Zen, truth is pursued through the discipline of meditation in order to realize enlightenment while in Tea we use training in the actual procedures of making tea to achieve the same end. (Sen Rikyū in Sen 1979b, 64)

Very few tea practitioners choose to follow Rikyū's difficult path, although most feel obliged to support the concept—at least in principle. Zen discipline is, nevertheless, absolutely fundamental to the practice of seeking salvation through the practice of transformatory (somewhat deceptively known as "*wabi*") tea ritual.[3]

The element of salvation in tea ritual

Whether the intent of the individual is to satisfy the desire for salvation—"original wholeness, health, or holiness" (Girardot 1983, 7)—through transformatory or confirmatory means, the perceived presence of some threat or existential disjunction is implied. As N. J. Girardot has pointed out "Cosmos is the cultivated persona of chaos" (Girardot 1983, 5). Ordering and integrating behavior is meaningful precisely because the individual senses the presence of or potential for disorder.

The concept of impending Chaos has important implications for the interpretation of tea ritual: The ancient Chinese believed that Chaos reigned before the cosmos was ordered by a plethora of mythological figures and their sages remained wary of its destructive potential. Some responded by attempting to physically and spiritually reconcile the individual to the flow of active and passive elements in the universe. Practicing ritual (including esoteric forms of meditation), balancing the diet, and compounding medicine were central to the efforts of these Taoists.

The Japanese found Taoism appealing because it represented the wisdom of an older and more powerful civilization. They also recognized Chaos as an intrinsic factor in their own creation myths. In the *Nihon Shoki* and the *Kojiki*, for example, earth was originally represented as existing in a formless state which floated below heaven like drifting oil. The brother and sister gods, Izanagi and Izanami, succeeded in organizing the world coherently. Unfortunately their offspring let creation deteriorate once again.

Susano-o, the younger brother of the Sun Goddess, was particularly destructive. He broke up the dikes in the rice fields, released a colt in the fields at harvest time, and defecated on the floor of his sister's palace. In disgust, the Sun Goddess hid in a cave and had to be lured out by the other gods and goddesses. Order was briefly restored but only until Susano-o once again journeyed to earth.

The next place Susano-o descended to "had always been waste and wild. The very rocks, trees, and herbs were all given to violence" (Pelzel 1974, 8). This was the future home of the Japanese. Order was finally reestablished by the ancestor of the imperial line, the Master of the Land. But the ancient chronicles note that "Japan is still painfully uproarious" (Pelzel in Lebra and Lebra 1974, 11). Japanese living in the Heian to Muromachi periods probably suspected that Chaos had not been completely subdued. Their sense of impending disaster complemented the Buddhist belief in the *dharma* cycle. Rikyū was merely speaking for his contemporaries when he suggested *mappō*, the final, degenerate cycle of the Buddhist faith, was at hand. He is thought to have said: "Even the Great Way of the Buddhas and patriarchs, of the *bodhisattva* saints and sages, has its era, it prospers and declines" (Rikyū in Hirota 1980b, 44).

To the Japanese, bloody wars, disastrous fires, and frequent natural cataclysms were and are more than mythological themes. They are part of life in "a painfully uproarious land." Even in the modern era, large scale manifestations of Chaos coexist with less obvious, but equally devastating, sources of spiritual, social, economic, and environmental distress.

Individual Japanese combat Chaos in a variety of ways:

The majority dedicate themselves to work or educational objectives. Some drink heavily and others engage in sports. A surprising number seek relief in conventional religious behavior. The vitality of the so-called new religions is one powerful indicator of this phenomenon and the popularity of *chadō* is another.[4] In both instances, ". . . symbolic acts operate through their capacity to map changed or adjusted perceptions of the possibilities inherent in a situation onto the actor's orientation to it." (Munn 1973, 593)

THE FOUR INTEGRAL ORDERING PRINCIPLES OF *CHADŌ*

In much the same way Nancy Munn suggests, tea practitioners cope with Chaos by reordering their perceptions of life through ritual. They perceive four values, *wa* (harmony), *kei* (respect), *sei* (purity) and *jaku* (tranquillity), as major mediators between the Transcendent, the cultural system, tea ritual, and the individual. (See figure 16.1) As noted in chapter 5, this particular normative litany was adapted by Rikyū from a similar formula favored by Shukō.

The first term, "*wa*," represents a considerably more complex concept than its English translation, "harmony," would suggest: The ideograph ("*ho*" in Chinese, "*wa*" in Japanese) was originally employed by the Taoists to represent "universal harmony" (*ho li*). "*Ho*" acquired an ethical tone when the Confucians incorporated the idea into their vision of integrated natural and social hierarchies.

When the Chinese used the ideograph "*ho*" to designate Japan (the kingdom of "*wa*," known as *Yamato* to its inhabitants) around the third century A.D., a more limited, ethnically specific connotation was appended to its original meaning. Subsequently, "*wa*" became a component in compounds designating "native" Japanese phenomena. Finally, in A.D. 604, the brilliant Japanese Prince Shōtoku solidified his subjects' sense of identification with "*wa*" by touting the notion as "the thing most estimable" in Japan's "first constitution" (Suzuki 1959, 305).

Sustaining the tradition of intimately associating "*wa*" with his homeland, the great modern exponent of Zen, Daisetz Suzuki pointed out that the character can be read "*yawaragi*" or "gentleness of spirit" (Suzuki 1959, 274). Suzuki argued that "*yawaragi*" was inherent to Japan and integral to the Japanese personality, observing that teamen prefer a "soft, tender, concil-

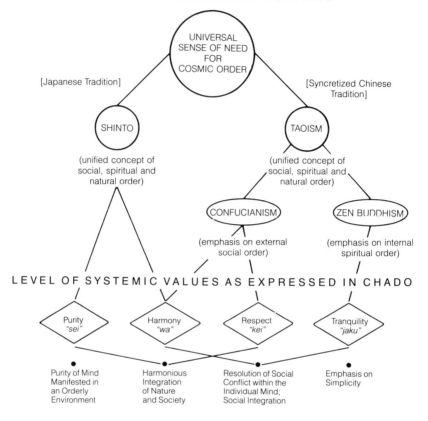

LEVEL OF RELIGIOUS SYSTEMS

UNIVERSAL SENSE OF NEED FOR COSMIC ORDER

[Japanese Tradition]

[Syncretized Chinese Tradition]

SHINTO

(unified concept of social, spiritual and natural order)

TAOISM

(unified concept of social, spiritual and natural order)

CONFUCIANISM

(emphasis on external social order)

ZEN BUDDHISM

(emphasis on internal spiritual order)

LEVEL OF SYSTEMIC VALUES AS EXPRESSED IN CHADO

Purity "sei"

Harmony "wa"

Respect "kei"

Tranquility "jaku"

Purity of Mind Manifested in an Orderly Environment

Harmonious Integration of Nature and Society

Resolution of Social Conflict within the Individual Mind; Social Integration

Emphasis on Simplicity

LEVEL OF INDIVIDUAL PRACTICE

1. Rituals of purification; 2. Ordering of mind and environment via cleaning routine.

1. Seasonal *tori-awase;* 2. Natural treatment of flowers; 3. Use of natural line and materials in architecture; 4. Respectful treatment of food in *kaiseki;* 5. Use of natural materials in tea utensils; 6. Respect for relationship between materials and craftsmen manifesting connoisseurship and curatorship.

1. Respect among actors manifested in etiquette; 2. Respect between master and disciple as manifested in school structure; 3. Respect for historic tradition of Tea manifested in conformity to established practice; 4. Respect for national identity manifested in boundary maintaining behavior.

1. Economy of desire manifested as frugality; 2. Economy of expression manifested as restraint; 3. Zen emphasis on enlightenment through direct experience — intellectual economy.

Figure 16–1

iatory" (and presumably indigenous) atmosphere, which bars "all the arrogant, individualistic, self-assertive spirit so characteristic of modern Japanese young men" (Suzuki 1959, 305).[5]

Combinations of utensils representing the Taoist five elements, drawing the trigram for "water" in the ash under the charcoal, the geomantic orientation of the tearoom, tea's special status as a "spiritual medicine", and even the aim of creating a mystic harmony between host and guest may be attributed to a desire for "*wa*."

Kei, the second element in Tea's quartet of major values, is a Confucian ethic. This particular kind of "respect" imposes order on the model of integration represented by harmony (*wa*). Its most important function is to validate the existing social hierarchy by convincingly reconciling it with the transcendent order. *Kei* is, however, ideally more than a superficial attitude; it is supposed to be a heartfelt sentiment that synthesizes important elements of reserve, reverence, and restraint. In the tearoom, *kei* is most strongly evident in the relationship between host and guests. Moreover, Sadler says that Zen monks were taught to regard their food with this attitude (Sadler 1962, 102). Probably for this reason, tea practitioners are encouraged to respect the physical objects they use.

The third element in *chadō*'s normative litany, *sei*, the Shintō concept of purity, is integral to Japanese perceptions of both natural and social environments. To the Japanese, something which is pure is also beautiful and satisfying to the senses. Host and guest must cleanse their minds of the conceptual refuse of daily life in order for the Tea ritual to be effective. Mental categories and attitudes toward life cannot be reordered in the context of a clutter of conflicting values.

Significantly, emphasizing the positive character of purity tends to obscure its boundary maintenance function. It should be noted that the concept is inextricably associated with ancient Japanese taboos aimed at preventing ritual pollution. As Mary Douglas points out, such beliefs reflect cultural intolerance of structural ambiguity "expressed by avoidance, by discrimination, and by pressure to conform" (Douglas 1972, 199). Her observations have important implications for the practice of confirmatory tea ritual and for understanding Japanese cognition in general.

Most of the rituals of purification, which take place in and around the tearoom, are manifestations of *sei*. Sprinkling the *roji* with water, using new utensils of unvarnished cedar, washing the hands at the *tsukubai,* and purifying the brazier with a feather all help define the ritual field and demonstrate the participants' state of ritual preparedness.

Jaku, the last of Tea's four central values, is a distinctively Buddhist concept. The same ideograph forms part of the Japanese word for Nirvana (the ultimate Buddhist endeavor, complete freedom from the limitations of existence), "*jakumetsu.*" While *wa, kei,* and *sei* contribute primarily to tea ritual's confirmatory character, *jaku* suggests its transformatory potential. It elicits a sense of lasting inner tranquillity, which transcends individual desire and arbitrarily imposed cognitive categories. Paradoxically, though it cannot exist in the absence of harmony with, and respect for, the social and natural orders or purity of mind and spirit, *jaku* ultimately connotes rejection of the kind of fragmented image of existence they contribute to creating. As Rikyū said:

> The garden path, the hut,
> The host and the guest—
> All are whipped together
> In the tea and are without distinctions.
>
> (Rikyū in Tsutsui 1980, 39)

Interestingly enough, though it is of equal if not primary importance, there is little in *chanoyu*'s symbolic repertoire pertaining directly to tranquillity (*jaku*). The completed bowl of tea is the only visual representation of this concept. This apparent anomaly may be attributed to the premium placed on direct experience in Zen philosophy: Symbols, like *sutras,* mediate between the individual and the *dharma.* The patriarchs insisted that the experiential fact and its symbolic expression recognized as separate phenomena.

INTEGRATING TEA INTO DAILY LIFE

Having suggested a few of the ways *chadō*'s axiomatic values mediate between higher order cultural concepts and immediate action, I would like to consider the way "Ritual adapts and periodically readapts the biopsychical individual to the basic conditions and axiomatic values of human social life" (Turner 1967, 43).

Japanese women's lives form the main subject matter of this discussion because, since the turn of the century, many more women than men have practiced *chadō.* An encounter with almost any large group of Tea *aficionados* is enough to convince the observer that while men continue to sit at the apex of the Tea pyramid and direct its change and development, women form the solid base of *chanoyu* today.

Japanese men are turning away from traditional Japanese leisure pursuits en masse and toward more western forms of recreation. Perhaps the progressive self-image of the modern salary-man precludes an after-hours shift from gray flannel to *kimono* and *hakama*.

Fortunately, the modern economy, which dominates men's interests, also generates more leisure time for women. Smaller family size, the increase in neolocal residence, family economies which do not require the wife's help in farm or shop, and the proliferation of laborsaving devices mean that more women have more time for themselves—at least before their children are born and after they are grown.[6] Not surprisingly it is women not yet or newly married and those whose children are grown who are most active in Tea.

The images of tea practitioners presented to the communications media are predominantly those of gracefully posturing, *kimono*-clad young women. The impression created is that of feminine subservience, uncompromisingly observed etiquette, and archaic art forms. These are *"kireigoto,"* "pretty things"— part of the cultural whitewash Japanese use to convince themselves that nothing has really changed since the Meiji era.

The truth is the women who practice tea are not all young and lovely. In fact, they are often much stronger, smarter, and more independent than many Japanese men would prefer. Most frequently, they are women who have raised their families (many through the privations of wartime), who seek intellectual stimulation, who enjoy relaxing among their peers in the tearoom, and who are relatively adventurous.

Takie Sugiyama Lebra's *Japanese Women: Constraint and Fulfillment* provides an excellent background for those who wish to understand the role that Tea can play in feminine life cycles. A woman's first encounter with Tea is likely to be made in the context of "bridal training" as part of what Lebra calls "a set of expressive specialties intended for femininity training" (i.e. flower arrangement, Tea, and instruction in classical music and dance). She also notes, quite accurately, that "... women seldom used these skills to entertain their husbands. The general goal was not so much to learn the specific technique of an art as to internalize proper manners and comportment through the art" (Lebra 1984, 59).

One important consequence of this early experience with Tea is the custom of making a lifetime commitment to a particular teacher (or at least school of Tea), which can continue unabated or be revived later in life. Often, such experiences also create a core of formal or informal female peer group associations of a lasting nature.

In my own interviews with young Japanese females, I have observed a pronounced tendency to de-emphasize *chanoyu*'s role in bridal training and a corresponding augmentation of its contribution to self-improvement. Lebra notes: "Young women today simply enjoy tea ceremony, find its theory sensible and intriguing, or participate in it only because they want to wear *kimono*" (Lebra 1984, 59). Her recognition of the fact that people may study Tea merely because they enjoy it is a real revelation in the anthropological literature. The subsequent observation that Japanese young women have the character and intelligence to find "its theory sensible and intriguing" is also an original and long overdue contribution to the literature.[7]

Japanese young people of both sexes prefer to organize their leisure around group activities. They also share the national predilection for engaging in leisure, which is at least nominally self-improving. Faced with an array of possibilities, which range from mountain climbing to celebrity fan clubs and *go* associations, it does not seem unusual that some young women would be attracted to the myriad charms of Tea. My subjects often commented that the hectic urban environment and its grueling pace of life rendered the tranquillity of the tea-room particularly appealing.

After marriage same-sex peer group activities may continue until the birth of the first child or be immediately curtailed by the demands of married life. I strongly suspect that young women in *mukoyōshi* or neolocal marriages (which do not result in a significant geographical relocation) are more likely to persist in their studies.[8] A bride who enters a traditional extended household immediately encounters a burden of housekeeping activities that precludes recreation. In addition, it may be felt by either the girl or her new family that expenditures for Tea lessons and gifts are inappropriate at this point in her life.

A marriage, which requires a tea student to move far from her natal home, may make it necessary to establish a new relationship with a tea teacher or study group. Making such contacts are likely to be assigned a low priority in a young household (unless it helps the husband's career). The wife is more apt to become involved with the novel responsibilities of decorating a home, and cooking regular meals. Discretionary capital is logically directed toward items both the husband and wife find necessary to their shared ideal life-style. Once a child arrives, the new mother is unlikely to have time or money for the study of Tea.

When children have finally left the home or are involved in adult activities to the extent that little time need be spent on their care (or a daughter-in-law has assumed the responsibility for household chores), the mature woman has the opportunity to reactivate her interest in Tea. Lebra says that this may sometimes be done for financial reasons. She writes of an impoverished aristocrat who founded her own school of Tea and flower arrangement in her sixties. This instance of converting "bridal training" to a profession is a somewhat risky economic strategy. The fees charged for lessons relate to expenditures (for equipment, etc.) in such a way that teaching Tea is probably lucrative only at the very top of the profession. Private tea instructors, who can support themselves on tuition and gifts alone, are rare.

In most cases, the return to Tea is related to the phenomenon that Lebra refers to as "age-peer grouping among middle-aged to elderly women." Such groups may be revivals of "alumni identity," (also Lebra's term), connected with specific geographical area women's associations or religious groups. Women meet to study Tea, practice, share equipment or facilities, and organize group *chakai*. They may also take tours to visit various places of interest such as famous teahouses, temples, kilns, or tea-growing areas.

Sociability and self-improvement are dominant themes. Group identity is strong and there is a definite sense of who is inside and outside a particular group. Stress is placed on consensual decision-making, careful accounting of financial responsibility, and shared labor. There is an emphasis on conformity within the group and individuals are discouraged from displaying expertise that is not commensurate with that of the group as a whole. Gossip is the primary mode of social control.

Lebra concludes that there are three possible future avenues of development for Japanese women in general: (1) professional domesticity, (2) the double and triple career, and (3) maximal freedom. She identifies professional domesticity as a "strategic extension of the traditional division of labor" where homemaking is raised to "a professional level of accomplishment" in order that a woman should "cultivate her feminine capacity toward her own fulfillment." I think that Tea will draw its future supporters from women who have chosen this avenue of self-fulfillment.

TEA IN A CULTURAL CONTEXT

Tea as a symbol of national identity

Both Japanese men and women seem to feel that attendance at a tea gathering is virtually mandatory for every visitor to their country. Almost no foreign head of state departs without being entertained at a tea ritual. The message is that Tea is something quintessentially Japanese, a tradition that guards deeply felt cultural values: It was no coincidence that Yasuhiro Nakasone, prime minister at the time, was photographed making tea on election day (*Time* [1984] 123 (1):64).

Nonetheless, *chanoyu* remains somewhat remote from the personal experience of many Japanese. Tea is a special area of the culture set aside as sacred and precious. Many Japanese seem to feel that individual experience with Tea is irrelevant as long as the institution is available to symbolize Japanese values and aesthetic sensitivity.

In her book, *Ethnic Identity*, Anya Peterson Royce makes the following statement: "No ethnic group can maintain a believable (viable) identity without signs, symbols, and underlying values that point to a distinctive identity" (Royce 1982, 7). This is precisely the reason that Japanese invite foreign heads of state and tourists to tea gatherings they would never attend on their own volition.

They are symbolically displaying the boundaries of their ethnicity. It does not matter that the guest has only a vague impression of ladies in lovely *kimono* moving gracefully through mysterious motions in preparing what many consider to be an unpalatable beverage. It would, in fact, be most disturbing to their hosts if they did claim to understand Tea. It is intended to be admired, not comprehended.

Ambivalent feelings and dissonant voices

A tradition of introspection   Paradoxically, the Japanese enthusiasm for *chanoyu* is anything but unqualified. Much of this ambivalence may be attributed to the Japanese predilection for melancholy self-criticism, a derivative of Japan's carefully cultivated tradition of philosophical introspection and poetic sensitivity.

Since Heian period, Japanese authors have won fame and fortune waxing nostalgic over the lost purity of earlier eras, lamenting the transience of life, and decrying the insensitivity of their peers. Yasunari Kawabata, Natsume Sōseki, and Yukio Mishima are internationally known exponents of this genre.

The concept of finite good   Coupled with the national passion for poetically expressed disillusionment is the suspicion that good fortune is finite: One individual's gain being interpreted as another's loss. The Tokugawa exploited this attitude by organizing the notorious "Five Man Groups" (*go nin gumi*), institutions that legally obliged Japanese to become "their brother's keepers."[9] Gossip and vicious criticism consequently became increasingly significant mechanisms for social control while abject self-depreciation developed into an indispensable survival skill. This intense and frequently self-righteous atmosphere gave rise to a class of literature devoted to criticizing anything or anybody suspected of failing to conform to the prevalent cultural standards.

Partially because Tea is perceived by both its proponents and detractors as the penultimate manifestation of some of Japan's most deeply valued beliefs, *chanoyu* has been the target of criticism for centuries. ("The nail that stands up gets pounded down.") But, whether incorporated into a Nobel prizewinning novel such as Kawabata's *Thousand Cranes* (1958), a gossip tabloid, or the International Edition of the New York Times (Weisman 1990); the contents of Tea critiques vary little.

Tea's negative image   Matsudaira Sadanobu (1758-1829), one of the greatest statesmen of the Tokugawa era and adviser to the *shōgun*, succinctly summarized national concerns about Tea when he wrote:

> Making Tea is a very worshipful performance, I can tell you. The host invites his guests and comes to meet them with an important and knowing air. Then it is "This scroll is by Kyōdō. I gave a huge sum for it. This kettle is Ashiya. It cost

me I don't know how much. This tea bowl was picked up cheap it is true, but I don't suppose there is another like it. And as I am an adept at the Zen philosophy, why should I need a famous teacher? You just take a little tea, and ladle up the water,—so—and then put it into the kettle—and it will croon its pine-breeze song, and a wonderful peace steals over you, and over the guests too—if they are the right sort of people (Matsudaira Sadanobu in Sadler 1962, 84).

Many of the points where Tea values seem to contradict one another and practice to fall short of the ideal are effectively summarized in this passage: Labeling Tea with the adjective "worshipful" and attributing a pompous manner to his imagined host highlights the common tendency to see Tea as overly formal—despite its claims to intimacy and naturalness. The air of pretentiousness attributed to tea practitioners in this passage also contrasts strongly with protestations that peace and simplicity are its goals.

Further, one might imagine that the fictive host, intent on impressing his guests with his erudition, has actually exercised very little in the way of personal creativity. His choices of utensils are both extravagant and orthodox. Raising the issue of the value of the utensils, also elicits the venerable question of expense *vs* an avowed commitment to frugality. And, finally, the host's concern with the reactions of the "right sort of people" emphasizes problems of relative rank and equality left unresolved since Rikyū's era.

"Inside" and "out"   Chadō's dual confirmatory and transformatory objectives do create a tremendous amount of confusion and emotional ambivalence about *chadō:* Non-practicing Japanese are bombarded with magazines, newspapers, and television shows that convey the message that tea ritual distills the essence of their national identity. Beguiled into thinking hard-earned skills are manifestations of native grace or inherent sophistication and unfamiliar with its complex etiquette, they feel awkward and unwelcome in the tearoom. Even more seriously, because they lack a fundamental understanding of its grammatical structure, they feel excluded from *chadō's* intricate spiritual dialogue.

Non-practitioners often react to the sensation of being "outside" (*soto*) Tea with puzzlement, anger, or both. Some decide that *chanoyu* is too frivolous, picayunish, or old-fashioned for their tastes. Others conclude that tea ritual has degenerated, frequently commenting that it is being practiced by the wrong kind (age, class, or sex) of practitioner.

Sexual prejudice   The idea that modern tea practice is in some-way "corrupt" may quite well be due in large part to sexual prejudice: Tanaka Senshō, (1875–1960), the founder of Dai Nihon Sadō Gakkai ("Great Japan Tea Society") was probably echoing his contemporaries' sentiments when he observed: "As times passed and conditions changed, the abuses of the way became renowned. The way became false, no more than a polite accomplishment, a casual pastime for women and children" (Tanaka in Kramer 1988, 13).

Perhaps it is time to consider the possibility that the phenomenal success of the modern tea schools results from their ability to provide intellectual stimulation and spiritual sustenance to a group of individuals generally denied such opportunities—Japanese women. There is, after all, more than a little justification for the notion that Japanese women, a historically repressed class, might feel a definite need to relieve the suspicion "that life is absurd and the attempt to make moral, intellectual, or emotional sense out of the experience in bootless" (Geertz 1973, 108). Indeed, Japanese culture provides few other socially acceptable opportunities for married women to participate fully (and without being assigned subordinate roles) in activities that both challenge their minds and refresh their souls.

Abuses and tea as a normative system   Japanese and Japanophiles alike appear to have charged the tea world with the responsibility of maintaining the spiritual purity of a "Golden Age" of Japanese culture that never really existed. The pressure to be "other-worldly" falls particularly heavily on the heads of the tea schools, for they are expected to function as the high priests of this inner shrine of ethnic identity.

While it is absolutely true that tea practitioners often do not live up to their ideals and must constantly guard against real and potential abuses of tea ritual, "The Way of Tea" is, after all, religion in practice. It incorporates a normative system precisely because people sometimes behave badly and need guidance to rectify the situation. The fault lies not with *chadō* but with "insiders" who falsely imply they have mastered it and "outsiders" who set standards of perfection they would never consider meeting. This is neither a modern phenomenon nor a problem that relates exclusively to Tea. It is generic to all cultural manifestations of religious belief.

Regrettably, tea practitioners have tended to respond to accusations of excessive formality, archaism, superficiality, and avarice by fortifying the boundaries of the ritual field. Criticized for engaging in an activity, which is harmless to others and deeply meaningful to them, they close the tearoom door behind them—justifying the charge of exclusivism. Too frequently, they also intensify their focus on the boundary maintenance features of confirmatory Tea, ignoring its integrative function.

TEA FOR THE TWENTY-FIRST CENTURY

Fortunately, in the last few decades a very remarkable tendency has been developing—tea practitioners are being stimulated to reject their former insularity and generate an unprecedented atmosphere of openness in *chanoyu*. Interestingly enough, the impetus for change has come from what might be thought to be bastions of conservatism, the *iemoto*. Through the publishing and broadcasting industries as well as the traditional tea school structure, the *iemoto* (particularly Urasenke) have begun to reach out to people of all sexes, ages, and walks of life. Even non-Japanese are being encouraged to practice Tea.

This trend has not been well received among cultural reactionaries. They fail to realize it is the boundaries of their cognitive model that are being challenged—not the coherence of Tea's ancient tradition. My own feeling is that *chadō* is once again demonstrating its wonderful adaptability: In the early days of tea history, the Japanese were intrigued by the splendid products of Chinese civilization but also vaguely threatened by the potential loss of cultural identity their adoption represented. The Japanese responded by integrating attractive features of the intrusive philosophies with indigenous beliefs and claiming the resultant synthesis as their own. They did this so successfully that one such amalgamation, tea ritual, became a symbol of "Japanese" culture recognized all over the world.

Today, Western technology and cultural artifacts seem to menace Japan's cherished traditions just as Chinese ideas did centuries ago. The response is much the same. Barricades are being raised around major symbols of Japanese identity such as tea ritual. But, *chadō* is more vital and functional than it has been in centuries. Blessed with a remarkable series of far-seeing leaders (epitomized by Urasenke's current grand master, Sen Sōshitsu), modern practitioners are being offered a unique opportunity to emulate Rikyū's egalitarian tea ritual in a refreshingly cosmopolitan atmosphere.

People are responding to this "invitation to Tea" with a renewed enthusiasm for this ancient form of religious practice. As Rikyū said:

> One must not be saddened in the least about tea. Neither is it the case that no Buddha will appear in this latter age. In the way of tea also, people with a true realization will come forth in later ages, and they will surely sense and share the aspiration that you and I have kept. If such a person extends a bowl of tea toward me—even though a hundred years have passed—it will moisten my bones; will not my departed spirit rejoice in accepting it? Without fail I shall become a guardian spirit of the way of tea. Surely the Buddhas and patriarchs will lend their power. (Sen Rikyū from the *Nampō Roku* in Nishibe 1981, 46)

The Temae *Appendix*

*T*here are a few basic elements common to almost every type of Tea preparation. The teacher may choose to separate out some of these often performed actions and have the student practice them separately. This is called *"warigeiko"* (divided practice). Emphasis is placed on the often repeated action sequences that combine to create *temae*. Some movements, which may be practiced individually, are walking, standing, opening and closing doors, carrying utensils, bowing, folding the *fukusa*, and handling the water ladle. It is important to note that a student never masters these basic arts. Even the most advanced students (teachers themselves) are exhaustively drilled in these skills when they take "master classes" from senior instructors (*gyōtei*). Tea study requires constant review at every stage of instruction.

RYAKU BON

The first tea procedure the student learns is usually one called *"ryaku bon,"* the abbreviated tray ceremony. This *temae* was created by Ennōsai, the thirteenth generation grand master of Urasenke. It is taught first because it is very useful and necessitates a minimum of equipment. Urasenke literature encourages a flexible approach to both the environment in which this *temae* is conducted and the equipment that may be used. Even the use of a Thermos bottle is permissible. It does not require the use of the water ladle (*hishaku*), something a bit complicated for beginning students.

Ryaku bon can be performed either indoors or outdoors. It is ordinarily used only to make thin tea (*usucha*), however, it incorporates many elements common to the preparation of thick tea (*koicha*). In preparation for the ritual, a small iron kettle with a handle and spout (*tetsubin*) is heated on a miniature brazier (*binkake*). As the water approaches a boil, the host kneels in the door of the room and greets the guests with a formal bow. He enters carrying a tray (usually the *yamamichi bon*, mountain road tray), which holds a tea bowl containing a damp linen cloth (*chakin*), a bamboo tea whisk (*chasen*), a tea

227

scoop (*chashaku*) and a tea container (*natsume*). The whole assemblage is placed in front of the brazier and the host returns to the preparation area (*mizuya*) for the waste water container (*kensui*). After he reenters and seats himself, he may elect to prepare the tea facing the hot water source or slightly turned toward the guests, a more intimate physical attitude.

The tea container and tea scoop are purified with a silk square (*fukusa*) that the host wears on his belt. The bowl is then filled with hot water. Next, the whisk is inspected for broken tines, rinsed, and the water in the bowl is discarded into the waste container. The bowl is subsequently wiped with the linen cloth and the host picks up the tea scoop. At the same time, he invites the guests to eat their sweets. The host then measures the tea into the bowl with the *chashaku* (tea scoop), adds hot water, and whisks it, placing the completed beverage in a location where it can be easily received by the guest. (Thin tea is about the consistency of a light broth, chartreuse green, and covered with froth.)

After the guests have drunk their tea, the bowl is cleaned and the whisk is once more inspected. The tea scoop is wiped and everything is replaced on the tray in its original position. If the tray has been placed to the right of the kettle, the host returns to a position directly in front of the brazier. Then he stands and exits with the waste container prior to returning for the tray. As in other *temae*, he kneels in the door to the preparation area to make final salutations.

This very abbreviated description of the *temae* makes it sound easy to perform—in fact, the strangeness of all these procedures tend to baffle a beginner. One Urasenke text illustrates this *temae* with over one hundred pictures, still inadequate to teach the process in the absence of a teacher. Compared to more advanced *temae*, however, *ryaku bon* is simple. The point to remember is that no *temae* is "below" the attention of even the most skilled Tea adept. This tray ceremony is a logical choice for performance under certain circumstances no matter what the skill level of the host might be—outdoor gatherings and the arrival of unexpected guests at home are two occasions on which this *temae* might typically be performed.

HIRADEMAE—THE MOST BASIC PREPARATIONS OF TEA

The *hirademae* essentially follow the same steps given for *ryaku bon:* Utensils are brought into the room and purified preparatory to making tea. Then, the equipment is cleaned and carried out again. Most disparities result from differences in the kinds of utensils required and in the techniques used to make thick tea. For example, the movements needed to incorporate water into the powder used for thick tea contrast to those used for thin tea because *koicha* (thick tea) is kneaded rather than whipped. The texture is very thick—like that of a thin pudding.

If the student learned only the *hirademae* for thin and thick tea, it would be possible to make tea correctly and in good taste under any circumstances (formal or informal). All other tea preparation procedures are variations of these basic *temae*. Thus, once a beginning student is comfortable with the methods of *hirademae*, the teacher may begin to teach him or her certain departures in technique. These allow for seasonal change and the use of different kinds of equipment (such as unusual bowls and tea containers, various tea stands, and different kinds of cold water jars). Commonly taught seasonal variations include using a leaf for a lid on the cold water jar (*habuta*) and rinsing out a damp *chakin* in the tea bowl to suggest coolness in summer (*araijakin*).

Nothing is taught out of the season in which it is actually performed. This means that the time for practicing a certain variation may pass before the student has mastered it—frustrating to beginners, but logical seen in the context of a lifetime study. Proper respect for seasonal variation is critical in *chanoyu*. After learning more advanced techniques of making tea, experts repeatedly return to the study of *hirademae* to polish and refine their style.

SUMIDEMAE, CHARCOAL PROCEDURES

Although the use of electric elements in the *furo* and *ro* is common outside of Japan (where the correct charcoal for Tea is scarce), it is absolutely necessary for the student to learn to lay a proper fire under the kettle. Like most other *temae*, *sumidemae* have seasonal variations. For example, disparate-sized pieces of charcoal are used for *ro* and *furo*. The utensils used reflect this difference. The *sumidemae* also include techniques for repairing the fire late in a *chaji*. As with other *temae*, the expert is never supposed to become complaisant. Charcoal procedures are practiced throughout a student's lifetime and are essential to making good tea. Nothing breaks the rhythm and carefully created atmosphere of a good *chaji* more abruptly than a cold fire!

It may take a student, who has but one weekly lesson (common outside of full-time studies in Kyōto), several years to become comfortable with the procedures just discussed. Once he or she has demonstrated an understanding of what is involved in the study of Tea and learned some basic skills, the teacher may suggest that the student apply for the *nyūmon* certificate. This is a formal request to begin the study of Tea with Urasenke. In effect, he or she is asking to join the *iemoto*. (There is a very small charge of applying.) The student will now begin the study of a series of *temae*, which provide an initial exposure to basic skills, tea history, and philosophy—the *konarai*.

THE SIXTEEN BASIC *KONARAI*

The word *konarai* is a contraction of *ko* meaning "small" and *narau*, the verb "to learn." The *konarai* are commonly seen at tea gatherings. They include procedures for making both thin and thick tea, laying charcoal, asking guests to help arrange flowers, hanging a special scroll in the *tokonoma*, and inspecting the jar used to store tea (*chatsubo*). The sixteen basic *konarai* of Urasenke were standardized in their present form by Gengensai. Each includes some lesson in Tea values as well as in technique.

Kinindate and *kinin kiyotsugu* are *temae* that can be performed for either *usucha* or *koicha*. They emphasize the rank of a noble guests (*kinin*) and their attendants (*tsugu* or [*o*]*tomo*, the person next in rank). The noble usually sits on the mat with his or her back to the alcove (*tokonoma*), a privileged position. Sweets are served individually to the noble on a special tray with a pedestal (*takatsuki*). The tea bowl is presented on a new, unlacquered wood stand (*kinindai*) indicative of purity. In theory, the tea bowl and its stand, tea scoop, linen cloth, and whisk are all new (and pure) and will only be used once. Tea stands (*tana*) are usually used because they indicate an appropriate degree of formality. While the guest drinks the tea, the host sits turned toward him or her with his knuckles on the *tatami* in an attitude of respect.

If an attendant has accompanied the noble into the tearoom, a second tea bowl with a specially folded linen cloth (*chidori-jakin*, a *chakin* folded to suggest a plover), and a smoked bamboo whisk is supplied for him or her. The *temae*, during which tea is prepared for both the noble and the attendant, is called "*kinin kiyotsugu*;" it emphasizes the difference in their ranks.

Obviously, these two techniques are a legacy of the *daimyō* era in Tea: Few modern students have the opportunity to serve tea to members of the imperial family. However, these *temae* are not considered anachronistic, because they teach important lessons about respect and prepare the student to perform more advanced *temae*. The Confucian element in *chadō* makes an awareness of social differentiation an inherent part of tea etiquette. Relationships within the tearoom are supposed to reflect those of an ideal society in microcosm.

Chaire kazari, chawan kazari, chashaku kazari, and *chasen kazari* are all procedures that focus on particular utensils used in the preparation of thick tea. For the first three *konarai*, the object to be featured is displayed in the alcove (*tokonoma*) at the beginning of the ceremony. The utensils are usually placed on a purple silk cloth (*fukusa*). In the case of tea scoop and the tea bowl, they are also placed in a bamboo case and silk bag, respectively. The thick tea container (*chaire*) is presented in its *shifuku,* a special fabric storage bag. *Chasen kazari* differs from the three procedures just discussed because it focuses on a more utilitarian object such as the water jar or kettle. The article to be emphasized is not placed in the alcove.

The purpose of these procedures is not to draw attention to the monetary values of the objects in question but to stress their emotional significance. Often something will be used because it has been a gift to the host and he wants to honor the donor. Alternatively, the item may relate to special interest of or have historical value for the main guest. Seeing something displayed in the characteristic *kazari* fashion cues the main guest to ask the host why he has chosen to use a particular article. All these *temae* are performed in both *ro* and *furo* seasons. There are some variations of these procedures that may be used when only thin tea is being prepared.

The next three *konarai temae* (*nagao, Ōtsubukuro,* and *tsutsumibukusa*) revolve around the use of different types of containers for thick tea powder. *Nagao* is a procedure where a large-mouthed *chaire* (*dai kai,* "big sea" or "inner sea" tea container) is used. It is believed that the first tea seeds brought to Japan arrived in such a receptacle. Because the mouth of the jar is so wide, the strings on the *shifuku* (bag) that contains it are particularly long and the student must learn to manipulate them correctly.

Ōtsubukuro is based on the use of a heavy silk (*chirimen*) bag shaped like that used to carry rice in Ōtsu province. It is interesting to note that this was the innovation of Sōon, Rikyū's second wife. The bag is tied around a type of plain, black-lacquered, medium-sized tea container (*natsume*) preferred by Rikyū. The procedure renders the use of the *natsume*, which is most frequently used for thin tea, proper for *koicha*.

A third *temae*, *tsutsumibukusa*, can be used if neither a *shifuku* or *Ōtsubukuro* is available for a *natsume* the host wishes to use in making thick tea. In this procedure, the tea container is wrapped in the host's own silk wiping cloth (*fukusa*) and tied.

Kasanejawan and *irekodate* are two more *konarai* of a very practical nature. The student learns *kasanejawan* so that he or she will know how to make *koicha* using two tea bowls (there are sometimes too many guests to use one). *Irekodate* is a thin tea procedure specially devised for children and those who are old or disabled. This *temae* reduces the frequency with which utensils are moved to and from the preparation area. For *irekodate*, the tea bowl and accompanying articles are carried into the room in a new, bent cedar, waste container (since it is new, it does not pollute the tea bowl the way a used waste container would). The other necessary utensils are already in place because a tea stand (*tana*) has been set up to display them prior to the host's entrance. This *temae* emphasizes the fact that there is room for everyone in the Tea world. The special needs of each individual can be accommodated, no matter what his physical ability.

As mentioned earlier, there are also two *konarai* that relate to charcoal procedures rather than to the actual preparation of tea: *bon kōgō* and *sumi shomō*. *Bon kōgō* focuses on the incense container (*kōgō*) in much the same way the *kazari konarai* featured other utensils. It can be used if the incense container has particular historical fame or is of great emotional significance to the host. Rather than being brought into the room in the charcoal basket as is the usual procedure, the incense container is carried in on a tray during the first charcoal preparation (*shozumi*).

Sumi shomō, the other charcoal *konarai*, and *hana shomō*, the *temae* where flowers are arranged in the tearoom, both involve and request a skilled guest's help in preparations. To be asked to participate in *sumi shomō* or *hana shomō* is a great compliment to one's skill as a Tea person. A host will ask a guest more skilled in tea than himself to arrange the charcoal either for *shozumi* (in *furo* or *ro* season) or *gozumi* (during the period when the *ro* is used). This demonstrates his own humility and respect for the superior abilities of the guest.

There are many reasons to perform *hana shomō*. For example, (1) the guest may be more experienced at arranging flowers for tea (*chabana*) than the host. (2) The flower vase or flowers may have been a gift of the main guest. (It is not considerate to take flowers to a tea gathering without prior consultation with the host. The flowers are carefully planned in advance to suit the event's seasonal theme. Bringing an unsolicited gift of flowers intended for the tearoom may have the effect of inducing the host to make unwelcome last minute changes.) (3) The host may have such a profusion of flowers that he wishes to share the enjoyment of arranging them. (4) The flower container may be a famous one in which the host humbly declines to arrange flowers. Or, (5) inclement weather during the middle break (*nakadachi*) of a full tea gathering (*chaji*) inspires the host to request *hana shomō* in order to provide the guests with the opportunity to stretch their legs without leaving the warm, dry tearoom. (It is interesting to note that the tray on which the flowers are carried into the room is unfinished cedar and resembles those used to make offerings at *Shintō* shrines.)

Tsubo kazari is another *temae* that requires a great deal of participation from the guests. Traditionally, after tea is picked in the spring, the tea leaves are aged in earthenware jars (*cha tsubo*). In the fall, these containers are opened and the tea removed in view of the guests. A little later during the gathering, the new tea is ground in a small stone mill set up in the preparation area. The special tea gatherings, where all this takes place, are called "*kuchikiri chaji.*" Unfortunately, they are seldom performed today because of the expense, equipment, and special skills required. The *tsubo kazari konarai* teaches students basic skills related to handling the tea jar and its wrapping materials—in case they are ever fortunate enough to attend this type of gathering.

The focus of the final *konarai temae* is the proper presentation of special scrolls (*jiku kazari*). At the beginning of the procedure, the rolled up scroll (*kakemono*, also called "*kakejiku*") is displayed on a purple silk cloth in the *tokonoma*. Its position on the floor of the alcove indicates its rank. The manner in which the host unrolls and hangs the scroll with the aid of a special fan reflects his respect for its meaning and creator as well as Tea's long tradition of curatorship.

It typically takes the part-time student several years to learn the sixteen basic *konarai* in both their *furo* and *ro* variations (when applicable). During this period, the student is also absorbing a great deal of information on Tea history, the nature of utensils, etiquette, and so forth. He or she has also begun to attend regular tea gatherings and participate in some of the varied activities of the Tea world. At the end of this time, the teacher may present the student with a certificate from the *iemoto* granting him or her permission to pursue Tea studies further.

SHIKADEN

Once the student has been thoroughly exposed to the *konarai*, he or she normally requests permission to study the *shikaden* (the first four orally transmitted or "secret" *temae*). The present forms of the *shikaden* were devised by Gengensai. They are normally not performed in the presence of those who have not received permission to study them, a practice designed to protect the *iemoto*'s control of its tradition. These *temae* include *satsubako, karamono, daitemmoku,* and *bondate*.

Satsubako is a restrained reminder of the ancient practice of tasting various teas. Only two teas are tasted, often because one has been a gift of the main guest. The host first makes thick tea with tea powder presented in a ceramic *chaire*. Afterwards, he prepares the tea brought by the guest. The second kind of tea is supplied from a black lacquer *natsume*. Both tea containers are carried into the room in a box like those used to contain medicine in ancient times.

Karamono, daitemmoku, and *bondate* focus on the respectful presentation of tea utensils that came from China to Japan in the early days of tea practice. *Karamono* means simply "Chinese thing." The procedure that bears this name was originally devised to feature precious Sung dynasty thick tea containers (*chaire*). *Daitemmoku* were similarly created to feature the *temmoku* tea bowls brought to Japan during the Kamakura period. *Temmoku* is a generic name for relatively deep tea bowls with dark glazes made in either China or Japan. They have wide mouths and narrow bottoms. Such bowls are associated with ceramics used for tea drinking in the Ch'an monasteries of northern Fujian. *Temmoku* is the Japanese pronunciation of Tien-mu, the range of mountains where these monasteries were located. They were originally used to take medicine. *Bondate* was created to feature Sung *chaire* that still have their original trays (or one of similar provenance). The trays vary in size, shape, and color.

These *temae* are introductions to the more advanced level of Tea. Three kinds of sweets should be served instead of the usual two. Very few people actually have the opportunity to make tea with such precious utensils. Students regularly practice with copies, however. The *shikaden* teach respect for objects important to tea history.

WAKIN, A KOICHA TEMAE
WITH EMPHASIS ON JAPANESE UTENSILS

After learning the four *temae* just discussed, the emphasis returns to Japanese utensils in another orally transmitted tea procedure created by Gengensai. It highlights a piece of Japanese cloth (*wakin*) that once belonged to the Emperor Kōkaku. From the material, Gengensai made both a *shifuku* for a paulownia wood *nakatsugi* (the wooden container for a *chaire* of Chinese origin) and a *kobukusa*. Both are used in the *wakindemae*. Tantansai altered the presentation by substituting an unlacquered *nakatsugi*-shaped container of mulberry wood.

CHABAKO, PREPARATIONS FOR TEA
MADE WITH UTENSILS CARRIED IN A BOX

In addition to the *wakindemae*, Gengensai created a wonderful series of tea preparations that use small utensils easily carried in a box. The portable character of the *chabako* (box for tea utensils) makes these *temae* ideal for outdoor tea gatherings (*nodate*). The boxes themselves can be made of various woods either lacquered or unlacquered (the most formal is plain black lacquer). The associated miniature utensils can be matched or disparate in material and design.

Unohana (*deutzia* blossom) *chabakodemae* is a basic procedure employing utensils without covers (*shifuku*). This *temae* is learned first in the series and may be performed at any time during the year. *Unohana* and *Wakeidate* are the only *chabakodemae* that may be studied without obtaining specific certificates. For the Moon (*tsuki chabako*), Snow (*yuki chabako*), and Flower (*hana chabako*), the utensils have covers that must be handled in a special way. They are performed only at specified times of the year. All four *temae* draw their inspiration from a poem on the four seasons by Zen master Dōgen.

The final two procedures in the *chabako* series were created by Tantansai. *Wakeidate* was created for the present (*o*)*iemoto* when he went to war. It was originally called by a name that indicated that it was a *temae* for the battlefield. (Sen Sōshitsu used it to prepare tea for the members of naval special attack units during World War II.) Today its name (*Wakeidate*) has been changed to mean "to make tea in harmony and respect. An unlacquered box was originally used to perform this *temae*. *Wakeidate* is fast and appropriate for two or more guests.

Shikishidate is the final *temae* in this series. It was invented to make use of a basketry letter box ordered by Ennōsai and associated with the imperial palace. *Shikishi* are the square poem boards on which calligraphy is written. They are sometimes placed on scroll-like hangers provided with threads for mounting them and hung in the tearoom. Most of the utensils used in this *temae* are placed on square pieces of board or fabric to recall the proportions of these cards.

THE HIGHER *TEMAE*

The *temae* of the advanced level are used mainly for presentations made at temples, shrines, and memorial services. They also recall the procedures used to prepare tea in the *shoin*. The *daisu* is often used and the utensils are mainly Chinese in origin. These orally transmitted *temae* are the most advanced studied by ordinary practitioners. They are not, however, formal (*shin*) *temae*. They are properly considered semiformal (*gyō*) *temae*. There are more advanced, formal *temae* above this level but only a very few extremely high-ranking practitioners ever learn them.

Gyō no gyō daisu is a procedure that uses an unlacquered semi-formal *daisu*. The *daitemmoku* tea bowl and *chaire* employed are supposed to be utensils brought from China during the Kamakura period through Momoyama period and classified *meibutsu* or famous objects during Rikyū's time (although copies are naturally used in practice). Both items are presented on a large tray about fourteen inches in diameter that is decorated with trigrams from the *I Ching*.

Shin no gyō daisu is a presentation that requires the use of a black lacquered *daisu* and a small tray like those used in *bondate*. Only the *chaire* is placed on the tray. The *chaire* and the *daitemmoku* tea bowl should be *ōmeibutsu*, very high-ranking tea objects identified as such during the Higashiyama period of Tea history. Sets of matched bronze utensils (*kaigu*), which include the water jar, ladle-holder, lid rest, and waste container, are used as they recall the style of tea practiced in ancient China.

Dai en no sō is a *temae* that uses no *daisu*. A large tray, two *chaire* (one Japanese container and one, ideally *ōmeibutsu*, Chinese container), and a *daitemmoku* bowl are used. *Dai en no shin* uses a formal *daisu*, a *daitemmoku* bowl, one tea container (again, ideally, *ōmeibutsu*), and a large tray.

SHICHIJI SHIKI, TEMAE
OUTSIDE THE FORMAL INSTRUCTIONAL HIERARCHY

As mentioned earlier, Ittō and Joshinsai invented seven *temae* designed to encourage cooperation among students in the tearoom. While they study regular *temae*, students are also exposed to these *shichiji shiki*.

All of *shichiji shiki* are group exercises requiring at least five students. The participants draw bamboo cards (*fuda*) to determine the roles they will play or functions they will perform in the drill. (The bamboo tablets were inspired by those used in incense appreciation games.) One drill centers on preparing rounds of *usucha* (*kagetsu*, flower moon *temae*). In another, each individual performs a different job such as preparing the fire, flowers, appreciating incense, and making both thick and thin tea (*shaza*). In others, students arrange charcoal or flowers in turn (*mawarizumi* and *mawaribana* respectively), taste five bowls of *koicha* (*chakabuki*), and judge one participant's performance (*ichi ni san*). More than five participants are required for the last exercise in the series (*kazu cha*). This is a relatively casual procedure involving making tea, drinking it, and eating sweets. It has also become the custom of each (*o*)*iemoto* to leave a signature performance of this type to be revealed posthumously. It may involve writing poetry in calligraphy on the subject of certain flowers, for example. All *shichiji shiki* involve great mental discipline and fine-tuned coordination. Everyone must know his job and how to move in a manner that avoids embarrassing "traffic jams" in the tearoom. People commonly say that one must practice each *shichiji shiki* one hundred times before it makes sense!

The Toriawase *Appendix*

*T*his appendix is intended to supplement previous chapters by providing the reader with a few examples of the *toriawase* of actual tea gatherings. I have selected them for the variety they represent and offer them as examples of the various ways in which the combination of utensils can be used to convey a message.

THE HŌJŌSAI EN YOTSUGASHIRA CHAKAI

This tea gathering is held annually on November 17, in the abbot's quarters of Tōfukuji (a Zen temple). It is considered a classic example of the kind of tea ritual performed in Japanese Buddhist temples.

A scroll with a picture of the temple founder, Shōichi Kokushi (Enni Ben'en, 1201–1280), hangs on one wall. It is flanked by other portrait scrolls that are treasures of the temple. On a low stand in front of the hangings, candles, incense, hot water, rice, and sweets are arranged. In the middle of the room, a higher table with an incense burner on top is located. The guests enter the room and sit in rows according to a prearranged seating scheme. The abbot enters and bows to the person sitting opposite him and the main guest. As he sits and places his cushion to one side, the other guests do the same.

The monk who is in charge of medicines (*jiyaku*) then comes into the room and waves his fan once. Everyone bows and puts their place cards to one side. The monk in charge of other people's belongings (*jie*) lights the candles and the monk in charge on incense (*jikō*) burns incense. Then the candles are extinguished. Exiting and reentering, the *jikō* and the *jiyaku* bow to the main position (*shui*) and go to their own places. The *jie* subsequently enters the room and removes the place cards of any absent guests. All fold their spread-cloths and place their rosaries to their right.

The guests at the ritual tea are next served a vegetarian meal. Trays are removed afterwards and sweets are brought in. For the four main guests, the serving monks bring sweets in lacquer containers (*fuchidaka*) with their right hands and *temmoku* tea bowls on stands (*dai*) with their left hands. The other guests receive their tea bowls and sweets from round trays that hold enough bowls and sweets for five or six people. (It is significant for comparison with other types of tea gatherings that the powdered green tea is already in the bowls when they are brought into the room.)

The serving monks reenter with ewers (*tōbyo*) of hot water. (The ewers look rather like western coffee pots.) A tea whisk (*chasen*) sits on the spout of each ewer. Taking the *chasen* in one hand, the monks pour water in each bowl and whisk the tea. When everyone has had tea prepared, the guests drink simultaneously. The serving monks then remove the tea bowls and sweet containers from the positions of the main guests from a kneeling position. The utensils of the main guests are removed individually. Those of the other guests are collectively gathered on trays by monks who perform this service from a standing position. When the room has been cleared of utensils, all the guests bow and exit following the main guests (Nishibe 1981).

MATSUDAIRA FUMAI'S FLOWER-VIEWING TEA

Matsudaira Fumai was a famous and well-respected *daimyō* tea master best known for his successful attempt to organize and preserve famous tea utensils in the collection of his family. He was also a spectacularly successful administrator. The gathering for which the *toriawase* is described was held in his villa in Shinagawa in 1816. It represents a balance of spectacular collector's items and more modest utensils. The reader should note that the character of the utensils do not compete with the beauty of the cherry blossoms that undoubtedly bloomed in the garden. Artistic themes pertaining to flowers are not in evidence. This *toriawase* is described in Kumakura Isao's article "Matsudaira Fumai: The Creation of a New World of Chanoyu" (Kumakura 1980).

The kettle was one that Fumai ordinarily used in the shrine, which he had built to Rikyū. The charcoal container was a simple basket of bamboo and the ash bowl was Raku. The *kōgō* was a copy of Ōhi ware with a whirlpool design and the *mizusashi* was a black-lacquered wooden bucket, a style considered very elegant and one preferred by Rikyū. The *chaire* was Ninsei and made in a shape that evoked the rice container used in a Zen temple. The main bowl was Karatsu and the waste water recep-

tacle was Imbe (Bizen). The gathering was, however, so large
that it had to be held in several rooms to accommodate all the
guests. In one hall hung a famous painting by Mu-ch'i (the
greatest painter of the Southern Sung Ch'an movement) and a
tea scoop made by a Momoyama period Zen monk (Kei Shuso)
was displayed. In one tearoom, a painting by the greatest
painter of the Northern Sung, Su T'ung P'o (1037–1101) was
hung. In another, two Chinese scrolls by L'iang K'ai (B.C. 1140),
a follower of Mu-Ch'i and a Korean Blue Ido tea bowl named
"Old Pine" were present. In yet another area, a *shikishi* (poem
card) by Fujiwara Teika was hung and in still more areas, a red
Raku tea bowl, a kettle that belonged to Sen Shōan, and a
chashaku made by Kobori Enshū were used.

This is an example of a really spectacular *toriawase* selected
by a man who was probably the greatest collector of tea utensils yet known. Notice, however, that only some of the utensils
are really famous. Fumai undoubtedly had well-known utensils
in every category which he could have used, but chose instead
to contrast his treasures with more obscure pieces. A final note
on the gathering is that there were many guests who over-
crowded the areas assigned to them, disrespectfully eating their
lunches in the shrine to Rikyū, and drinking *saké* that they had
heated in its kettle.

A MEMORIAL SERVICE FOR
GENGENSAI AND MUGENSAI HELD AT SANGEN'IN

This tea gathering was held on September 6 and 7 in 1976 to
honor the one-hundredth death anniversary of Gengensai (the
eleventh generation grand master of Urasenke) and the thirteenth death anniversary of Mugensai (also known as Tantansai, the fourteenth generation grand master of Urasenke). It
was also a large scale gathering with five thousand guests
attending in a period of several days. It was held at a subtem-
ple of Daitokuji. The gathering was described in the Winter
1976 issue of the *Urasenke Newsletter*.

The scroll was written by Engan Kokushi (Shun'oku Sōen,
1529–1611). He explains that Rikyū contributed to the building
of the San mon Gate. The historical associations of this letter
make it a priceless object and very famous. It was once owned
by Matsudaira Fumai. Rose of Sharon and Japanese pampas
grass were arranged in an ancient Persian container with a

flower-shaped mouth. The *kōgō* was made by Sen Sōtan himself of lacquer papier-mâché and has a box inscribed by Gengensai. It is in the shape of a lion. The kettle used was made by a maker who supplied Rikyū and was a favorite of Sen Shōan, the second in the Sen line. It has a design of clouds and dragons. Its box was signed by Tantansai. The *furo* used was a rust-colored one of a type favored by Jōō; the *tana* was one signed by Gengensai called *"Kanundana,"* "cold clouds." The *mizusashi* was Bizen with an arrow-notch type mouth and was a favorite of Sōtan. Tantansai had inscribed its box. The *chaire* was of the type known as Oribe ware and had square shoulders. A letter was found in its box that was written by a *daimyō*, who had been Tokugawa Ieyasu's sword bearer as a child. The *chashaku* was one made by Sen Sōtan and called "Wind in the Pines." The first tea bowl was made by Chōjirō, the first in the line of famous Raku potters, and is called "Distant Mountains" (*Tōyama*). It is a very famous black Raku bowl. Gengensai was one of the tea masters who had signed its box. Gengensai had also inscribed the box of the second tea bowl, a Korean ware whose name describes the flower forms made by waves breaking on the beach. The lid rest was a trefoil-shaped also preferred by Gengensai. The tea used was called "The Way of Buddha" and the sweets named "The Grass of Memories." The sweets were served in black-lacquer boxes.

This is another example of a large and magnificent tea gathering designed to honor the memory of two famous tea masters. Notice that a great many of the utensils used were particularly liked or designed by the individuals being remembered and that the poetic names are solemn and selected to evoke a sense of remembrance.

RIKYŪKI AT URASENKE

Sen Rikyū is honored on March 28 by Urasenke students and teachers all over the world. At Urasenke in Kyōto a variety of different events honor him. Private offerings are made by the (*o*)*iemoto* in the Rikyūdō and a large gathering is subsequently held in the Totsutotsusai, an important tearoom within Konnichian. A memorial portrait of Sen Rikyū hangs (a copy of one drawn from life by Hasegawa Tōhaku [1539–1610] is most often used) in the *tokonoma*. Also present is a low mulberry stand, designed by Rikyū, decorated with a bronze vase, candlestick, and Raku incense burner. The flower characteristically found in the vase is *nanohana*, the rape flower. It is always used at *Rikyū-ki* because it is said to have been the flower arranged by Rikyū for his last tea. Several other vases of flowers are arranged during the gathering as part of the service.

The *(o)iemoto* builds the fire and makes *koicha*. The kettle used is usually one in a hanging-style called *"tsurigama."* A kettle called *"Unryugama,"* which has a design of a dragon in clouds and was a favorite of Shōan, Rikyū's son-in-law, is often used. A red Raku tea bowl on a tall stand of the same material is used. This type of bowl and stand are only used for memorial presentations. An unlacquered *daisu* with bamboo supports is also used. Later, students and other members of the tea family may have the chance to participate in *shichiji shiki*, the collective tea exercise where participants draw cards to determine their respective duties. A typical sweet served at this event is called *"Hanagoromo,"* "Flower Robe" a name that suggests the cherry blossoms that bloomed around the time of Rikyū's death.

THE NEW YEAR AT URASENKE

The New Year is a time for joyous celebration and magnificence. Symbols of good fortune and the use of happy colors and gorgeous gold and silver decorations are appropriate for the occasion. The utensils described in the following paragraph were selected for a gathering conducted during the first six days of 1979 and detailed in the Spring 1979 issue of the *Urasenke Newsletter*.

The scroll in the *tokonoma* was one done by the Emperor Gomizuno-o (1596–1680), the husband of Sen Sōtan's pupil Tōfukumon'in. He wrote about the marvelous joy of being the ruler of such a dignified country as Japan. The frame which surrounded the *ro* was made especially for the gathering of formal black-lacquer with *makie* designs in gold of shrine gates. It was supposed to represent the gates of the shrine of Miwa in the hills near Nara. The emperor's poetic theme for the year was *"saka,"* "hill." The *chashaku* was the first one carved by the *(o)iemoto* that year. It was named *"Fukuju kai,"* "Sea of Happiness." The tea bowls used were a nested pair (*Shimadai*) which evoke the image of the island home of the Immortals. They were made by the eleventh generation of the Raku family in red raku. The top bowl was lined inside in gold and the bottom one, in silver. The base of the top bowl is made in a pentagon shape, which evokes the five sacred mountains surrounding Kyōto. The lower bowl has a six-sided foot that represents the shape of the tortoise. A paired set such as this symbolizes "*tsuru kame*," "crane-tortoise," emblematic of longevity. A *kōgō* called the "*Buri buri kōgō*" is always used at Konnichian during the New Year. It was made from a child's toy used in the imperial palace and subsequently given to the Sen family who had it made into a *kōgō*. It is a painted, eight-sided wooden block. As a toy, it was pulled along on wheels by a string and made a "buri buri" sound. A formal, black-lacquer *daisu* was used and the *Hōraizan kazari*, a special display of objects having felicitous meanings, decorated the alcove.

A *SHŌGO CHAJI* GIVEN BY A TEACHER
FOR HER STUDENTS

The following *toriawase* is that of a gathering given by a teacher for her students. The teacher lives in California and has a western-style house with an eight-*tatami* mat tearoom. By giving several tea gatherings a year, she instructs her pupils in the etiquette of full tea gatherings, seasonal *toriawase*, and the spirit of Tea.

The students assembled in the teacher's living room and were served cups of hot water with dried chrysanthemum in them. The youngest member of the group passed the cups around. Afterwards, the guests lined up in the order in which they would ultimately be seated in the tearoom. They then went around the outside of the house and entered the gate to the *roji*. A bench with *enza* and *tabako bon* was located around the corner from the tearoom entrance and the guests waited there until invited to enter the tearoom. After washing at the *tsukubai* in the garden, the students enter the tearoom as if there were a *nijiriguchi*. (Actually, a bamboo screen had been lowered over a sliding glass door to approximate the dimensions of the crawling-in entrance.)

The scroll in the *tokonoma* had been done by an amateur calligrapher who visited a nearby town; its theme was the beginning of Fall. The poem was originally included in an anthology of the tenth century. The *tana* used was the *Yoshinonodana*. The *mizusashi* was Egaratsu with a design of fall grass and a cicada. The *kōgō* was similar to the Tamukeyama *kōgō* but was shaped like a maple leaf and lacquered black with red leaves. The *futaoki* used had a design of red leaves that suggested those along a river near Nara. The *chaire* was Tambayaki in the "thrusting shoulders" shape. The fabric of its bag was one preferred by Oribe. The bowl used for *koicha* was the gift of a student, who had traveled to the "Stone Garden" temple in Kyōto. Small white stones from the famous Zen garden were embedded in the white *raku* bowl. The brazier was a bronze *Dōanburo* and the kettle was in the "crane's neck" shape. The name of the *chashaku* used for *koicha* was *"Mu Ichi Butsu"* "No One Thing" and the scoop used for *usucha* was called *"Nowaki"* "Storm."

During the break, the scroll was replaced by an arrangement of five fall grasses and chrysanthemum in a basket-shaped *hanaire* like one favored by Sōtan. The *natsume* used for thin tea was black-lacquer with a design of mother and baby quails. The first bowl was painted in the Kyōto style and had a motif of fall leaves. The second bowl was in a style preferred by Oribe.

A *HANGO CHAJI* PRESENTED IN OCTOBER

This *toriawase* was created by a non-Japanese Urasenke instructor who resides in Kyōto. October *chaji* are called *"nagori chaji"* because the intent is to use the remainder (*nagori*) of the year's tea supply. The sense of barest sufficiency is reflected in the choice of utensils that are considered *sabi* in character. The weather is growing colder and the *furo* is placed in the center of the preparation *tatami* to provide more warmth for the guests. The host describes this *toriawase* as one of which he is proud but considers "perhaps too much covering all the bases of alliteration, allusion, and fantasy."

The four guests were Midorikai students and a Japanese friend. The gathering began at nine in the morning. The *machiai* was a ten mat room with a large *tokonoma*. In the *tokonoma* a painting of the brushwood gatherer was displayed with a blue and white Korean incense burner, and a *biwa* (a classical Japanese musical instrument). Hot water was served in cups with peony decorations on a tray made by a friend of the host. The tray was cherry wood with worm holes filled with gold lacquer. An ink stone, ink stick, bronze brush rest, and a water dropper made by Joseph Justice were provided.

The guests progressed to a four mat *daime* tearoom. The scroll in the *tokonoma* was written by Konoe Nobuhiro. The

246 JAPANESE TEA RITUAL

hanging displayed in the tearoom was a letter thanking a friend for the loan of some books. It was lent to the host by his sponsor. It was written between 1647 and 1649.

The kettle and brazier used at this gathering had recently been retrieved from the ruins of a burned house. The *furo* was cracked but was appropriate for October gatherings for this reason. The kettle was cylindrical and carried a "cloud-dragon" pattern favored by Rikyū. The brazier rested on the severed end of a roof tile, which had been found by the host near Yatadera in Nara. It had a characteristic trefoil shape, which accommodated the three-legged *furo* perfectly. The charcoal was carried into the room in a tall, red folk basket shaped like a Chinese painter's brush holder. The basket was a *"karahitsu kago."* The feather used to purify the brazier was that of an osprey and the *hibashi* were long roof nails found at the Hompōji temple, which adjoins the Urasenke property. The *kan* were made of old horse bits and the *kōgō* was a turned wood *shari* (relic case) from India. It contained mixed incense, another October custom that makes use of the leftovers from the previous Tea year.

The flowers were arranged in a bamboo *hanaire* made from material found near the Byakkōji, a temple near Nara. *"Byakkō"* is the name for the tuft of white hair that grows on the *ushnisha* lump on Buddha's forehead. The temple itself is famous for its bush clover (*hagi*). The flowers placed in the vase were *hototogisu* ("toad lily," *Tricyrtis macropoda*), *yamagobō* (Indian poke, *Phytolacca esculenta*), and *yabu myōga* (*Pollia japonica* Thumb). The *mizusashi* was in the shape of a *sutra* case (*kyozutsu*) and had been made by an American friend of the host. *Koicha* was presented in a small *natsume* (*konatsume*) wrapped in the host's *fukusa* (the *tsutsumibukusa temae*). The main bowl was a Chinese "ash fall" (*kenzan haikatsuki*) *temmoku* and it rested on a stand favored by Tantansai, which is red inside and black outside. An ivory tea scoop named *"Kokū,"* "the Ultimate Void" was used for *koicha*.

A bamboo *chashaku* made by the host was employed to scoop *usucha*. The thin tea container was a black piece of American Indian pottery purchased by the host at the Santa Maria pueblo in Arizona during an archaeology field trip. Two bowls were used for thin tea. One was a red *raku*. The previous owner had been the host's landlord. Since the landlord had disposed of the tea bowl's box, its name was unknown. The host renamed it after the owner's grandfather, *"Yūzan,"* "friend mountain." The other bowl was Korean *katade* made during the *Yi* period (1392–1910).

Since the gathering was a *hango chaji* (one presented after breakfast or after the noon meal), the full *kaiseki* was not presented. The host offered his guests food on a brown lacquer tray (*shunkei*) with abalone shells used as *mukōzuke*. The shells contained *katsuotataki*, a mixture of grilled bonito, garlic, ginger, green onions, *shiso* ("beefsteak plant", *Perilla frutescens*), *wakame* seaweed (*Undaria pinnatifida*), and *myōga* shoots. It was dressed with *konbu katsuo shoyu*, a sauce made of dried bonito, *konbu* seaweed (genus *Laminaria*), and soy sauce. The *nimonowan* contained a fried cornmeal mush with ginkgo nuts, a green vegetable called "*okahijiki*," and ground chicken. The soup was thickened with *kuzu* (arrowroot). It was decorated with a curl of *sudachi* (a small and fragrant, green citrus) skin. *Namasu* was offered only to first time guests. It consisted of grated *daikon* (*Raphanus sativus*), vinegar, and red pepper. The *hassun* was presented on a ceramic box lid. The mountain element was egg yolks pickled in red *miso*. The sea component was jellyfish and codfish eggs wrapped in *nori* seaweed.

Since the *koichademae* was *daitemmoku*, three sweets were served. They were *warabi mochi* (fern root jelly), fresh crabapples, and a combination of fresh persimmons and fresh chestnuts bound with *tōfu* (soy bean) cream.

Notes

CHAPTER 2: THE BEGINNING OF THE ROAD

1. In the *Erh ya*, China's earliest known dictionary (perhaps prepared in pre-Han times), tea was referred to as *chia* and defined as "bitter" *t'u*. The author called the earliest gatherings of this camellia-like plant "*t'u*" and the latter crop, "*ming*." As *ming*, it was included in both the *Shuo wen chien-tzu*, a dictionary presented to Han Emperor An Ti in A.D. 121, and the *Po ya* compiled by Chang I in the third century. In addition, Tea's utility as a medicine was noted in the *Dialects* of Yang Hsiung written during the Han dynasty (Carpenter in Lu Yü 1974, 12–13).

2. Lu Yü is also said to have written additional works on the proper water used for boiling tea, and so forth, but these have been lost (Carpenter, Introduction to Lu Yü 1974, 52).

3. It is important in comparing the utensils Lu Yü used to those of today to note that the tea that he discussed preparing is tea molded into a dense, dry brick not powdered or leaf tea as we know it.

4. The original was supposedly lost but a work (the *Pai-chang ch'ing-kuei* or *Hyakujō Shingi*) based on Pai-chang's text that was compiled in Japan by imperial order in 1335 (Fujikawa 1957). Martin Collcutt asserts that this work is actually a Yüan dynasty (1264–1368) synthesis of some major Sung codes (960–1279). He says it contains nothing that can be traced directly to Pai-chang (Collcutt 1981, 137).

CHAPTER 3: TEA COMES TO JAPAN

1. Murai Yasuhiko (1989) thinks that Eisai could have brought powdered tea, saplings, or seeds.

2. When Nampo's *daisu* fell into disuse after his death, it was stored at Daitokuji.

3. The calligraphy he hung was the work of Yüan Wu, a Chinese Zen master. It was a gift from Ikkyū and it emphasized the relationship between Buddhism and Tea (Nishibe 1981, 23).

4. Daisetz T. Suzuki defined *wabi* as "transcendental aloofness in the midst of multiplicities" (Suzuki 1959, 22). He went on to say that it has the implication of poverty and being out of fashion (Suzuki 1959, 23). Takeno Jōō preferred to express it by evoking the image of a soli-

tary, thatched hut standing by the seashore in the autumn dusk. Sen Rikyū evoked the image of young grasses pushing up through the snow (Sen 1979, 72–73). All these images and definitions stress the positive virtues of the sense of insufficiency. The glamour of bright fall leaves and spring flowers is missing, but a deeper, more subtle tranquillity pervades the scene. This aesthetic has been translated into a style of Tea where both the atmosphere and spiritual attitudes created by the *toriawase* communicate these qualities. The emphasis is on material and spiritual purity and a deep respect for what is natural. Since this attitude is often identified with that of the philosophical recluse, *wabi* is sometimes translated "rustic simplicity."

5. *Yūgen* is best understood by evoking a vision of the moon shrouded by clouds, a sight that the master was known to prefer.

CHAPTER 4: THE *SAMURAI* AND THE MERCHANT TEA MASTERS

1. Some of Hideyoshi's strange behavior may have been due to his illness—tuberculosis. Communicated by Allan Palmer, September 1983.

2. Furuta Oribe and Hosokawa Sansai were the only two of Rikyū's seven important disciples (Oribe, Hosokawa, Makimura Hyōbu, Gamō Ujisato, Seta Kamon, Shibayama Kenmotsu, and Takayama Ukon) who had the courage to go down to the Yodo River to see him off when he left on the brief exile, which preceded his *seppuku*. Oribe was criticized by his contemporaries as the least talented of Rikyū's students. (Authorities disagree on the composition of this list.)

CHAPTER 5: SEN RIKYŪ'S ACHIEVEMENTS IN TEA

1. A few extant tea utensils bearing "cross" motifs predate Hideyoshi's and Ieyasu's anti-Christian purges (Haga 1981, 12).

CHAPTER 6: SEN RIKYŪ'S LEGACY

1. Sōon was a very remarkable woman. She is said to have shared Rikyū's sense of taste (Sadler 1962, 114) and to have been the first of the female "tea masters" (Iguchi 1976, 11). She is also credited with the inspiration for various tea articles (the *fukusa*, silk wiping cloth, and the *Ōtsubukuro*, a silk bag for the *natsume*, tea container). It was probably the influence of Sōon's faithful memory of Rikyū's ideals and his own Zen training that made Sōtan a faithful supporter of the *wabi* tradition in Tea.

2. By the end of her life, Hamamoto Sōshun had achieved such respect that she was recognized by all as one of the very highest-ranking *gyōtei*.

3. Another group was established in New York in the 1920s. The members were Japanese but the group gradually grew to include Americans as well. The next overseas branch of Urasenke was started in Boston, a sister city of Kyōto.

CHAPTER 7: TEA SCHOOL STRUCTURE

1. While investigators agree on the central importance of the *ie* in Japanese thought, they do not all concur on its definition. Harumi Befu argues that the *ie* is essentially an economic organization rather than a kinship group. Certainly, there is no question that unrelated individuals such as new brides, adopted-in sons-in-law, and apprentices are considered part of the house. Daughters who marry out become part of their husband's *ie*. In contrast, Ronald Dore believes kinship is central to the *ie*. He reminds us that the *ie* was legally recognized during the Meiji period as a unit of living individuals defined by kinship and recorded in local government offices—regardless of residential location or occupation. Residence and occupation were discounted because sons recorded as members of the *ie* had the potential for forming economically independent branches or going to town to work in factories (Dore 1958, 103). Chie Nakane stresses the "frame of residence" as primary (Nakane 1970, 5).

2. The term *dōzoku* is used by ethnologists to refer to similar institutions that occur throughout Japan. Regional nomenclature varies.

3. Although the rooms are probably too small to accommodate everyone, attendance at the last (*uzumebi*) and first teas (*Ōbukucha*) of the solar year held in Konnichian are good indicators of *ie* membership.

4. The families are those of Nakamura Sōtetsu (twelfth generation, lacquer), Okumura Kichibei (eleventh generation, scroll mountings, screens, and paper goods), Eiraku Zengorō (sixteenth generation, ceramics), Nakagawa Jōeki (eleventh generation, repoussé and cast metal), Raku Kichizaemon (fifteenth generation, ceramic utensils), Ōnishi Seiemon (fourteenth generation, cast metals), Kuroda Shōgen (thirteenth generation, bamboo objects), Tsuchida Yūkō (twelfth generation, textile crafts), Hiki Ikkan (eighth generation, papier mâché utensils), and Komazawa Risai (fifteenth generation, wooden objects).

5. I find it suggestive that the wooden statue of Rikyū was installed in the memorial chapel at Urasenke. If Sōtan had intended Omotesenke to assume the major responsibility for ancestor worship, one would think that an object so central to Rikyū's memorial cult would have been enshrined there.

6. Robert J. Smith says that the care of elderly parents and the ancestor tablets has classically been considered the responsibility of

the oldest son (Smith 1974, 119). He also notes that, unlike the Chinese, the Japanese do not put marks on tablets that allow one to tell the difference between the original and duplicates (Smith 1974, 186).

7. Each family's gravestones can be identified by a separate distinctive shape.

8. This indicates that the Urasenke (o)*iemoto* alone may venerate as many as three sets of ancestor tablets (*ihai*): (*a*) those at Jukō'in, (*b*) those in the *butsuma* (family chapel) at Konnichian, and (*c*) those in Chadōzan Kyōshinan, the meditation hall at the *Chadō* Research Center. This multiplicity of tablets leads one to conclude that such tablets are more evocative of departed souls than unique embodiments of their presence.

The tablets at the family sub-temple at Daitokuji (Jukō'in) represent all three branches of the Sen family while those at Konnichian memorialize only the Urasenke branch (which counts Rikyū as its first generation). The *ihai* at Kyōshinan are dedicated to Rikyū "followers of tea throughout the world," and some former abbots of the temple (personal communication from Gary Cadwallader, 1989).

9. The Sen (o)*iemoto* must sometimes attend events of national or civic importance at the same time and the Omotesenke grand master appears to take precedence. For this reason many Japanese consider Omotesenke the *honke*. When questioned more closely informants respond that they base their opinion on Omotesenke's position as the front house or say that it was established by "the oldest son" (actually it was founded by the oldest son of Sōtan's second marriage). Also, when the patriarchs of the Senke Jūshoku, the ten crafts families, which have traditionally served the three schools, make their New Year's greetings, they do go to Omotesenke first. Even so, the (o)*iemotos*' relative ages are probably more important in determining precedence than branch affiliation.

10. For example, when the present (o)*iemoto*'s (Sen Sōshitsu) younger brother wished to take the surname "Naya" (after the old *nayashu* families of Sakai from which Rikyū came), his announcement mentioned seeking the approval of all three families. The identical form was used by Mr. Izumi, the younger brother of the present *waka sōshō* (Sen Sōshi, Zabōsai, the heir to Sen Sōshitsu).

11. The relationship between Urasenke and the Tankōsha publishing house, a corporation run by the (o)*iemoto*'s brother, Naya Yoshiharu (Sōtan) provides an interesting example of successful diversification in the modern *ie*. Tankōsha publishes a large variety of magazines, texts, and so forth, related to Urasenke's style of *chanoyu*.

12. Grand masters have been criticized throughout tea history for decisions they have made in the course of evaluating and authenticating tea utensils. An (o)iemoto's signature on the box of a utensil can increase its value astronomically. Typically the owner or creator of the item provides an unsolicited gift in gratitude for the evaluation. This is perceived as an inappropriately commercial activity by some. Grand masters are frequently suspected of abusing this privilege by approving too many or inferior objects. Nevertheless, connoisseurship and artistic creativity have been an essential aspect of tea master's responsibilities since the time of the dōbōshū. Indeed, the sheer volume of high quality tea utensils that a leading master handles in the course of his lifetime must qualify him as an expert.

There is no question that the value of some tea utensils has been artificially inflated, however, I am not convinced tea masters have created the situation. The simple truth is that no one is forced to buy these things. People buy them for prestige, out of affection for the signer, because they like the item, and/or because they are reassured about its quality by the signature. Purchasers are aware that they are subsidizing the activities of the tea master when they purchase signed utensils. They are often members of the master's tea school and would support it anyway. The difference is that they have something to show for their contribution which, unlike a form letter of thanks, can be used and will increase in value.

CHAPTER 8: LEARNING THE GRAMMAR OF TEA RITUAL

1. If the student can no longer study with the original teacher (due to a change of residence, for example), the student must ask permission of his teacher to study with another instructor. Ideally, then, the two teachers will formally greet each other in person or by letter and pass the responsibility for the student's instruction between them.

2. I suspect that the strong emphasis on learning "with the body" is related to the kind of cognitive processes Japanese have traditionally relied on to aid them in the memorization of Chinese characters. The collective experience of generations of Japanese has been that this difficult learning experience is best mastered by repeatedly copying the characters. There are no short cuts. The subconscious pathways in the brain formed by the endless drill of copying characters aid the process of conscious memorization. This approach is common to the teaching techniques of Japanese arts such a swordsmanship, archery, and drama. It is, of course, also deeply rooted in the philosophical systems of Japan.

3. The reason practicing Tea is perceived as expensive is because a great number of utensils are required to practice the basic temae.

And, as the student's connoisseurship develops, his or her desire for quality inevitably increases. One could practice quite simply and effectively for a minimal investment but, human nature being what is it, most people spend as much on it as they can reasonably afford. Practicing *chanoyu* is only as expensive as the individual practitioner chooses to make it. Those who do not study Tea usually have little appreciation for tea utensils and no need for them, so they quite understandably judge them over-priced.

4. Ash formation (*haigata*) is a art form unique to *chanoyu* and "the way of incense" (*kōdō*). Tea practitioners sculpt the light ash used in the *ro* or *furo* into specified shapes. The style of formation created is determined by the type of *ro* or *furo* used, the degree of formality associated with the *temae* to be performed, and the season. Good *haigata* are much admired and require years of practice.

5. The tobacco tray used in the tearoom is supplied with a packet of Japanese thread tobacco, a container which holds one lighted charcoal in a bed of ash, a section of green bamboo with water in the bottom (for smoking residue), and two traditional pipes. Since such pipes hold but a thimble full of tobacco, they provide for only a few puffs of smoke. Although few people smoke in this fashion today, the *tabako bon* has been retained for its aesthetics and as a symbol of relaxation. Smoking modern forms of tobacco such as cigarettes in the tearoom is generally prohibited.

6. Flowers from a florist shop are always considered poor taste for *chanoyu* as they lack the natural qualities necessary for good *chabana* (the art of preparing flowers for tea gatherings).

CHAPTER 9: BEHIND THE SCENES

1. Once learned, the meanings of some symbols may not be consciously activated by every ritual participant under all circumstances. For example, one may handle one's fan in greeting as if it is a sword, but one does not think of a sword every time one manipulates a fan.

2. Sprinkling was originally and continues to be a practice of purification at *Shintō* shrines. Today some nice Japanese stores, particularly those that sell tea equipment, have shop girls sprinkle the sidewalk in front of their doors regularly throughout the day as a sign of welcome. Sweeping, too, is laden with *Shintō* implications as sweeping with a branch of *sasa* (bamboo grass) is purificatory. Further, the sound recalls wind in the bamboos, evoking a restful feeling for Japanese. Finally, in a practical sense, it keeps the dust down and clearly distinguishes the house where a *chaji* is about to take place from others on the street.

CHAPTER 10: THE EVENT BEGINS

1. Straightening and smoothing one's *kimono* in the tearoom is considered poor form. It draws too much attention and is reminiscent of the mannerisms of *geisha*.

2. "Bride schools" specialize in teaching proper *kimono* wearing, but tea teachers (particularly at Urasenke headquarters) avoid the subject. Tea students must learn the fine points of *kimono* wearing from other students or in the home.

3. Gary Cadwallader believes that this story has been fairly thoroughly discredited. He believes that it may somehow be related to an incident that took place in 1789. Most of Kyōto from Rokujō north to Daitokuji and from Horikawadōri to Kawaramachi burned at that time. It is said that the famous statue of Sen Rikyū was saved by being thrown into a backyard pond and covered with wet *tatami* (Personal communication from Gary Cadwallader, March 1984).

4. Money may also be folded in the *kobukusa* and presented in a similar manner.

5. I have seen some inspired by Peruvian textiles and European tapestry motifs.

6. The manufacture of good paper is one of many traditional Japanese art forms whose preservation has been stimulated by its association with the tea world. It is an interesting fine point of tea etiquette that some instructors prefer their students to use the stiffer *kaishi* to wipe lacquer bowls clean after the *kaiseki* meal than the more pliable tissues available today. They feel that there might be additives in the paper of the tissues that might damage fine lacquer.

7. If the gathering takes place at night, the guests will find special guest candlesticks (*teshoku*) on a rock outside the *yoritsuki* with which to light their way through the garden.

8. In the *Nampō Roku*, it is written that Rikyū discouraged wearing *geta* in the *roji* because so few people could walk in them properly (Hirota 1980b, 35).

CHAPTER 11: PHYSICAL ASPECTS OF THE
RITUAL ENVIRONMENT

1. The question of the polite nomenclature for the washing basin in the *roji* is colored by the insistence of some that *chōzubachi* is used for the basin outside a toilet and is, hence, too indelicate for use at a tea gathering. They suggest the use of the word *tsukubai*, which refers

to the whole washing area in the *roji*. Others prefer to use *chōzubachi* as a more specific and older word for the basin.

2. There are numerous styles of both basin and lanterns. Some are the *konomi* of particular tea masters.

3. There is debate on this based on the Taoist geomantic influence. The present directional orientation in construction may represent a historical change from original preferences. (Per. comm. from Allan Palmer, September 1983.) Traditional Japanese beliefs about auspicious and inauspicious directional influences also exist and may predate the Chinese influence.

4. The most formal hangings (*shin*) are calligraphy (*bokuseki*) done by respected Zen priests or (*o*)*iemoto*. These are usually works of an inspirational or didactic character. The works may be mounted horizontally or vertically and sometimes consist of a single character. Less formal (*gyō*) examples of calligraphy include *kaishi* (with characters larger than ordinary calligraphy, they usually present *waka* poetry), *shikishi* and *tanzaku* (poetry written on long or square papers mounted on a hanging scroll), and *kohitsugire* (ancient writing). *Shōsoku* (letters, usually by people important to Tea) are considered informal (*sō*). Paintings are usually divided into three classes: *kaiga* (Chinese paintings), *emakimono* (fragments of long scroll paintings that have been remounted), and *esan* (paintings and poems that complement each other).

5. Mounting must be suited to the rank of the calligrapher and to the message. Painting done by Japanese are generally mounted in what is known as the *yamato*-style as opposed to Chinese mountings. Proper material must be chosen for the borders to suit the rank of the calligrapher. Works by imperial authors should be mounted in brocades or white twill (as worn by the emperor). Nobles' works are appropriately surrounded by purple cloth with gold-stamped or woven patterns. *Samurai*'s calligraphy is best found with plain satin weave or twill mounting. Finally, works of people of lower ranks should be surrounded with correspondingly plain cloth or paper. In addition, the relative widths and dispersal of mounting strips are ranked. Obviously, the mounter must exercise discretion when, for example, a highly inspirational work is done by someone of no great social rank, such as that done by a merchant tea master who has taken holy orders. If the painting or calligraphy is of a seasonal nature that, too, must be reflected in the mounting's aesthetic character.

6. Takeno Jōō was the first to use ceramic *furo*. However, the style was repeatedly modified by later tea masters. In doing away

with metal, Jōō was rejecting a symbol of money. Ceramic provided the earth element that held fire and over which boiled water in a metal kettle. Fire needs air to burn so, all the Taoist elements were represented.

7. This incense is used by Urasenke people at all standard *furo chaji*.

8. In *shoin*-style rooms, nobles sit in the place of honor with their backs to the *tokonoma*. But, in a *yojōhan*, this would correspond to taking a seat on the mat corresponding for the trigram for "peril." Since *kinin* are normally received in *shoin*-style rooms, this potential for conflict between status and symbolism has probably seldom arisen.

9. In 1983, Allan Palmer provided me with a diagram showing the correspondence between trigrams of the *I Ching* and the mat segments of the *yojōhan*. He did not, however, suggest that his paradigm be applied to Yūin or describe the relationship between trigrams and symbol suggested in C. A. S. Williams' *Outlines of Chinese Symbolism and Art Motives* (Williams 1974, 149). Palmer instead identified the mat segments with the Chinese zodiacal signs and the Taoist elements. No doubt this cosmological scheme must also be considered as part of the geomancy of the *yojōhan*. The application of William's interpretation of the trigrams to Yūin is my own. It is, however, entirely possible that Sōtan had access to the scheme reported by Williams and applied it to Yūin's architecture. The number of points of correspondence between the symbols described by Williams and the architecture of the tearoom would suggest that they did.

Allan Palmer has also suggested that the same directional scheme applied to the teahouse is pertinent to the manipulations of the *daisu* (per. comm. from Allan Palmer, 1983). Certainly, on the bottom (earth board) we find the brazier located in the section identified with fire in Rikyū's time and the water jar in the area associated with that element. The four posts are also frequently identified with the Buddhist guardians of the four directions (*shi tennō*). Both Allan Palmer and Ron Nado, two senior non-Japanese tea practitioners, should be credited for the important research they have done on the Taoist elements in *chadō*.

CHAPTER 12: *SHOIRI*—THE FIRST HALF OF THE *CHAJI*

1. These dishes are known as *ichijū sansai*, one soup and three dishes. The dishes are supposed to consist of the *mukōzuke, nimono,* and *yakimono* courses. Gary Cadwallader feels that rice and pickles may have originally been included but were considered too basic to mention. Sweet cakes would fall under another classification, *kashi,* and would not have been mentioned for that reason.

2. Red lacquered utensils are used by Buddhist monks because the color red is believed to have prophylactic value, protecting the food from pollution. The custom has its roots in Taoist alchemic practice: Cinnabar, the red pigment originally used in vermilion lacquer, was considered an essential ingredient in the elixir of immortality. It was, in fact, very successfully used in ancient China to embalm the bodies of the elite.

3. Presenting rice in the form of *ichi mon ji* is not common to all the Sen schools of Tea but it is the practice at Urasenke. At a tea gathering, the top part of the rice arrives at the perfect consistency first, so a small scoop full is put in the initial serving to the guest. It is taken from the top of the rice near the edge of the cooking vessel. Steamed rice is served three different times during the *kaiseki* and each time, the texture is a little different. Omotesenke presents the first rice as a rounded-shape serving.

4. The fire is built before serving the *kaiseki* meal in *ro* season in order to warm the room.

5. The feather used in *furo* season is wider on the right side than the left. A different feather with the opposite arrangement is used in *ro* season.

6. A finer type called *jinkō*, Aquilaria agallocha, is used in incense braziers in Konnichian.

7. In *ro* season, it would be appropriate to use a ceramic *kōgō* with kneaded incense, *nerikō*. *Nerikō* is considered to be a Japanese form of incense and more useful in masking the smell of the heavier charcoal used with the *ro*. A ceramic *kōgō* is used because the oily, kneaded incense may stain the lacquer. Bits of leftover *byakudan* and kneaded incense are blended together in October and cemented together with honey (*tsukeboshi*) for use in the *furo*. This is a symbol of the end of the tea year and anticipates the opening of the *ro*.

8. *Fuchidaka* and *meimeizara* are most common at *chaji* while *kashibachi* are found almost exclusively at *chakai*. If a cake bowl is used, an uneven number of sweets will be found in it (no matter what the number of guests) probably because of the Japanese aesthetic preference for asymmetry reflected in odd numbers. Guests are never offered four pieces of any food since the word for "four" is a homonym with the verb "to die" When a cake bowl is placed in front of him, each guest shows appreciation by raising the bowl, takes a sweet with special moistened chopsticks provided, admires the bowl, and passes it on. The guests will use the picks they have brought with them to eat the sweets. Sweets may also be served on individual plates that have *kuromoji* with them. Etiquette is generally the same as being served a tray of food.

CHAPTER 13: THE BREAK AND THE RETURN

1. The *dora* is considered to have a *yang* sound while the *kanshō* is *yin*. According to Taoist belief, the great Tao has both active (*yang* in Chinese, *yō*, in Japanese) and passive components (*yin* in Chinese and *in* in Japanese). *Yō* things are active, bright, and male. *In* things are passive, dark, and female.

2. Some flower containers made by Rikyū from sections of bamboo survive today.

3. The imaginary host of this October gathering has chosen not to use *hagi* in the arrangement because it has already been used as a *toriawase* component in the name of the moist sweets. Each symbol normally appears but once. The seven grasses of fall were first identified as such in the *Man'yō shū*.

4. Taoism and associated wind-and-water type geomancy were probably more central to *chadō* during the early years of tea practice than they are today.

5. The *tsurube* is most commonly used in the hottest months of the year to suggest coolness. It is moistened and may be decorated with *Shintō* ropes (*shimenawa*) and papers (*gohei*) if it contains water from a sacred or famous spring or well (*meisui*).

CHAPTER 14: THICK TEA PREPARATION

1. As one can see by examining a piece of bamboo, the wood is divided in sections with the location of the septum at each joint indicated on the outside by the node (*fushi*). If a cut section of bamboo with a septum at one end is held upside down (opposite the natural direction of growth), it can hold water and is *in* (female) in Allan Palmer's interpretation of the Taoist symbolic paradigm. If held right side up, the piece can function as a stand and is male, *yō*. The *chasen* is a male symbol. It enters the tea bowl (which as a container is female) creating a cosmic union. For this reason, the tines must be made from the section of bamboo that would be located below the *fushi* in nature. The whisk is right side up when it is in the position of use, that is, whisking tea.

2. The color of *chasen* has come to symbolize allegiance within the Tea world by emphasizing differences between schools. The Omotesenke part of the Sen family uses mainly smoked bamboo *chasen* while Urasenke uses plain "white" ones.

3. When serving nobles, gorgeously decorated *temmoku*-shape *kyōyaki* bowls are used. Plain white bowls are employed for practice.

4. This allowed the user to determine if the scoop had been correctly carved: According to *chadō*'s Taoist symbolic paradigm, the handle end of the scoop ought to "grow" out of the tea in the same direction bamboo grows from the ground. This "outwardness" identifies it as a male utensil.

5. One of the most famous was supposedly given to Furuta Oribe by Rikyū at the time of Rikyū's death. It is called *"Namida"* or *"Tears."* This is only one story explaining the name—there are others.

6. In the extended Taoist paradigm, the *chakin* is designated is *in* (female, wet). It contrasts with the other cloth used for purification, the *fukusa*. The *fukusa* is considered *yō* (active and male).

7. Because of the way in which it is used (opposite the direction of growth), the *futaoki* is considered a stand and is male in the Taoist symbolic paradigm.

8. The host ideally cuts a new green *futaoki* from bamboo for *chaji* to give a feeling of freshness and purity. This is particularly appropriate for the Tea New Year in November and for *Hatsugama*. The *futaoki* may continue to be used for informal gatherings. By October they are very faded and convey a *wabi* feeling particularly appropriate for that month.

9. Rikyū was known to have been particularly fond of seven different types designs. One was a bronze copy of an incense brazier. Another was an iron trivet. Still others represented a circle of three children, a crab, a shell, a trefoil-shaped ink stick rest, and a man looking into a well.

10. The *hishaku* is considered female because it is like a vessel in that it contains water.

11. Walking and turning is the tearoom is strictly choreographed. The specific style of walking used in the tearoom is supposed to emulate that of the actors in the *Nō* drama.

12. *"Mi te"* or three-handling is a way of lifting a utensil with one hand, holding it on the opposite side with the other, and then readjusting the grasp of the first hand before placing the item on the mat. It is both graceful and secure.

13. The "five key relationships" of Confucianism are father/son, ruler/subject, brother/brother, husband/wife, and friend/friend. I suspect that brother/brother and friend/friend are subsumed under the same category in the tea school's *ie* based social structure. A fictive kin organization equates brothers and friends almost by definition. The husband/wife relationship is also rendered irrelevant in *ie-*

based fictive kin organizations such as *iemoto*. This is because everyone but the reproductive pairs at the apex of the *iemoto* structure (i.e. the grand master and his wife and the heir and his wife) relate as subjects, children, or brother/friends (fellow practitioners). Collapsing two categories (brother/brother and friend/friend) and eliminating one (husband/wife) creates the opportunity to insert the critical teacher/student relationship category.

14. Gold leaf is believed to have been originally applied to the underside of lids because a change in color was supposed to be indicative of poison in the tea. Ideally, new gold foil is applied to the underside of the lid before each *chaji*, although few people follow this practice today. The foil is particularly interesting to see on an old *chaire* because it takes on a distinctive character with age.

CHAPTER 15: THE PREPARATION OF THIN TEA

1. *Tsuyu* is a term used for the tip of all *chashaku*. It means "dew." The "three dews" in Tea are the dew found on the flowers in the alcove, the threads on streamers that are found hanging from the top of some scrolls, and the "dew" shape of the *chashaku* tip.

2. The door to the tearoom is closed during thin tea in winter. This is done to keep the room warm.

3. The fact that the host makes a semiformal bow while the guest makes a formal bow does not indicate a difference in status. The host abbreviates his bow (not placing his hands flat on the mat) to keep his hands pure for tea preparation and because the utensils in front of him leave little room for a full bow.

CHAPTER 16: INTERPRETING TEA RITUAL

1. In Lu Yü's day, tea was sometimes mixed with salt and onions and took on the character of a soup. In Chinese food ritual, a thicker type of soup called *"keng"* fell into the marginal area between soup and food. Interestingly enough, *keng* was commonly served at ancestor rituals. Thick tea resembles it in texture. That *keng* may have provided a symbolic model for early preparations of tea is suggested by the quotation from the *Tso Chuan* included in Girardot's *Myth and Meaning in Early Taoism*:

> Harmony may be illustrated by soup [*keng*]. You have the water and the fire, vinegar, pickle, salt, and plums, with which to cook fish and meat. It is made to boil by the firewood, and then the cook mixes the ingredients, harmoniously

equalizing the several flavors, so as to supply whatever is deficient and carry off whatever is excess. The master eats it, and his mind is made equable. (From the *Tso Chuan* in Girardot 1983, 29)

A mixture of coarse tea, vegetables, and hot water called "*botebote cha*" is drunk in present day Shimane prefecture (Kumakura 1984, 42).

2. The phrase "Die while alive, and be completely dead," comes from a Tokugawa era *waka* by Shidō Bunan Zenji (d. 1676):

> Die while alive and be completely dead,
> Then do whatever you will, all is good.
>
> (Shidō Bunan quoted in
> Shibayama 1970, 46)

Shibayama says "to die while alive" means to "become the self of no-mind, and no-form and then revive as the True Self of no-mind and no-form" (Shibayama 1970, 46).

3. Although Rikyū himself called his kind of tea ritual "*wabi,*" people have used the term so often to describe his aesthetic taste that they forget it was a vehicle for communicating his religious ideals. In other words, using *wabi* utensils is not always indicative of the practitioner's commitment to the great tea master's ideals.

Also, it should be noted that Zen is a broad philosophy that should not be exclusively associated with one kind of Buddhism. As Shibayama said: "There can be Christian Zen, or Taoistic Zen; there can be Zen interpretations of Christianity or Taoism." (Shibayama 1970, 16)

4. While *chadō* is a form of religious practice, learning tea ritual within the *iemoto* system is distinctly different from joining a religious sect or "cult." Tea is a form of Zen based on the fundamental premise that each person must develop his or her own religious convictions on the basis of personal experience. In contrast, most of the groups popularly identified as religious sects (including those of Japan's "new religions") require converts to accept specific spiritual beliefs on faith.

Some analysts have recently begun to revive the use of the term "cult" to describe tea ritual (See Kramer 1987, 1988). I feel this is somewhat misleading as both popular and scholarly concepts of what constitutes a "cult" have changed rather dramatically in the eighty years since Okakura Kakuzō first called *chanoyu* "a cult founded on the adoration of the beautiful" (Okakura [1906] 1956, 3). Therefore, in the interests of academic rigor, I would like to suggest theoreticians refrain from using this emotionally loaded term unless prepared to demonstrate that the *iemoto* and the kind of organizations recognized as "cults" today share a significant number of common characteristics.

5. Daisetz Suzuki's discussion is particularly fascinating because, like Rikyū, he appeared intent on convincing his contemporaries to pursue strategies for attaining salvation based on transformatory rather than confirmatory models.

6. "Neolocal residence" means that the bride and groom establish their own household, independent of either set of parents.

7. I question the assertion that anyone would stay involved in Tea for long simply to wear *kimono*. The effort involved in wearing and maintaining *kimono* coupled with the physical and mental discipline necessary to the study of Tea are not likely to hold the attention of individuals with such frivolous motives for very long. Moreover, *kimono* are worn with diminishing frequency to both tea lesson and tea gatherings in Japan today.

8. A *mukoyōshi* marriage is one where a son-in-law is adopted to be heir of his wife's *ie*.

9. The *go nin gumi* were groups of five household heads held collectively responsible under Japanese law for the actions of their fellows and their families. If, for example, one member failed to pay his taxes or committed a crime, all were held responsible. Mutual aid and mutual surveillance were the main functions of these institutions. George Sansom suggests that villagers created very rigid regulations for the *go nin gumi* to impress the authorities; they actually dealt with offenders in their own ways (Sansom 1963, 103).

Glossary

赤蜻蛉   *akatonbo*—Red dragon fly

暁茶事   *akatsuki chaji*—A standard type of tea gathering that begins at about 4:00 A.M. in *ro* season

秋の蟬   *aki no semi*—Autumn cicada

洗い茶巾   *araijakin*—An *usucha* procedure that includes the practice of wringing the *chakin* out in a bowl of cool water in front of the guests. It suggests coolness and is undertaken in the hottest part of the year.

朝茶事   *asa chaji*—A standard type of full tea gathering held during the hottest part of the summer beginning at about 5:00 or 6:00 A.M. in *furo* season

跡見茶事   *atomi chaji*—A type of tea gathering requested by guests who have heard that the host is holding a full gathering and wish to see the utensils he had used

瓶掛   *binkake*—A brazier used for heating water for tea in a small spouted pot. It is smaller in size than the *furo* more commonly used.

墨蹟   *bokuseki*—The calligraphy of Zen priests

盆点   *bondate*—A tea procedure featuring Chinese *chaire* such as Sung ware or famous early Seto. The *chaire* should be paired with trays of the same general provenance. (This *temae* and others featuring utensils of great historic significance are most frequently practiced using replicas of the original objects.)

盆香合   *bon kōgō*—A charcoal preparation that features a *kōgō* with special meaning that is presented on a tray

分家   *bunke*—A subsidiary house in a *dōzoku*

仏間   *butsuma*—A special room where a family venerates its Buddhist ancestor tablets

白檀   *byakudan*—Sandalwood incense (*Santalum album*) used in *furo* season. It consists of thin chips of wood about one centimeter square.

茶合せ   *cha awase*—An activity conducted by the nobility and *samurai* in early eras of tea where guests competed in identifying different kinds of tea

茶箱   *chabako*—A box of standard size used to carry tea utensils and to present the *temae*. It is employed primarily for outdoor gatherings.

茶花   *chabana*—the art of preparing flowers for tea gatherings

茶道   *chadō*—The "way" of Tea, the spiritual path followed by those who practice *chanoyu*

茶菓子   *chagashi*—The class of sweets served for tea gatherings

茶入   *chaire*—A ceramic container for thick tea modeled on Chinese medicine containers

茶入荘   *chaire kazari*—A specific thick tea procedure that features a *chaire* with special meaning for the host. Usually the *chaire* has been a gift from a respected friend.

茶人   *chajin*—An ideal tea personality, one who really loves tea and has internalized its spiritual ideals such that he or she can prepare tea generously and without ostentation. The ideals of Tea permeate his or her everyday existence.

茶かぶき　*cha kabuki*—A modern type of *cha awase*, one of the *shichiji shiki*

茶会　*chakai*—a tea gathering, the term is usually applied to informal, social gatherings where only thin tea is served

茶巾　*chakin*—A white linen cloth used for wiping the tea bowl at a tea gathering. It is usually about 15 cm. by 27 cm. in size. The long edges are loosely hemmed and the short edges bordered only by the selvage of the material itself.

茶名　*chamei*—The "tea name" bestowed on the student by the *iemoto* directly or through his or her teacher. Usually not awarded until after reaching age thirty and completing some degree of formal tea studies.

茶湯　*chanoyu*—Those things and/or behaviors related to the "formal" consumption of powdered tea

茶礼　*charei*—The ritualized communal sharing of tea among Buddhist monks

茶筅　*chasen*—The bamboo whisk used to knead or whip tea

茶筅荘　*chasen kazari*—A specific thick tea procedure that features a particular utensil, usually the *mizusashi* or *kama* with special meaning for the host

茶筅とおし　*chasentōshi*—An act undertaken in every tea

preparation during which the *chasen* is examined and rinsed

茶杓   *chashaku*—The scoop used to remove powdered tea from the tea container. The most commonly used are bamboo although they may be made a various materials such as ivory, silver, various woods, and so forth. Some shapes are the *konomi* of specific tea masters.

茶杓荘   *chashaku kazari*—A particular thick tea procedure that features the *chashaku*

茶室   *chashitsu*—The teahouse

茶壺   *chatsubo*—A ceramic jar in which tea is stored for one month during the year-long aging process. When presented in the tearoom, *chatsubo* are often decorated with a carrying net and a complicated set of decorative knots.

茶碗   *chawan*—The tea bowl

茶碗荘   *chawan kazari*—A particular thick tea procedure that features a tea bowl with special meaning for the host

千鳥の盃   *chidori no sakazuki*—The path taken by the *saké* saucer of the main guest as it travels between host and guests. It is filled and emptied in an act of commensal exchange, which takes place during the *kaiseki* meal.

千鳥茶巾   *chidorijakin*—An ordinary *chakin* folded in a special manner said to resemble a plover. It is used for wiping the tea bowl of the retainer in the *kinin kiyotsugu* tea procedures in Urasenke *temae*.

塵穴   *chiriana*—The symbolic refuse pit in the garden

縮緬 — *chirimen*—A special, heavy weight silk used to make an *Ōtsubukuro*

千歳盆 — *Chitose bon*—A round box with a lid used to carry utensils into the tearoom, designed by Sen Kayoko to honor Tantansai's sixtieth birthday. The inside is lacquered red and decorated with gold ginkgo leaf designs. It is inscribed with the phrase "live a thousand years."

手水鉢 — *chōzubachi*—The name for the stone water basin found in the *roji*. *Chōzubachi* were originally tall enough to use in the standing position. Sen Rikyū redesigned them so that the user would have to use them in a stooped posture. Some prefer to call these basins "*tsukubai*" as the word *chōzubachi* can also be applied to the basin outside the toilet.

中門 — *chū mon*—The gate between inner and outer *roji*

台 — *dai*—Stands for tea bowls, *saké* saucers, displays for the *tokonoma*, and so forth. They may be of plain wood, lacquered, or of ceramic as is appropriate for the character of the particular presentation. *Dai* for tea bowls are shaped like a saucer sitting on a pedestal. The tea bowl rests on an attached cup-shaped stand on top of the saucer.

台円の真 — *dai en no shin*—A formal tea presentation using a large black lacquer tray and one Chinese tea container. The *shin daisu* is used.

台円の草 — *dai en no sō*—A formal tea presentation using one Chinese and one Japanese tea container and a large tray

大海茶入 — *dai kai chaire*—A thick tea container of the

"great inner sea" type. The mouths of such containers are wider than most *chaire* and the total shape is broader and shorter.

大根 *daikon*—Giant white icicle radish, commonly used in Japanese cooking

大名 *daimyō*—A lord ruling a clan or fief

台子 *daisu*—A rectangular stand of standard dimensions having two levels and two or four legs that is used in many formal preparations of tea. It may be lacquered or plain.

台天目点前 *daitemmokudemae*—A tea procedure featuring tea bowls brought from T'ien mu in China to Japan during the Kamakura period with their associated stands. See *dai*.

だし *dashi*—A stock made of dried bonito flakes and *konbu*, a type of kelp. Both first and second infusions of the dry ingredients are used. This stock forms the basis of *kaiseki* cooking.

田宝 *denbo*—Balls of earth from the Inari mountain that were tossed into the rice fields to please the gods

道安風炉 *Dōanburo*—A style of ceramic *furo* that was the *konomi* of Rikyū's son, Dōan

同朋衆 *dōbōshū*—Retainers of the *shōgun* who functioned as their artistic advisors

道場 *dōjō*—A place for the practice of tea, judo, Zen, and so forth

同好会 *dōkōkai*—The individual, small tea group consisting of people who regularly practice tea with one teacher

同門   *dōmon*—"Same gate." A term used to indicate students who have entered the same artistic and spiritual discipline.

緞子   *donsu*—A type of satin weave silk material comparable to damask. It is used to make *shifuku* and *kobukusa* and in scroll mountings. It is considered formal.

銅鑼   *dora*—The gong used to call guests back to the tearoom after the middle break. Used in daytime only.

同族   *dōzoku*—A type of extended family organization

絵讃   *e san*—A class of hanging scroll found in the tearoom that consists of poems and paintings integrated on a single scroll in a complementary fashion

枝炭   *edazumi*—White branch charcoal made from branches covered with gesso

餌畚   *efugo*—A shape of *kensui* modeled after a falconer's pouch

絵巻物   *emakimono*—A class of hanging scrolls sometimes found in the tearoom that consists of fragments of long scroll paintings that have been remounted

円座   *enza*—Round straw cushions used in the *koshikake machiai*

縁高   *fuchidaka*—A set of stacked boxes, often lacquered, used to contain sweets for formal tea gatherings

不時茶事   *fuji chaji*—"No time" tea gathering. (See *rinji chaji*.)

藤灰   *fujibai*—Fine white wisteria ash sprinkled on the other ash arranged in the *furo*. It is decorative.

袋棚   *fukurodana*—A tea stand made of unlacquered wood that was created by Takeno Jōō. It is also called the "*shinodana*" because of a similar stand used by the Shino incense school.

帛紗   *fukusa*—A silk cloth used by the host at tea gatherings to purify utensils and grasp the metal knob on top of the kettle if it is made of particularly heat-conductive material such a gold, silver, or iron. Standard size is 28 cm. by 27 cm. Men usually use purple while red is more characteristic of women.

帛紗捌き   *fukusa sabaki*—The act of folding the *fukusa* in a special way prior to purifying utensils at a tea gathering

帛紗挟み   *fukusabasami*—A flat purse of fabric used to carry *fukusa, kobukusa,* sweet pick, and papers into the tearoom when wearing western dress. Used by both men and women.

風炉   *furo*—A brazier constructed of metal (usually iron or bronze) or ceramic in which the fire is contained. Water is boiled over this fire with which to make tea.

風炉中の拝見   *furo chū no haiken*—The practice of guests individually viewing the contents of the *furo* early in the *asa chaji* or during *gozumi* during other *furo* season gatherings

節   *fushi*—The naturally created line where two sections of bamboo meet

蓋置   *futaoki*—The lid rest used in tea gatherings. They are of various shapes and materials such as metal and ceramic. The most common (and the style preferred by Rikyū) is a bamboo cylinder about 5.5 cm. tall and 5 cm. in diameter. *Futaoki* are usually cut from a piece of bamboo that includes the *fushi*.

芸者   *geisha*—A special class of skilled, female Japanese entertainers. They are often experts in traditional music and dance.

下駄   *geta*—Outdoor footgear worn by the Japanese, usually made of wood and raised on platforms

義理   *giri*—The unfulfillable obligation to repay *on*

御幣   *gohei*—Sacred white papers folded in a special way. They indicate the proximity of an area or objects sacred to *Shintō*. They are often found twisted into ropes or evergreen boughs.

後入   *goiri*—The second part of a *chaji*, usually including the preparation of thin and thick tea

五徳   *gotoku*—A three-pronged, iron trivet usually used to support the *kama* in the *furo* or *ro* so that it does not rest directly on the charcoal or the ash

後炭   *gozumi*—The procedure during which the charcoal is repaired and replenished for the second portion of the tea gathering

行   *gyō*—The semiformal component of the *shin, gyō, sō* system of classifying objects and behaviors according to their degree of formality

行の行台子   *gyō no gyō daisu*—an advanced tea preparation using any four-legged *daisu*, which is not lacquered black. The *chaire* and *daitemmoku* bowl should be Chinese *meibutsu*. A tray decorated with trigrams from the *I Ching* is used to present both items.

業躰 *gyōtei*—Senior instructors of the Urasenke tea school. The name literally means "those who have learned with their bodies." The term is particular to Urasenke.

羽箒 *habōki*—The feather used to purify the *ro* or *furo* during *sumidemae*

葉ぶた *habuta*—Literally, "leaf lid." It is the practice of using a fresh green leaf as a lid for the *mizusashi* during the hot period of the year.

萩 *hagi*—Bush clover, used in *chabana*

盃台 *haidai*—A black lacquer stand similar to the *dai* used for tea bowls. This *dai* is used to present shallow, *saké* saucers to the guests at the *kaiseki* meal.

灰形 *haigata*—The act, result of, or specific method of arranging the ash in the *furo*

拝見 *haiken*—The portion(s) of a gathering during which guests have an opportunity to closely examine and handle tea utensils. The word is also used to indicate the actual actions involved in doing so.

灰器 *haiki*—A shallow ceramic bowl that is filled with ash when used in the charcoal *temae*

灰匙 *haisaji*—A metal spoon with a non-heat conductive handle used to sprinkle white ash over the other ash form in the *furo* and to create a slight imperfection in it after arrangement. Also used to sprinkle damp ash over dry in the *ro*.

袴

hakama—Large, baggy trousers worn over *kimono* as an article of formal Japanese men's attire. They are often worn when formally preparing tea.

蛤端板

hamaguriba ita—A black, lacquer board with an edge shaped like the front edge of a clam shell. Used under semiformal *hanaire*.

半月

han getsu—Literally, "half-moon." In Tea, the gesture of holding a utensil, usually the *natsume*, from the top with the pointer finger extended and the others gently curled around the lid.

花所望

hana shomō—A standard procedure whereby the host asks the guest to arrange flowers

花寄

hana yose—A procedure sometimes used in the formal act of offering flowers to the memory of the deceased at a memorial service. It is similar to one of the *shichiji shiki*. Guests draw tiles to determine the order in which they will go forward and select flowers to arrange in vases in the *tokonoma*.

花入

hanaire—The flower container

飯後茶事

hango chaji—A tea gathering presented either before or after the noon meal during either *ro* or *furo* season. It offers only the barest rudiments of the *kaiseki* meal. It is also called "*tokihazure*" meaning "off time" or *kashi chaji*, if the emphasis is on the sweets.

半東

hantō—The host's assistant

箸洗

hashiarai—A course of very lightly-flavored *dashi* with one or two small food items, served in tall lidded cups at the *kaiseki* meal. The name means "chopsticks wash," and it is used to do this and to purify the palate.

八寸 *hassun*—A square, usually unlacquered cedar tray modeled after one used to present offering at the Hachiman Shrine. It is approximately eight inches across and has a small rim around the perimeter. The course of the *kaiseki* meal served on this tray is also called "*hassun.*" It consists of small amounts of carefully arranged mountain and sea delicacies.

初釜 *Hatsugama*—Literally "first kettle," the first Tea festivities of the Japanese New Year

火鉢 *hibachi*—A container for lighted charcoal used in the *machiai* to warm the guests in winter

火箸 *hibashi*—The metal chopsticks used to arrange charcoal during charcoal *temae.* The size used during *ro* season is larger than those used for *furo* and has wooden handles.

冷え *hie*—The aesthetic concept of "chilled" used in *renga* poetry

干菓子 *higashi*—Dry sweets traditionally eaten before drinking thin tea

火入 *hiire*—A small vessel of clay used in the *tabako bon* to hold ash and a hot coal to light the *kiseru*, the Japanese pipe

引柄杓 *hikibishaku*—A gesture used when returning the *hishaku* to the top of the *kama* after drawing cold water. It is said to resemble drawing a bow. It is used only in *furo* season.

引盃 *hikihai*—The shallow red saucer from which *saké* is formally consumed at the *kaiseki* meal

平点前 *hirademae*—The most basic presentations of thin and thick tea for either *ro* or *furo* season

平仮名   *hiragana*—A system of characters used to designate the syllables of native Japanese words and other grammatical elements

柄杓   *hishaku*—The bamboo water ladle used to move water between the kettle, the cold water container, and the tea bowl in most presentations of tea

宝珠   *hōju*—Literally, "treasure jewels." Round containers with pointed lids made for offering sacred water at *Shintō* shrines. These vessels are depicted in the *tsubo tsubo mon*.

本家   *honke*—The main house in a *dōzoku*

一期一会   *ichigo ichie*—Best translated "once chance in a lifetime," a phrase coined by Ii Naosuke (1815–1860) and frequently used in Tea. It has the sense that there is but one chance and one time for each tea gathering. The opportunity should be used to the fullest since it cannot be repeated.

一汁三菜   *ichijū sansai*—Literally, "one soup and three dishes." It is the framework suggested by Rikyū for the *kaiseki* meal.

一文字   *ichimon ji*—Literally, the character "one." The long, narrow portion of rice served in each bowl at the beginning of the *kaiseki* meal.

一族郎党   *ichizoku rōtō*—one family group and its retainers

家   *ie*—The house. (See pages 78–80.)

家元   *iemoto*—A traditional school of instruction in the classical arts

位牌   *ihai*—Ancestor tablets

陰陽   *in-yō*—The Japanese terminology for the system of opposed cosmic principles of light and darkness, male and female, active and passive, which is called *"yin-yang"* in Chinese

入子点   *irekodate*—A specific tea procedure whereby the host enters the room but once. He carries the utensils in a new, bent cedar *kensui*. The procedure was developed for children, the aged, and the disabled to eliminate frequent trips to the *mizuya*. There is no *haiken*.

寂   *jaku*—An important concept in Tea indicating the value of achieving selfless tranquillity

直心の交   *jikishin no majiwari*—The Zen concept of correspondence in direct mind

軸荘   *jiku kazari*—A special procedure for displaying a prized scroll to the guests and hanging it in the *tokonoma*

沈香   *jinkō*—A type of fine incense made from *Aquilaria agallocha*, aloes wood

浄土   *jōdo*—The "Pure Land," enlightenment

十徳   *juttoku* (also *jittoku*)—A loose, black silk jacket worn by tea masters

鏡柄杓   *kagamibishaku*—The host's gesture of holding the *hishaku* up like a mirror with a handle. He is said to reflect his thoughts on the *hishaku*. It is also said that one's heart should be reflected as one's face would be reflected by a mirror.

絵画   *kaiga*—Chinese paintings, a class of hanging found in the tearoom

皆具   *kaigu*—Matched sets of tea utensils originally brought from China. They were originally bronze and are considered very formal.

懷石   *kaiseki*—The formal meal that accompanies a full tea gathering

懷紙   *kaishi*—Special Japanese paper. Packs of *kaishi* are carried in the bosom of the *kimono* and used as disposable plates for tea sweets and to wipe bowls clean after the *kaiseki* meal.

掛字書   *kakeji sho*—Calligraphy

掛け軸   *kakejiku*—Another word for *kakemono*

掛物   *kakemono*—Literally, "hung or suspended thing." The name by which the long scroll hanging in the *tokonoma* is usually known.

書絵   *kaki e*—Paintings. An informal class of hanging found in the tearoom.

釜   *kama*—The kettle used to boil water for tea. They are usually cast iron.

梭魚   *kamasu*—Barracuda

紙釜敷   *kami kamashiki*—A thick pad of Japanese paper used as a hot pad for the kettle during *shozumi*. They are also used underneath *kōgō* in a display that indicates that charcoal *temae* will not be performed.

関白   *kampaku*—The title designating the emperor's chief advisor

鈒   *kan*—Open spirals of heavy metal wire in circular shape that are twisted into the lugs of the kettle and used to lift it

金棒   *kanabō*—(also *nyōi*)—An iron rod about fifty cm. long carried by Zen priests of high rank. It is sometimes used in the course of Zen instruction to gesticulate or as a visual aid.

Zen texts also relate incidents where it has been used to beat spiritual aspirants. It probably derives from the Hindu *vajra* ("diamond" or "thunderbolt" mace), a symbol of truth and the power of the Buddhist faith. It is also said to mean "as one thinks" in Sanskrit.

寒梅粉   *kanbaiko*—Flour made from sweet rice used in making dry sweets

燗鍋   *kannabe*—A vessel resembling a small western tea pot, usually iron, used to serve *saké* during the *kaiseki* meal

喚鐘   *kanshō*—The clapperless bell struck with a mallet to call guests back to the tearoom after a middle break at a night time tea gathering

漢東   *kantō*—A plain or satin weave fabric with stripes as the pattern. The original *kantō* was cotton but silk is now common. It is used for *shifuku* and *kobukusa*. It is considered very informal.

花押   *kaō*—A distinctive calligraphic cipher used to identify the *konomi* of specific individuals

唐糸草   *karaito sō*—Burnet, used in *chabana*

唐物点前   *karamonodemae*—A procedure featuring a Sung period Chinese-made *chaire* (or copy thereof)

枯れ   *kare*—The aesthetic concept of "withered" used in *renga* poetry

重茶碗点前   *kasanejawandemae*—A procedure for making thick tea using two bowls in order to accommodate a large number of guests

菓子鉢   *kashibachi*—A bowl used to serve moist sweets at a *chakai*

片仮名   *katakana*—An angular system of characters used by the Japanese to designate syllables of foreign words

刀掛   *katanakake*—The sword rack sometimes found outside a teahouse

桂籠   *Katsura kago*—A type of flower basket used for tea gatherings

河原撫子   *kawara nadeshiko*—A flower known in English as a "pink." It is used in *chabana*.

敬   *kei*—The concept of respect important in Tea values

結界   *kekkai*—Divider. The model was probably the sacred ropes that delineate the holy places of *Shintō*. In Tea, the fan is used as such a symbolic divider defining the space of the guest. Further, a low divider of wood or bamboo may be set behind the tea preparation mat to separate that space from its context in a large, *shoin*-style room or at a outdoor gathering.

献茶   *kencha*—The act of formally preparing tea as an offering at a *Shintō* shrine or Christian church

建水   *kensui*—The waste water container used at tea gatherings

着物   *kimono*—A loose, wrapped garment worn by both men and women in Japan

貴人台   *kinin dai*—A stand of unlacquered wood used to present a tea bowl to a noble. It is ideally only used once.

貴人清次点前   *kinin kiyotsugudemae*—A specific procedure for preparing tea for a noble accompanied into the tearoom by his or her retainer(s)

貴人点   *kinindate*—A specific procedure for preparing tea for a nobleman (or woman)

金襴   *kinran*—A type of satin-weave Japanese silk material often having gold threads throughout it. It is used in *shifuku* and *kobukusa* and for scroll mounting. It is considered semiformal.

金団   *kinton*—A type of tea sweet consisting of a ball of bean paste covered by more sweetened bean and/or potato paste (frequently white paste which has been tinted). The outer layer is pressed through a sieve to give it an interesting texture. It is subsequently applied to the inner ball of paste.

綺麗寂び   *kirei sabi*—The aesthetic quality of beautiful, worn elegance. It is often associated with the taste of Kobori Enshū.

裂地   *kireji*—Fabric. The term is used when inquiring as to the name of a fabric used in *shifuku* or *kobukusa*.

切柄杓   *kiribishaku*—The gesture of placing the handle of the *hishaku* back on the top of the *kama* as if one is framing an archery target with a flat hand and thumb. It is used only in *furo* season.

香合せ   *kō awase*—Competitions where different types of incense are identified and judged as to quality

公案   *kōan*—A puzzling phrase given as a problem to consider during meditation to students of Zen by their spiritual masters

古帛紗   *kobukusa*—A square of material 15.5 cm. by 16 cm. used to present especially precious tea utensils to the guest or to present a tea bowl that conducts heat particularly easily. At Urasenke, this usually means any bowl that is not *raku*. It protects the guests' hands from heat. The materials used vary and are often famous or associated with particular personalities in tea. Omotesenke uses a bigger size of *kobukusa*.

香合   *kōgō*—The incense container

古筆切   *kohitsugire*—Ancient writing, a class of hanging found in the tearoom

濃茶   *koicha*—Tea prepared with a large amount of tea powder so that the texture is viscous

石   *koku*—A measurement of dry volume that differed according to locale and time but is generally standardized as 5.12 American bushels. One *koku* was theoretically deemed adequate to feed one person for a year.

独薬紋   *koma mon*—The *mon* worn by the (o)*iemoto* of the three Sen families. It represents the "flaming jewel of enlightenment."

小習   *konarai*—Sixteen basic tea preparations learned at the beginning stage of tea

昆布   *konbu*—Giant kelp. Used in dry form as an ingredient in *dashi*.

好み   *konomi*—The personally preferred designs of individuals, often items created to their own specifications

香物   *kōnomono*—Pickles

腰黒薬鑵   *koshiguro yakan*—A water supplier used to add water to *mizusashi* which have been used with four-legged *tana*. It is also used to carry water to replenish the kettle during *gozumi* and *bon kōgō*.

腰掛待合   *koshikake machiai*—The waiting arbor located in the tea garden between outer and inner *roji*

小吸物   *kosuimono*—The *hashiarai* ("chopstick washing") broth at the *kaiseki* meal served in tall, lidded cups (*kosuimono wan*)

供茶   *kucha*—The act of formally preparing tea as an offering at a Buddhist temple

口切茶事   *kuchikiri chaji*—A tea gathering where the host presents the new crop of tea in its storage jar and subsequently grinds and prepares it for the enjoyment of his guests

汲み出し   *kumidashi*—Cups used to serve a hot beverage in the *machiai*

椚   *kunugi*—A type of Japanese oak

黒文字   *kuromoji*—Spicewood (*Lindera umbellata*) picks used to remove sweets from *fuchidaka* and eat them. They are about 18 cm. long. Guests may take them home to remind them of a particular gathering. In this case, they may be inscribed by the guest with the date of the *chaji* at which they were used and the host's name.

許状   *kyōjō*—A certificate issued by the the *iemoto* granting a student permission to study a new *temae* or group of *temae*

京焼   *kyōyaki*—Ceramics made in Kyōto

待合   *machiai*—The waiting area where guests gather previous to entering the tearoom

名物   *meibutsu*—A tea utensil, often of Chinese origin, classified as famous during Rikyū's time

銘々皿   *meimeizara*—Small plates used to serve moist sweets to the guests on an individual basis

味噌汁   *miso shiru*—A staple kind of Japanese soup made from dried bonito flakes and seaweed stock to which *miso*, fermented soy bean paste, has been added

水引草   *mizuhiki sō*—Smartweed, used in *chabana*

水指   *mizusashi*—A cold water container used at tea gatherings. They come in a great variety of sizes, shapes, and materials. Some containers have black, lacquer lids.

水屋   *mizuya*—An area where preparations to make tea take place. It is outside the tearoom itself and is ideally provided with a water source and a storage area for utensils.

水屋見舞   *mizuya mimai*—The contribution given by the guests to the host by leaving money in a white envelope in the changing area

水屋先生   *mizuya sensei*—Young tea teachers who work directly under the supervision of the (o)iemo-to and the *gyōtei* to take care of *Konnichian* and its associated utensils. They are considered to be in training to become *gyōtei*.

餅   *mochi*—Cakes of steamed Japanese glutinous rice, pounded in a mortar and mixed with water. The resulting dough is then formed into shapes. Sometimes the dough is wrapped around balls of sweet bean paste or other fillings. The formed cakes may also be fried, toasted, or boiled.

物合せ

mono awase—Competitions held by court nobles involving identifying, comparing, or judging the quality of various items such as poems, shells, tea, incense, birds, iris rhizomes, and so forth

紋付き

montsuki—Formal *kimono*, displaying the family emblem

諸飾

morokazari—The practice of displaying the flowers and the scroll in the *tokonoma* at the same time. It is done at an *atomi chaji* so that the guests have a chance to see these two important elements of the previous gathering. *Morokazari* is also done at *chakai*.

毛氈

mōsen—Heavy felt mats, usually red or blue, sometimes used to cushion the floor during *usucha* at *chakai* or in the *machiai*. They are most properly used for outdoor tea gatherings.

向付

mukōzuke—A dish, generally raw fish, served at the beginning of the *kaiseki* meal

長緒

nagao—A thick tea procedure based on the use of the *dai kai chaire*. The *shifuku* used has a particularly long cord due to the width of the bag's mouth.

投入れ

nageire—A technique of flower arranging that influenced *chabana*. It means "thrown in" style.

中立

nakadachi—The middle break in a tea gathering taken between the *kaiseki* meal and the preparation of tea. The guests leave the tearoom at this time and return to the waiting area in the garden.

中次

nakatsugi—A class of wooden containers used to hold powder for thin tea. They are thought to have originally functioned as containers for *chaire* of Chinese origin. Black lacquer (*shin nuri*) *nakatsugi* are used for display only. Mulberry *nakatsugi* are used for the *Wakinde-mae*. Others maybe used for ordinary thin tea preparations.

菜の花   *nanohana*—Rape flower, *Brassica napus*

直会   *naorai*—A *Shintō* ritual during the course of which celebrants once consumed food and *saké* with a deity in the belief that they could thus share in its divinity. More recently, the food consumed has been different than that offered to the divinity. Sacred *saké* is still shared, however.

棗   *natsume*—The standard container for thin tea powder. It is modeled after the shape of the jujube fruit. The type preferred by Rikyū is lacquered in a plain black color. Various finishes and shapes may be used. It is sometimes used for thick tea.

納屋衆   *nayashū*—The name by which the thirty-six families, who controlled the warehouses in early Sakai, were collectively known

練香   *nerikō*—Kneaded incense. Used during *ro* season, it is considered to be a native Japanese form of incense. It is presented in a ceramic *kōgō* or on a leaf in other types of *kōgō*.

躙口   *nijiriguchi*—The small, "crawling-in" entrance to the tearoom. It is approximately 1.2 meters high, almost square, and has a sliding door.

二文字   *nimon ji*—A particular way of forming the ash in the *furo* so that two long, parallel "mountains" of ash are created

煮物   *nimono*—The class of boiled (or simmered) foods in Japanese cooking

煮物碗   *nimono wan*—The bowls with lids in which *nimono* are served at *kaiseki* meals. They are often beautifully lacquered.

能   *Nō*—A form of drama accompanied by chanting, which was started in the fourteenth century

野点   *nodate*—Outdoor tea gatherings

入門   *nyūmon*—A certificate giving the student permission to begin the formal study of tea with the *iemoto*

帯   *obi*—A wide belt worn over the *kimono* by both men and women. The width, material, and style of tying varies for men and women.

帯締   *obijime*—A thin cord tied over the top of the *obi* by women

お盆   *Obon*—The Japanese festival honoring the Dead, which takes place in July or August

皇服茶   *Ōbukucha*—The first tea of the solar year celebrated by all of the tea families

お家元   *(o)iemoto*—The head of an *iemoto*

お菓子   *(o)kashi*—The general category of Japanese sweets

大名物   *ōmeibutsu*—Tea utensils, mostly of Chinese origin, traditionally classified as very famous during the Higashiyama period of tea history

主菓子   *omogashi*—Moist sweets traditionally eaten before drinking thick tea

恩   *on*—The social debt owed one's benefactors

お白湯   (o)sayu—Literally, "honorable hot water." The term is used most often in Tea to refer to cups of plain hot water served as a beverage in the *machiai.*

押板   oshiita—An alcove featured in a Kamakura era Zen temple believed to be the forerunner of the *tokonoma*

折敷   oshiki—Food tray

大津袋   Ōtsubukuro—A silk bag, modeled after of the rice bags of the Ōtsu region in Japan, which is used to wrap the *natsume* when it is used for the preparation of thick tea. The bag is usually purple and made of *chirimen*-type silk. It was created by Rikyū's wife Sōon and has two pointed extensions at the top that are tied over the tea container.

お詰   (o)tsume—The last guest at a *chaji*

楽   raku—A type of ceramic that is hand-formed and fired at low temperature. The technique was developed by the Raku Chōjirō family under Sen Rikyū's direction. Many other people now employ similar techniques.

連歌   renga—The art of linked verse

立花   rikka—A very formal, structured technique of flower arranging used on Buddhist altars

利休忌   Rikyūki—The memorial service for Sen Rikyū

臨時   rinji or *fuji chaji*—A spontaneously presented tea gathering held on short notice. Skilled guests may help the host with various aspects of this rather informal event.

淋汗茶の湯   *rinkan chanoyu*—A form of tea gathering that included bathing, supported by the Furuichi clan in the early days of tea practice

炉   *ro*—A firepit cut in the floor of the tearoom near the area where the host prepares tea. It is a deep (50 cm. or more) box of wood or metal, lined with clay, and partially filled with ash. The *ro* used in Tea is modeled on larger such features in Japanese farm houses. The most common size is the size preferred by Rikyū, approximately 42.2 cm. square. A larger *ro* is sometimes used in the coldest season of the year. It is called the "*dai ro*" and is about 54.5 cm. square. It is unique to Urasenke and was devised by Gengensai.

露地   *roji*—The path to the tearoom, symbolic of the road to spiritual enlightenment

露地行灯   *roji andon*—Special portable lanterns made of paper, wood, and bamboo used to light the *roji* at night and in very early morning

露地傘   *roji gasa*—A special kind of umbrella without a handle used in the *roji* to protect the guests from rain. They resemble large straw hats.

露地下駄   *roji geta*—Wooden sandals provided by the host as rain footwear

露地草履   *roji zōri*—Specially made, soft straw sandals made from the sheathing of bamboo stalks for wear in the *roji*. They are most likely to be found where the physical layout of the hosts house and tearoom is such that guests have left their shoes at the main door of the house and subsequently must move through an internal courtyard to the tearoom.

略盆   *ryaku bon*—A *temae* created by Ennōsai, the thirteenth generation grand master of

Urasenke. Most of the utensils are brought into the tearoom on a tray. The bamboo water ladle is not used as a kettle shaped like a western teapot with a spout (*tetsubin*) makes it unnecessary. It is considered a very basic tea preparation.

立礼棚   *ryūreidana*—The class of tables at which the host makes tea sitting on a stool

立礼点前   *ryūreidemae*—*Temae* conducted by a host seated at a table for guests who are not seated on *tatami*. The first such procedure was created by Gengensai to serve guests in western clothing in 1872.

茶道口   *sadōguchi*—The door between the tearoom and the *mizuya* from which the host enters and exits the tearoom when making tea

酒   *saké*—Japanese rice wine

侍   *samurai*—The warrior class

悟   *satori*—Enlightenment

茶通箱   *satsubako*—A plain unlacquered box of paulownia wood that holds a *natsume* and *chaire* used during a specific procedure for tasting two teas

清   *sei*—The concept of purity important in Tea

精中円能
無限忌   *Seichū-Ennō-Mugenki*—The combined memorial services for Gengensai, Ennōsai, and Tantansai. Usually held July 5.

清花   *seika*—A technique of flower arranging preferred by the nobility for decorating their *shoin*-style rooms

席   *seki*—The term applied to the various seatings of guests at a large tea gathering. Guests must be seated in succeeding groups to avoid crowding the tearoom.

関守石   *sekimori ishi*—The heart-sized stones tied with black string that block off paths in the *roji* which the guest should not follow

先輩後輩   *senpai-kōhai* system—A component of organizational structure according to which seniors owe juniors protection and aid and juniors owe seniors obedience and assistance

先生   *sensei*—Teacher. This term of address is used throughout Japanese culture. It implies deep respect.

扇子   *sensu*—Fan

切腹   *seppuku*—Suicide conducted according to strict rules of etiquette

雪隠   *setchin*—The now largely symbolic privy located near the *koshikake machiai*

支部   *shibu*—Local chapters of Urasenke tea practitioners

渋い   *shibui*—The aesthetic value of simple elegance

七事式   *shichiji shiki*—Tea procedures involving a number of participants performing various tasks related to tea preparation. (See the *Temae* appendix for a complete listing.)

仕覆   *shifuku*—The fabric bag that holds a utensil

椎茸   *shiitake*—A type of mushroom (*Lentinus edodes*) commonly used in Japanese cooking

四ケ伝   *shikaden*—Four orally transmitted *temae*

色紙   *shikishi*—A white or lightly colored square of paper on which a poem can be written. One may be mounted and hung in the *tokonoma*

色紙点   *shikishidate*—A tea procedure making use of a rectangular basket originally used as a letter box at the imperial palace. The way in which the utensils are laid out is reminiscent of that of *shikishi* poem cards.

注連縄   *shimenawa*—Special sacred ropes used to indicate *Shintō* sacred precincts

真   *shin*—The formal component of the *shin, gyō, sō* method of classifying objects and behaviors according to their degree of formality

真の行台子   *shin no gyō daisu*—A very advanced tea procedure conducted with the use of a black lacquer *daisu* and small tray such as that used in *bondate*. The *chaire* and *daitemmoku* tea bowl should be *ōmeibutsu*, very high-ranking utensils from China.

真塗   *shin nuri*—Very formal black lacquer finish. The grain of the wood does not show through.

下火   *shitabi*—The three lighted pieces of charcoal initially placed in the *ro* or *furo* to start the charcoal

正午茶事   *shōgo chaji*—The standard type of full tea gathering that begins at noon

書院   *shoin*—Formal, Japanese reception rooms. Usually eight *tatami* mats in size or larger and having a *tokonoma*. Often a writing desk was set into the *tokonoma* area.

初入   *shoiri*—The first half of a *chaji*, generally including the first charcoal preparation and the meal

障子   *shōji*—Sliding wooden frames with translucent paper panels

精進料理   *shōjin ryōri*—The special vegetarian cooking style of the Buddhist temple

正客   *shōkyaku*—The main guest at a tea gathering. He or she is responsible for communicating with the host on behalf of the other guests.

消息   *shōsoku*—A class of hanging found in the *tokonoma*. These are letters, usually written by people important to Tea, which have been mounted.

初炭   *shozumi*—The first charcoal preparation at a tea gathering. (It is actually the second since three "starter" charcoal are characteristically in place when it is performed.)

出張所   *shutchōjo*—Overseas branches of Urasenke directly representing Konnichian

草   *sō*—The informal component of the *shin, gyō, sō* system of classifying items or behavior according to their degree of formality

草庵   *sōan*—The informal, four-and-one-half mat (or smaller) teahouse modeled on the humble dwelling of a recluse

宗旦忌   *Sōtanki*—The memorial service for Sen Sōtan. Usually held November 19

卒啄同時   *Sottaku dōji*—A Zen phrase originally appearing in the sixteenth chapter of the *Hekigan Roku*. It represents the spontaneous understanding of student and teacher. The image evoked is of a mother bird and her hatching chick pecking at the egg shell simultaneously. *"Sotsu"* means "noise," *"taku"* is a word for pecking, and *"dōji"* means "at the same time."

外露地   *soto roji*—The outer *roji*

簾   *sudare*—Rush blinds often hung outside tearoom windows to soften the light and provide a cooling effect. They are sometimes dipped in water and are then called *"tama sudare,"* "jewel blinds."

吸物   *suimono*—A light broth of *dashi* with various ingredients artfully arranged in it

数寄屋   *sukiya*—A *wabi* teahouse

炭所望   *sumi shomō*—A procedure whereby the host asks a guest to help arrange the charcoal

炭手前   *sumidemae*—The class of *temae* that relate to charcoal preparation and repair

墨絵   *sumie*—Brush and ink painting

炭斗   *sumitori*—The container in which unlighted charcoal is carried into the tearoom. Gourds and baskets are very common and are often lacquered black inside when used as *sumi tori*. The sizes differ for use with *ro* and *furo*.

寸   *sun*—A traditional Japanese unit of measurement, about one inch

薄   *susuki*—Japanese pampas grass, used in *chabana*

経   *sutra* (Sanskrit, *kyō* in Japanese)—Buddhist scriptures.

煙草盆

tabako bon—A box or tray with several Japanese pipes, a container of ash with a lighted coal centered in it, and a section of bamboo used for discarding used ashes. Some feel that tobacco should also be provided although it seldom is today because of the relative lack of availability of the particular type of Japanese thread tobacco (*kizami*), which was traditionally smoked in the *kiseru*, the Japanese pipe. Few smoke this type of tobacco today.

足袋

tabi—Split-toed Japanese socks. White ones are always worn in the tearoom.

高杯

takatsuki—A tray with a pedestal made of wood used to present sweets to a noble. It is ideally only used once.

沢庵

takuan—A pickle made from the giant white icicle radish believed created by a Zen priest of the same name

棚

tana—A stand used to hold some of the utensils used to make tea. They come in myriad designs and materials with corresponding differences in seasonality and formality.

短冊

tanzaku—long paper strips with calligraphy written on them that are sometimes hung in the *tokonoma,* most commonly in the *machiai*

畳

tatami—Very thick straw mats about six by three feet in size with edges bound in cloth. It is the standard measure in Japanese architecture although the size may vary slightly from area to area. The mats found in tearooms are usually bound in black cloth.

手焙リ

teaburi—Individual hand warmers provided to guests for their use in the *machiai* and *koshikake machiai* in cold weather

亭主   *teishu*—The host

点前   *temae*—Specific procedures related to tea preparation. Among the individuals associated with *iemoto,* only the (o)*iemoto* may create *temae.*

天目   *temmoku*—Capitalized, a tea bowl from China of a type originally used to drink tea at a Buddhist temple on T'ien Mu in China. Not capitalized, a Japanese copy of similar shape and character.

天下こ茶頭   *tenka gosadō*—Tea master of all Japan

手桶   *teoke*—In tea, the bucket used to carry water to the basin in the *roji.* A similar lacquered vessel is used as a *mizusashi.*

手燭   *teshoku*—A special candlestick used by the guest at night gatherings

鉄瓶   *tetsubin*—A small iron tea kettle shaped like a western teapot with a spout

闘茶   *tōcha*—See *cha awase.*

特攻隊   *tokkōtai*—Special naval attack unit formed toward the end of the war in the Pacific

床の間   *tokonoma*—An alcove in a *shoin*-style room or more informal tearoom where a scroll, flowers, or other appropriate articles may be displayed. The standard size for *yojōhan* is one *tatami* mat in area.

止め炭   *tomezumi*—The procedure whereby charcoal is added to the fire at the end of an evening tea gathering in *ro* season to encourage the guests to linger for further conversation

取合せ   *toriawase*—The combination of utensils and symbolic elements chosen by the host to characterize an individual tea gathering or the style in which a particular host regularly makes such combinations

壺荘   *tsubo kazari*—The tea procedure for opening the tea jar and displaying it to the guests

つぼつぼ紋   *tsubo tsubo mon*—An emblem representing three sacred water vessels used at *Shintō* shrines. Various configurations are used by the three branches of the Sen family as decorative motifs and to designate their followers who have *chamei.*

次
お供   *tsugi* or *(o)tomo*—The retainer of a noble person

付け干し   *tsukeboshi*—A type of incense created for use in the *furo* during October by sticking leftover incense from the previous year together with honey

月   *tsuki*—Moon. *Tsuki chabako* is a *chabako* used for moon viewing *temae* or in the autumn in general.

突上窓   *tsukiage mado*—The skylight in a tearoom

蹲踞   *tsukubai*—The area around the basin in the *roji,* including specially placed stones and the lantern. The term is also used to refer to the basin itself.

蹲踞柄杓   *tsukubaibishaku*—A wooden ladle used at the basin in the *roji* to spill water over the hands and cleanse the mouth

釣瓶   *tsurube*—Special, square wooden well-buckets with lids used as *mizusashi* during the hottest months of the year. They are considered very informal but very pure. It may also be used at the New Year to express the Zen directness of water coming from the well to the guest.

包帛紗

tsutsumibukusa—A tea procedure for wrapping (the verb is *tsutsumu*) a *natsume* in the host's *fukusa,* which permits the *natsume* to be used as a container for thick tea

露

tsuyu—Dew. The term is applied to a special shape at the end of a *chashaku* and to the threads at the end of the streamers hanging from a scroll mounting in Tea.

続き薄茶

tsuzuki usucha—Sometimes shortened to *tsuzukiusu.* The preparation of thick tea immediately followed by the preparation of thin tea without the repair of the charcoal fire.

打水

uchi mizu—The water sprinkled from outside the gate to the changing area and down the *roji.* It suggests coolness and purity to the guest

内露地

uchi roji—The inner *roji*

梅干し

umeboshi—Pickled plum

卯の花

unohana—Deutzia blossom. *Unohana chabako* is the basic model for the *chabakodemae.*

薄茶

usucha—The preparation of powdered tea in a thin consistency; or, the tea itself

渦巻紋

uzumaki mon—The *mon* worn by the women of the Sen family, representing the spinning motion of water or a top

埋火

uzumebi—The act of burying the last charcoal of the solar year in the ashes of the *ro* in the

Ryūseiken tearoom of Konnichian. They are recovered very early the next morning and used to kindle the first fire of the subsequent year.

和

wa—The value of harmony important in Tea

侘び

wabi—See note chapter 3, note 4, pg. 249.

和歌

waka—A Japanese verse form in which thirty-one syllables are arranged in lines of five, seven, five, seven, and seven syllables

若宗匠

waka sōshō—The (o)*iemoto*'s heir

和敬点

wakeidate—A *chabako* tea procedure created for use on the battle field by Tantansai for his son. A particular set of utensils was created for such use. The name is now said to mean "to make tea in harmony and respect."

和巾

wakin—A particular type of Japanese cloth. A *koichademae*, using such cloth, was created by Gengensai.

椀盛

wanmori—Literally, "piled up in the bowl." A course in the *kaiseki* meal wherein a beautiful arrangement of simmered foods is placed in the bottom of a bowl with *dashi* and present-ed to the guest. It is considered the heart of the *kaiseki* meal.

割稽古

warigeiko—"Divided practice." The teaching technique whereby certain action units com-mon to many tea procedures are practiced by students out of the context of individual *temae*.

失筈板

yahazu ita—A board used under formal flow-er containers which is lacquered black and has a V-shaped indentation cut in the edge similar to the top of the fletching on a tradi-tional Japanese arrow

焼物   *yakimono*—The class of grilled foods in Japanese cooking

薬石   *yakuseki*—Literally "medicinal stones." A light snack eaten by Zen priests at a break in evening meditation. Only two meals a day were allowed by temple regulations so this meal was called "medicine."

山道盆   *yamamichi bon*—"mountain road tray." A black, lacquer tray about 26 cm. in diameter with an undulating rail around the edge, which resembles a mountain road. The top of the undulating edge is painted in red.

大和   *Yamato*—The ancient name for Japan. It is often used to refer to something done in native Japanese style (as opposed to things done in Chinese, Korean, western style, etc.).

夜咄茶事   *yobanashi chaji*—A standard type of full tea gathering held during *ro* season in the evening

四方捌き   *yōhō sabaki*—Literally, "four-direction handling." A special way of folding the *fukusa* before using it to purify the *chaire* during *koichademae*. Examining four sides of the material symbolizes showing respect four the Buddhas of the four cardinal direction, deities of the four directions, and/or the four main relationships of Confucianism.

四畳半   *yojōhan*—Four-and-one-half mat tearoom modeled on the size of the room of Vimalakīrti

寄付   *yoritsuki*—An area where a guest may remove his/her street wear and change into clothing for tea

洋種山牛蒡   *yōshu yamagobō*—Pigeonberry, used in *chabana*

幽玄 *yūgen*—The aesthetic quality of ethereal mystery

雪 *yuki*—Snow. The *yuki chabako* is a *chabako* procedure used for snow-viewing teas. The utensils are first presented in bags and a tray stored inside the tea equipment box is also used.

湯斗 *yutō*—A broth made by mixing toasted bits of rice that stick to the inside of the rice kettle with salt and water. A common item in Buddhist monasteries, it is symbolic of the desire to waste no food.

柚子 *yuzu*—A Japanese variety of citrus that is generally used green. It is about the size of a lime and is treasured mainly for the fragrance of its peel. It is often used in *kaiseki* cooking.

座布団 *zabuton*—Cushions provided for the guests during *usucha* (and sometimes *kaiseki*)

前茶 *zencha*—A large, shared bowl of *usucha*. It is most often presented before charcoal preparation and *kaiseki* at night gatherings.

前礼 *zenrei*—The act of notifying the host of one's intention to attend a tea gathering

Tea Bibliography

ENGLISH LANGUAGE SOURCES

Anderson, Jennifer. 1985. "Chanoyu: An Anthropological Approach to Tea." Doctoral Thesis, Stanford University.

———.1987. "Japanese Tea Ritual: Religion in Practice." *Man* 22:475–498.

1970. "Chadogu—Tea Utensils." *Chanoyu Quarterly* 11:81–86.

1976a. "Chadogu—Tea Utensils: Ceramics." *Chanoyu Quarterly* 13:54–59.

1976b. "Chadogu—Lacquerware." *Chanoyu Quarterly* 15:54–58.

1976c. "Chadogu—Chaire." *Urasenke Newsletter* (Spring).

1977. "Chadogu—Tea Utensils: Chaire." *Chanoyu Quarterly* 19:59–63.

1981. "Temae: Tea Procedure: Otsubukuro." 1981. *Chanoyu Quarterly* 26:61–73.

Birnbaum, Alfred, trans. 1981. "Exerpts from the Chanoyu Kojidan." *Chanoyu Quarterly* 29:50–53.

Bodart, Beatrice M. 1977. "Tea and Counsel: The Political Role of Sen Rikyu." *Monumenta Nipponica* 32:49–74.

Castile, Rand. 1971. *The Way of Tea*. New York: Weatherhill.

Chikamatsu Shigenori. 1982. *Stories from a Tearoom Window*. 1804. Reprint. Edited by Toshiko Mori and translated by Kozaburo Mori. Tokyo and Vermont: Charles E. Tuttle Company.

Cohen, Kenneth. 1976. "T'ai Chi Chu'an and Chanoyu: Steps Along the Way." *Chanoyu Quarterly* 12:13–23.

Cooper, Michael. 1975. "The Early Europeans and Chanoyu." *Chanoyu Quarterly* 11:36–50.

Cort, Louise Allison. 1979. "Tea in Japan from the Late Sixteenth Century to the Present." In *Chanoyu: Japanese Tea Ceremony*. Edited by Hayashiya Seizo. 25–29. New York: Japan Society, Inc.

———.1982a. "Gen'ya's Devil Bucket." *Chanoyu Quarterly* 30:31–40.

———.1982b. "The Great Kitano Tea Gathering." *Chanoyu Quarterly* 31:15–20.

Covell, Jon Carter. 1975. "The Zen Tea Bowl." *Chanoyu Quarterly* 11:28–36.

————.1976. "Kanamori Sowa and Teigyokuken." *Chanoyu Quarterly* 16:7–19.

Fujikawa Asako. 1957. *Chanoyu and Hideyoshi.* Tokyo: Hokusaido Press.

Fujioka Ryoichi with Masaki Nakano, Hirokazu Arakawa, and Seizo Hayashiya. 1973. *Tea Ceremony Utensils.* New York and Tokyo: Weatherhill/Shibundo.

Fukukita Yasunosuke. n.d. *The Tea Cult of Japan: An Aesthetic Pastime.* 3rd Ed. Tokyo: Board of Tourist Industry, Japanese Government Railways.

Haga Koshiro. 1981. "The Sen Family Tradition of Chado." *Chanoyu Quarterly* 29:7–15.

Hamamoto Soshun. 1984a. "A Tea Master's Vision of the Ten Oxherding Pictures, Part 1." *Chanoyu Quarterly* 37:28–40.

————.1984b. "A Tea Master's Vision of the Ten Oxherding Pictures, Part 2." *Chanoyu Quarterly* 38:36–44.

————.1985. "Reflections on the Buddhist Name 'Rikyu'." *Chanoyu Quarterly* 43:7–13.

Hammitzch, Horst. 1980. *Zen in the Art of the Tea Ceremony.* New York: St. Martin's Press.

Hata Kohei. 1976. "Sen Rikyu: The Last Man of the Middle Ages." *Chanoyu Quarterly* 16:47–53.

Hayakawa, Masao. 1973. *The Garden Art of Japan.* New York and Tokyo: Weatherhill/Heibonsha.

Hayashiya Seizo. 1976. "Honami Koetsu—His Ceramic Works." *Chanoyu Quarterly* 14:34–53.

————.1979. *Chanoyu: Japanese Tea Ceremony.* New York: Japan Society, Inc.

Hayashiya Tatsusaburo, Masao Nakamura, and Seizo Hayashiya. 1974. "Japanese Arts of the Tea Ceremony." New York and Tokyo: Weatherhill/Heibonsha.

Hayashiya Tatsusaburo. 1970a. "Historical Review of Chanoyu, Part I—The Realization of Furyu and Vision for an Elixir of Life." *Chanoyu Quarterly* 2:33–39.

———.1970b. "Historical Review of Chanoyu, Part II—Tea Amongst the Heian Aristocracy." *Chanoyu Quarterly* 3:37–50.

———.1970c. "Historical Review of the Arts of Chanoyu, Part III—The Varja and the Tea Contests." *Chanoyu Quarterly* 4:50–56.

———.1971a. "Historical Review of the Art of Chanoyu, Part IV—The Elegant Culture of the Eastern Hill." *Chanoyu Quarterly* 5:28–42.

———.1971b. "Historical Review of the Art of Chanoyu, Part V—Zen and the Samurai." *Chanoyu Quarterly* 6:48–60.

———.1971c. "Historical Review of Chanoyu, Part VI—The Fragrance of Nature in the City." *Chanoyu Quarterly* 7:37–54.

———.1971d. "Historical Review of the Art of Chanoyu, Part VII—Chanoyu and the Social Reformation of Japan." *Chanoyu Quarterly* 8:48–67.

———.1976. "Historical Review of the Art of Chanoyu, Part VIII—Changing Times." *Chanoyu Quarterly* 12:24–26.

Hirota, Dennis. 1979. "Heart's Mastery: The Kokoro no Fumi: The Letter of Murata Shuko to his Disciple Choin." *Chanoyu Quarterly* 22:7–24.

———.1980a. "The Wabi Tea of Takeno Joo: The Letter on Wabi and Related Documents." *Chanoyu Quarterly* 23:7–24.

———.1980b. "Memoranda of the Words of Rikyu: Nampo Roku Book I." *Chanoyu Quarterly* 25:31–47.

Hisamatsu Shin'ichi. 1987. "The Significance of the Nampo Roku." *Chanoyu Quarterly* 52:7–17.

Iguchi Kaisen. 1976. "Sen Sotan and Yuin." *Chanoyu Quarterly* 13:7–13.

Ishikawa Soji. 1970. "An Invitation to Tea." *Chanoyu Quarterly* 11:54–58.

Itoh Teiji. 1976. "Sen Rikyu and Taian." *Chanoyu Quarterly* 15:7–20.

———. 1983. The Lights of Chanoyu. *Chanoyu Quarterly* 36:26–32.

Kato Shuichi. 1970. "Esthetics in the Way of Tea: Three Approaches." *Chanoyu Quarterly* 11:24–28.

Kawabata Yasunari. 1958. "Snow Country and Thousand Cranes." Harmondsworth, Middlesex, England: Penguin Books.

Kida Taiichi. 1970. "The Science of Tea, Part 1." *Chanoyu Quarterly* 1 (2):47–54.

Kondo, Dorinne. 1985. "The Way of Tea: A Symbolic Analysis." *Man* 20: 287–306.

Kramer, Robert W. 1987. "The Cult of Sen Rikyu in Tokugawa Japan: Eighteenth Century Interpretations of the Legacy." Paper presented at the Conference of Asian Studies on the Pacific Coast, Salem, Oregon, June 19, 1987.

————.1988. "Discourse Formation in the Edo Period Tea Cult." Paper Presented at the Association for Asian Studies Annual Meeting, San Francisco, California, March 26, 1988.

Kumakura Isao. 1980. "Matsudaira Fumai: The Creation of a New World of Chanoyu." *Chanoyu Quarterly* 25:22–30.

————.1984. "Chasen: The Tea Whisk." *Chanoyu Quarterly* 37:41–49.

Kumamoto Kenjiro. 1976. "Confluence of East and West: Okakura Kakuzo and Tea." *Chanoyu Quarterly* 12:8–12.

Kurokawa Kisho. 1983. "Rikyu Grey: An Open-ended Aesthetic." *Chanoyu Quarterly* 36:33–51.

Kuwata Tadachika. 1976. "Men of Power and Their Tea Masters." *Chanoyu Quarterly* 14:7–20.

Lee, Sherman E. 1976. *Tea Taste in Japanese Art*. New York: Arno Press.

Lu Yü. 1974. *The Classic of Tea*. Eighth Century. Reprint. Translated and Introduced by Francis Ross Carpenter. Boston: Little, Brown and Company.

Mittwer, Henry. 1974. *The Art of Chabana: Flowers for the Tea Ceremony*. Tokyo and Vermont: Charles E. Tuttle Company.

Murai Yasuhiko. 1971. "Chanoyu and the Early Christian Missionaries and Converts in Japan." *Chanoyu Quarterly* 7:27–36.

————.1989. "Development of Chanoyu Before Rikyu." In *Tea in Japan: Essays on the History of Chanoyu*. Edited by Paul Varley and Kumakura Isao. 3–32. Honolulu: University of Hawaii Press.

Nakamura Shosei. 1970. "Aspects of the Development of Tearoom Design: Joo to Modern Times." *Chanoyu Quarterly* 9:30–39.

————.1977a. "Furuta Oribe and Ennan." *Chanoyu Quarterly* 17:9–19.

————.1977b. "The Tearooms of Hosokawa Sansai." *Chanoyu Quarterly* 18:7–20.

————.1980. "Katagiri Sekishu and Korin An." *Chanoyu Quarterly* 23:25–36.

Nishibe Bunjo. 1976. "Zen Priests and Their Concepts of Tea." *Chanoyu Quarterly* 13:14–26.

———.1981. "Zen Monks and the Formation of the Way of Tea." *Chanoyu Quarterly* 28:7–46.

Oba Takemitsu. 1976. "An Introduction to Mounting." *Chanoyu Quarterly* 15:21–34.

Okakura Kakuzo. 1956. *The Book of Tea.* 1906. Reprint. Tokyo and Vermont: Charles E. Tuttle Company.

Okuda Naoshige. 1981. "The Temmoku Teabowl." *Chanoyu Quarterly* 26:7–32.

Plutschow, Herbert E. 1986. "Historical Chanoyu." Tokyo: The Japan Times, Ltd.

Rhodes, Daniel. 1970. *Tamba Pottery: The Timeless Art of a Japanese Village.* Tokyo: Kodansha.

Sadler, A. L. 1962. *Chanoyu: The Japanese Tea Ceremony.* 1933. Reprint. Tokyo and Vermont: Charles E. Tuttle Company.

Saint-Gilles, Amaury. 1978. *Earth n' Fire: A Survey Guide to Contemporary Japanese Ceramics.* Tokyo: Shufunotomo.

Sen Soshitsu. 1976. "Notes on the Way of Tea." *Chanoyu Quarterly* 12:6–7.

———.1977a. "Classic of Tea: The World of Lu Yü." *Chanoyu Quarterly* 18:5–6.

———.1977b. "The Green Oasis." *Chanoyu Quarterly* 20:5–6.

———.1979a. *Chado: The Japanese Way of Tea.* New York and Tokyo: Weatherhill/Tankosha.

———.1979b. *Tea Life, Tea Mind.* New York and Tokyo: John Weatherhill, Inc.

———.1980a. *Urasenke Chanoyu, Handbooks One and Two.* Kyoto: Urasenke Foundation.

———.1980b. "Form in Chanoyu." *Chanoyu Quarterly* 24:5–6.

———.1981. "A Wider Realm." *Chanoyu Quarterly* 27:5–6.

Sen Soshitsu, ed. 1988. *Chanoyu: The Urasenke Tradition of Tea.* New York: Weatherhill.

Tachihara Masaaki. 1977. "The Path to the Tearoom: An Expression of the Tea of Quiet Taste." *Chanoyu Quarterly* 18:47–58.

Tanaka Seno. 1977. *The Tea Ceremony.* New York: Harmony Books.

Tanihata Akio. 1981a. "Men of Tea: An Evaluation by Yamanoue Soji, Part I." *Chanoyu Quarterly* 26:50–60.

——1981b. "Men of Tea: An Evaluation by Yamanoue Soji, Part II." *Chanoyu Quarterly* 27:51–58.

———.1981c. "Men of Tea: An Evaluation by Yamanoue Soji, Part III." *Chanoyu Quarterly* 28:48–56.

Tanikawa Tetsuzo. 1976. "Four Elements of Tea." *Chanoyu Quarterly* 15:35–41.

———.1980a. "The Esthetics of Chanoyu: Part I." *Chanoyu Quarterly* 23:37–47.

———.1980b. "The Esthetics of Chanoyu: Part II." *Chanoyu Quarterly* 25:7–21.

———.1981a. "The Esthetics of Chanoyu: Part III." *Chanoyu Quarterly* 26:33–49.

———.1981b. "The Esthetics of Chanoyu: Part IV." *Chanoyu Quarterly* 27:35–50.

Tierney, Lennox. 1975. "Chanoyu as a Form of Non-Literary Art Criticism." *Chanoyu Quarterly* 11:12–16.

Tsuji Kaichi. 1972. *Kaiseki: Zen Tastes in Japanese Cooking.* Tokyo and Palo Alto: Kodansha.

Tsutsui Hiroichi. 1980. "The Transmission of Tea Traditions Through Verse." *Chanoyu Quarterly* 24:35–44.

———.1981. "The Role of Anecdotes in the Transmission of Tea Traditions." *Chanoyu Quarterly* 29:28–36.

———.1982. "The Essence of Chanoyu Lies Precisely in What Isn't Chanoyu." *Chanoyu Quarterly* 32:58–61.

1978. "Midorikai Program Handbook." (Urasenke Foundation.) Mimeo.

Varley, Paul and Kumakura Isao, eds. 1989. *Tea in Japan: Essays on the History of Chanoyu.* Honolulu: University of Hawaii Press.

Weisman, Steven R. 1990. "As High Priests of Tea Meet, a Cool Breeze Builds." *New York Times International*, 9 April 1990.

Yashiroda Kan, ed. 1968. *Handbook on Japanese Herbs.* Special Ed. of Plants and Gardens, vol. 24, no. 2. Brooklyn: Brooklyn Botanic Garden.

Yoneda Soei. 1982. *Good Food From a Japanese Temple*. Tokyo: Kodansha.

Young, John. 1970. "Tea for the West." *Chanoyu Quarterly* 1:28–38.

JAPANESE LANGUAGE SOURCES

Azegami Chikara, Hayashi Yasaka, and Hishiyama Chuzaburo. 1983. *Nihon no Yaso (Wildflowers of Japan)*. Tokyo: Yamakei Publishers.

———.1985. *Nihon no Jumoku (Woody Plants of Japan)*. Tokyo: Yamakei Publishers.

Harai Toshiko, Okuyama Kazuko, and Okuyama Haruki. 1985. *Chabana Shokubutsu Zukan (Illustrated Dictionary of Tea Flowers)*. Tokyo: Shufu no Tomosha.

Koga Kenzo. 1980. *Cha no Kireji (Tea Fabrics)*. Kyoto: Tankosha.

Kuwata Tadachika. 1976. *Sen Rikyu Kenkyu (Sen Rikyu Research*. Tokyo: Tokyodo Shuppan.

Murai Yasuhiko. 1985. *Sen Rikyu*. Tokyo: Nihon hoso shuppan kyokai (Japan Broadcasting Publishing Company).

Nakamura Masao. 1984. *Chashitsu no Mikata (A Way of Looking at Teahouses)*. Tokyo: Shufuno Tomosha.

Naya Yoshiharu. 1975. *Genshoku Chado Dai Jiten (Big, Full-Color, Illustrated Dictionary of Tea)*. Kyoto: Tankosha.

———.1981. *Kaiseki Zensho (Everything about Kaiseki*, volumes 1–4). Kyoto: Tankosha.

Sen Sosa, Sen Soshitsu, Sen Soshu, eds. 1989. *Sen Rikyu Dai Jiten. (Great Dictionary on Sen Rikyu)* Kyoto: Tankosha.

Sen Soshitsu. 1976–1977. *Urasenke Chado Kyoka (Urasenke Tea Curriculum)*. Volumes 1–17. Kyoto: Tankosha.

———.1984. *Shogo no Chaji—Ro" (Noon Tea Gathering—Ro Season)*. Kyoto: Tankosha.

———.*Urasenke Chado no Oshie (Urasenke Tea Textbook)*. Tokyo: Nihon Hoso Shupan Kyokai.

———.1985. *Shogo no Chaji—Furo (Noon Tea Gathering—Furo Season)*. Kyoto: Tankosha.

———.1986. *Yobanashi no Chaji (Evening Tea Gathering)*. Kyoto: Tankosha.

———.1987. *Asa no Chaji (Morning Tea Gathering)*. Kyoto: Tankosha

Sasaki Sanmi. 1985. *Chado Saejiki (Annual Cycle of Tea)*. Kyoto: Tankosha.

Sato, Takashi. 1988. *Chanoyu no Nyumon (Introduction to Tea)*. Tokyo: Heibonsha.

Tsuji Yoshiichi. 1982. *Anata no Kaiseki (Your Kaiseki)*. Tokyo: Fujingahosha.

Urasenke staff. 1987. *Mizuya no kokoro (Preparation Room Knowledge)*. Kyoto: Tankosha.

Yamafuji Sozan. 1985. *Chabana no Ire Kata (How to Arrange Tea Flowers)*. Kyoto: Tankosha.

————.1987. *Furo no Haigata (Brazier Ash Formation)*. Kyoto: Tankosha.

Japanese Culture Bibliography

Agency of Cultural Affairs. 1972. *Japanese Religion*. Tokyo: Kodansha.

Anesaki Masaharu. 1963. *History of Japanese Religion, with Special Reference to the Social and Moral life of the Nation*. Tokyo and Vermont: Charles E. Tuttle Co.

————.1970. *Religious Life of the Japanese People*. Tokyo: Kokusai Bunka Shinokai.

Aoki Michiko Y. and Margaret B. Dardess, eds. 1981. *As the Japanese See It: Past and Present*. Honolulu: University of Hawaii Press.

Austin, Lewis. 1975. *Saints and Samurai, The Political Culture of the American and Japanese Elites*. New Haven: Yale University Press.

————.1976. *Japan: The Paradox of Progress*. New Haven: Yale University Press.

Beardsley, Richard K., John Hall, and Robert Ward. 1959. *Village Japan*. Chicago: University of Chicago Press.

Befu, Harumi. 1962. "Corporate Emphasis and Patterns of Descent in the Japanese Family." In *Japanese Culture: Its Development and Characteristics*, Edited by Robert J. Smith and Richard K. Beardsley. 34–41. Chicago: Aldine Publishing Co.

————.1963. "Patrilineal Descent and Personal Kindred in Japan." *American Anthropologist* 65:1328–41.

————.1964. "Ritual Kinship in Japan, Its Variability and Resiliency." *Sociologus* 14:150–169. Also in Yamamoto, George K. and Tsuyoshi Ishida, eds. 1971. *Selected Readings in Modern Japanese Society*. 49–63. McCutcheon Publishing Corporation.

————.1966. "Duty, Reward, Sanction, and Power." In *Modern Japanese Leadership*, edited by B. Silberman. 25–49. Tucson: University of Arizona Press.

————.1968. "Gift-giving in Modernizing Japan." *Monumenta Nipponica* 23:445–446. Also in Lebra, Takie Sugiyama, and William P. Lebra, eds. 1974. *Japanese Culture and Behavior*. 208–221. Honolulu: The University Press of Hawaii.

————.1970. "Studies in Japanese Kinship." Reprint. *Rice University Studies* 56:4.

———.1971. *Japan: An Anthropological Introduction*. San Francisco: Chandler Publishing Co.

———.1980. "A Critique of the Group Model of Japanese Society." *Social Analysis* 56:29–41.

Bellah, Robert. 1957. *Tokugawa Religion*. Glencoe, Illinois: The Free Press.

———.1965. "Japan's Cultural Identity." *Journal of Asian Studies* 24:4.

Benedict, Ruth. 1946. *The Chrysanthemum and the Sword*. Boston: Houghton Mifflin.

Bennett, John W., and Leo A. Despres. 1953. "The Japanese Critique of the Methodology of Benedict's *The Chrysanthemum and the Sword*." *American Anthropologist* 55: 404–411.

Berry, Mary Elizabeth. 1982. *Hideyoshi*. Cambridge, Massachusetts: Harvard University Press.

Bloom, Alfred. 1965. *Shinran's Gospel of Pure Grace*. Tucson: University of Arizona Press.

Brown, Keith. 1966. "Dozoku and the Ideology of Descent in Rural Japan." *American Anthropologist* 68:1129–1151.

———.1968. "The Content of Dozoku Relationships in Japan." *Ethnology* 7:113–38.

Burks, Ardath W. 1981. *Japan: Profile of a Postindustrial Power*. Boulder, Colorado: Westview Press.

Collcutt, Martin. 1981. *Five Mountains: The Rinzai Zen Monastic Institution in Medieval Japan*. Cambridge, Massachusetts: Harvard University Press.

Cooper, Michael, ed. 1965. *They Came to Japan: An Anthology of European Reports on Japan, 1543–1640*. Berkeley: University of California Press.

Crane, Gene A., and Kojima Setsuko, eds. 1987. *A Dictionary of Japanese Culture*. Tokyo: The Japan Times.

Davis, Winston. 1980. *Dojo: Magic and Exorcism in Modern Japan*. Stanford: Stanford University Press.

DeVos, George A. 1973. *Socialization for Achievement: Essays on the Cultural Psychology of the Japanese*. Berkeley: University of California Press.

Devos, George A. and Hiroshi Wagatsuma. 1961. "Value Attitudes Toward the Role Behavior of Women in Two Japanese Villages." *American Anthropologist* 63:1204–1230.

———.1973. "Status and Role Behavior in changing Japan." In *Sex Roles in Changing Society*, edited by G. Steward. 334–370. New York: Random House, 1973.

Devos, George A., and Keiichi Mizushima. 1967. "Organization and Social Function of Japanese Gangs: Historical Development and Modern Parallels." In *Aspects of Social Change in Modern Japan*, edited by Ronald P. Dore. 289–325. Princeton: Princeton University Press.

Doi Takeo. 1962. "Amae: A Key Concept for Understanding Japanese Personality Structure." In *Japanese Culture: Its Development and Characteristics*, edited by Robert J. Smith, and Richard K. Beardsley. 132–139. Chicago: Aldine Publishing Co. Also in Lebra, Takie Sugiyama, and William P. Lebra, eds. 1974. *Japanese Culture and Behavior*. Honolulu: The University Press of Hawaii.

Dore, Ronald P. 1958. *City Life in Japan: A Study of a Tokyo Ward*. Berkeley: University of California Press.

———.1967a. *Aspects of Social Change in Modern Japan*. Princeton: Princeton University Press.

———.1967b. "Mobility, Equality, and Individuation in Modern Japan." In *Aspects of Social Change in Modern Japan*, edited by Ronald P. Dore. 113–153. Princeton: Princeton University Press.

———.1978. *Shinohata: A Portrait of a Japanese Village*. New York: Random House.

Dower, John W., ed. 1965. *Origins of the Modern Japanese State: Selected Writings of E. H. Norman*. New York: Pantheon Books.

Dumoulin, Heinrich. 1988. *Zen Buddhism: A History*. Vol. 1. Translated by James W. Heisig and Paul Knitter. New York: MacMillan.

———.1990. *Zen Buddhism: A History*. Vol. 2. Translated by James W. Heisig and Paul Knitter. New York: MacMillan.

Dunne, Charles J. 1972. *Everyday Life in Traditional Japan*. Tokyo and Vermont: Charles E. Tuttle Company.

Duus, Peter. 1969. *Feudalism in Japan*. 2d ed. New York: Alfred A. Knopf.

Embree, John F. 1939. *Suye Mura: A Japanese Village*. Chicago: University of Chicago Press.

———.1941. "Some Social Functions of Religion in Rural Japan." *American Journal of Sociology* 47:184–189.

Frager, Robert and Thomas P. Rohlen. 1976. "The Future of a Tradition: Japanese Spirit in the 80's." In *Japan: The Paradox of Progress,* edited by Lewis Austin. 255–278. New Haven: Yale University Press.

Frederic, Louis. 1973. *Daily Life in Japan.* Tokyo and Vermont: Charles E. Tuttle Company.

Fukutake Tadashi. 1962. *Man and Society in Japan.* Tokyo: Tokyo University Press.

————.1967. *Japanese Rural Society.* Tokyo: Oxford University Press.

————.1974. *Japanese Society Today.* Tokyo: University of Tokyo Press.

————.1980. *Rural Society in Japan.* Tokyo: University of Tokyo Press.

————.1982. *The Japanese Social Structure.* Tokyo: University of Tokyo Press.

Gibney, Frank. 1975. *Japan, The Fragile Superpower.* (Rev. Ed.). New York: The New American Library, Inc.

Hall, John Whitney. 1959. "The Confucian Teacher in Tokugawa Japan." In *Confucianism in Action,* edited by David S. Nivison and Arthur F. Wright. 268–301. Stanford, California: Stanford University Press.

————.1970. *Japan: From Prehistory to Modern Times.* New York: The New American Library, Inc.

Haring, D. G. 1953. "Japanese National Character: Cultural Anthropolgy, Psychoanalysis and History." *Yale Review* 42:375–402.

Hendry, Joy. 1981. *Marriage in Changing Japan.* New York: St. Martin's Press.

Hsu, Francis L. K. 1975. *Iemoto: The Heart of Japan.* New York: John Wiley and Sons.

Ishida Eiichiro. 1961. "A Culture of Love and Hate." *Japan Quarterly* 8:394–402. Also in Lebra, Takie Sugiyama, and William P. Lebra, eds. 1974. *Japanese Culture and Behavior.* 27–36. Honolulu: The University Press of Hawaii.

Ishino Iwao. 1953. "The Oyabun-Kobun: A Japanese Ritual Kinship Institution." *American Anthropologist* 55:695–707.

Ito Teiji. 1969. "Iemoto Shido o Kangaeru" (A Study of the Iemoto System). A series of articles published in the Tokyo *Asahi Shimbun,* 22 April to 27 March.

Kawabata Yasunari.1958. *Japan the Beautiful and Myself.* Translated by G. Seidensticker. Tokyo and Palo Alto: Kodansha.

Keene, Donald. 1969. *The Japanese Discovery of Europe 1720–1830* Rev. ed. Stanford, California: Stanford University Press.

———.1976. *World Within Walls: Japanese Literature of the Pre-Modern Era, 1600–1867.* New York: Grove Press.

Kitano, S. 1962. "Dozoku and the Ie in Japan: The Meaning of Family Geneological Relationships." In *Japanese Culture: Its Development and Characteristics,* edited by Robert Smith, and Richard K. Beardsley. 42–46. New York: Viking Fund Publications in Anthropology 34.

Kitagawa, Joseph M. 1964. "Religious and Cultural Ethos of Modern Japan." *Asian Studies* II:3:334–352. Also in Yamamoto, George K. and Tsuyoshi Ishida, ed. 1971. *Selected Readings in Modern Japanese Society.* Berkeley: McCutchen Publishing Corporation, 186–198.

———.1966. *Religion in Japanese History.* New York: Columbia University Press.

Kojima Setsuko and Yamaguchi Momoo, eds. 1979. *A Cultural Dictionary of Japan.* Tokyo: The Japan Times.

Koyama Takashi. 1961. *The Changing Social Position of Women in Japan.* Paris: UNESCO.

Lebra, Joyce, and Elizabeth Powers. 1976. *Women in Changing Japan.* Boulder, Colorado: Westview Press.

Lebra, Takie Sugiyama. 1969. "Reciprocity and the Asymmetric Principle: An Analytical Reappraisal of the Japanese Concept of On." *Psychologia* 12:129–138. Also in Lebra, Takie Sugiyama, and William P. Lebra, eds. 1974. *Japanese Culture and Behavior.* 90–116. Honolulu: University Press of Hawaii.

———. 1974. "Intergenerational Continuity and Discontinuity in Moral Values Among the Japanese." In *Japanese Culture and Behavior,* edited by Takie Sugiyama Lebra and William P. Lebra. pp. 90–116. Honolulu: The University Press of Hawaii.

———.1976. *Japanese Patterns of Behavior.* Honolulu: The University Press of Hawaii.

———.1984. *Japanese Women: Constraint and Fulfillment.* Honolulu: The University of Hawaii Press.

Lebra, Takie Sugiyama and William P. Lebra, eds. 1974. *Japanese Culture and Behavior.* Honolulu: The University Press of Hawaii.

Linhart, Sepp. 1975. "The Use and Meaning of Leisure in Present Day Japan." In *Modern Japan: Aspects of History, Literature, and Society,* edited by W. G. Beasley. 198–208. London: George Allen and Unwin, Ltd.

Marsh, Robert M. and Hiroshi Mannari. 1971. "Lifetime Commitment in Japan: Role Norms and Values." *American Journal of Sociology* 76:795–812.

Matsumoto, Y. Scott. 1960. "Contemporary Japan, the Individual and the Group." *Transactions of the American Philosophical Society* 50 (Part 1): 1–75.

Minami Hiroshi. 1971. *Psychology of the Japanese People.* Tokyo: University of Tokyo Press.

Moore, Charles A., ed. 1967. *The Japanese Mind.* Honolulu: University of Hawaii Press.

Morris, Ivan. 1974. *The World of the Shining Prince.* New York: Penguin Books.

Morse, Edward S. 1961. *Japanese Homes and Their Surroundings.* New York: Dover.

Najita Tetsuo. 1974. Japan: *The Intellectual Foundations of Modern Japanese Politics.* Chicago: University of Chicago Press.

Nakane Chie. 1970. *Japanese Society.* Berkeley: University of California Press.

Nishiyama Matsunosuke. 1962. *Gendai no Iemoto (Iemoto Today).* Tokyo: Kobundo.

Norbeck, Edward. 1962. "Common Interest Associations in Rural Japan." In *Japanese Culture: Its Development and Characteristics,* edited by Robert J. Smith, and Richard K. Beardsley. 73–85. Chicago: Aldine Publishing Co.

———.1970. *Religion and Society in Japan.* Houston: Tourmaline Press.

Norbeck, Edward and Harumi Befu. 1958. "Informal Fictive Kinship in Japan." *American Anthropologist* 60:102–117.

Norbeck, Edward and Susan Parman. 1970. "The Study of Japan in the Behavioral Sciences." *Rice University Studies* 56:(4).

Ono Sokyo. 1962. *Shinto: The Kami Way.* Tokyo and Vermont: Charles E. Tuttle Company.

Ortolani, Benito. 1969. "Iemoto." *Japan Quarterly* 17 (3): 297–306.

Papinot, E. 1972. *Historical and Geographical Dictionary of Japan.* Rutland, Vermont and Tokyo: Charles E. Tuttle Company.

Pelzel, John C. 1974. "Human Nature in Japanese Myths." In *Japanese Culture and Behavior,* edited by Takie Sugiyama Lebra and William P. Lebra. 3–26. Honolulu: The University Press of Hawaii.

Peterson, Gwenn Boardman. 1979. *The Moon in the Water: Understanding Tanizaki, Kawabata, and Mishima.* Honolulu: University of Hawaii Press.

Pharr, Susan J. 1976. "The Japanese Woman: Evolving Views of Life and Role." In *Japan: The Paradox of Progress,* edited by Lewis Austin. 301–328. New Haven: The Yale University Press.

Plath, David W. 1964. *The After Hours: Modern Japan and the Search for Enjoyment.* Berkeley: University of California Press.

———.1967. "The Enjoyment of Daily Living: Some Japanese Popular Views." *Journal of Asian Studies* 22:3.

———.1980. *Long Engagements.* Stanford: Stanford University Press.

Reischauer, Edwin O. 1978. *The Japanese.* Cambridge, Mass.: Belnap-Harvard University Press.

———.1971. *Japan: Past and Present.* 1946. Reprint. New York: Alfred A. Knopf.

Robins-Mowry, Dorothy. 1983. *The Hidden Sun: Women of Modern Japan.* Boulder, Colorado: Westview Press.

Rohlen, Thomas P. 1970. "Sponsorship of Cultural Continuity in Japan." *Journal of Asian and African Studies* 5:3. Also in Lebra, Takie Sugiyama, and William P. Lebra, eds. 1974. *Japanese Culture and Behavior.* 332–341. Honolulu: The University Press of Hawaii.

———.1974. *For Harmony and Strength.* Berkeley: University of California Press.

Rudofsky, Bernard. 1982. *The Kimono Mind.* New York: Van Nostrand Reinhold Company.

Sansome, George. 1958. *A History of Japan: To 1334.* Stanford: Stanford University Press.

———.1961. *A History of Japan: 1334–1615.* Stanford: Stanford University Press.

———.1963. *A History of Japan: 1615–1867.* Stanford: Stanford University Press.

————.1978. *Japan: A Short Cultural History.* Stanford: Stanford University Press.

Seward, Jack. 1968. *Hara-Kiri: Japanese Ritual Suicide.* Rutland, Vermont and Tokyo: Charles E. Tuttle Company.

Singer, Kurt. 1973. *Mirror, Sword, and Jewel: The Geometry of Japanese Life.* San Francisco: Kodansha.

Shibayama Zenkei. 1970. *A Flower Does Not Talk: Zen Essays.* Tokyo and Vermont: Charles E. Tuttle Company.

Shibusawa K. 1958. *Japanese Life and Culture in the Meiji Era.* Tokyo: Obunsha.

Shimizu Akitoshi. 1987. "Ie and Dozoku: Family and Descent in Japan." *Current Anthropology* 28 [4]:S85–90.

Smith, Robert J. 1974. *Ancestor Worship in Contemporary Japan.* Stanford, California: Stanford University Press.

————.1978. *Kurusu: The Price of Progress in a Japanese Village, 1951–1975.* Stanford: Stanford University Press.

Smith, Robert J., and Richard K. Beardsley, eds. 1962. *Japanese Culture: Its Development and Characteristics.* Chicago: Aldine Publishing Co.

Smith, Robert J. and Ella Lury Wiswell. 1982. *The Women of Suye Mura.* Chicago: University of Chicago Press.

Smith, Thomas C. 1959. *The Agrarian Origins of Modern Japan.* Stanford: Stanford University Press.

————.1977. *Nakahara: Family Farming and Population in a Japanese Village, 1717–1830.* Stanford: Stanford University Press.

Sofue Takao. 1960. "Japanese Studies by American Anthropologists: Review and Evaluation." *American Anthropologist* 62:306–317.

Suzuki Daisetz. 1956. *Zen Buddhism.* New York: Doubleday.

————.1959. *Zen and Japanese Culture.* New York: Pantheon Books.

————.1964. *An Introduction to Zen Buddhism.* New York: Grove Press.

————.1967. "An Interpretation of Zen Experience." In *The Japanese Mind,* edited by Charles A. Moore. 1967. 122–142. Honolulu: University Press of Hawaii.

Tiedman, Arthur. 1962. *Modern Japan.* 1955. Reprint. New York: D. Van Nostrand Company, Inc.

Totman, Conrad. 1981. *Japan Before Perry: A Short History.* Berkeley: University of California Press.

————.1983. *Tokugawa Ieyasu: Shogun.* South San Francisco: Heian International Inc.

Trager, James. 1982. *Letters from Sachiko.* New York: Atheneum.

Trewartha, Glenn T. 1965. *Japan.* Madison, Wisconsin: University of Wisconsin Press.

Tsunoda Ryusaku, William Theodore DeBary, and Donald Keene, eds. 1964. *Sources of Japanese Tradition, Volumes I and II.* New York: University of Columbia Press.

Tsurumi Kazuko. 1970. *Social Change and the Individual.* Princeton: Princeton University Press.

————.1977. "Women in Japan: A Paradox of Modernization." *Japan Foundation Newsletter* 5:1.

Vogel, Ezra F. 1967. *Japan's New Middle Class: The Salary Man and His Family in a Tokyo Suburb.* Berkeley: University of California Press.

————.1979. *Japan As Number One.* New York: Harper and Row.

Von Siebold, Philipp Franz. 1973. *Manners and Customs of the Japanese in the Nineteenth Century.* Tokyo and Vermont: Charles E. Tuttle Company.

Wimberly, Howard. 1972. "On Living with Your Past: Style and Structure Among Contemporary Japanese Merchant Families." *Economic Development and Cultural Change* 21:423–428.

————.1973. "Conjugal Role Organization and Social Networks in Japan and England." *Journal of Marriage and the Family* 35:125–130.

World Fellowship Committee of Tokyo. Young Women's Christian Association. 1955. *Japanese Etiquette: An Introduction.* Tokyo and Vermont: Charles E. Tuttle Company.

Yamamoto, George K. and Tsuyoshi Ishida, eds. 1971. *Selected Readings in Modern Japanese Society.* Berkeley: McCutchen Publishing Corporation.

Selected General Bibliography

Bachofen, J. J. 1861. *Das Mutterrecht*. Basel: Benno Schwabe

Brinker, H., R. P. Kramers, and C. Ouwehand, eds. 1985. *Zen in China, Japan, East Asian Art*. New York: Peter Lang.

Chai, Ch'u and Winberg Chai, eds. and trans. 1965. *The Humanist Way in Ancient China: Essential Works of Confucianism*. New York: Bantam Books.

Cheek, Neil H., Jr., and William R. Burch Jr. 1976. *The Social Organization of Leisure*. New York: Harper and Row.

Cohen, Abner. 1977. "Symbolic Action and the Structure of the Self." In *Symbols and Sentiments*, edited by Ioan Lewis. 117–128. New York: Academic Press.

Cohen, Abner, ed. 1974. *Urban Ethnicity*. New York: Tavistock Publications.

Comte, A. 1830–1842. *Cours de Philosophie Positive*. Paris: Bachelier.

Dolgin, Janet L., David S. Kemnitzer, and David M. Schneider, eds. 1977. *Symbolic Anthropology: A Reader in the Study of Symbols and Meanings*. New York: Columbia University Press.

Douglas, Mary. 1966. *Purity and Danger*. London: Routledge and Kegan.

————.1972. "Pollution." In *Reader in Comparative Religion: An Anthropological Approach*. 3rd ed., edited by William A. Lessa and Evon Z. Vogt. 196–202. New York: Harper and Row.

Duncan, Hugh Dalziel. 1961. *Language and Literature in Society*. New York: The Bedminster Press.

————.1962. *Communication and Social Order*. New York: The Bedminster Press.

————.1969. *Symbols and Social Theory*. New York: The Oxford University Press.

Durkheim, Emile. 1912. *Elementary Forms of the Religious Life*. Translated by J. W. Swain. London: Allen & Unwin.

Eliade, Mircea, ed. 1987. *The Encyclopedia of Religion*. New York: MacMillan.

Evans-Pritchard, E. E. 1937. *Oracles and Magic Among the Azande.* Oxford:Clarendon Press.

————.1940. *The Nuer.* London: Oxford University Press.

Feleppa, Robert. 1986. "Emics, Etics, and Social Objectivity." *Current Anthropology* 27(3):243–255.

Firth, Raymond. 1973. *Symbols: Public and Private.* Ithaca, New York: Cornell University Press.

Frazer, J. G. 1958. *The Golden Bough.* 1890. Reprint. New York: Macmillan.

Freud, Sigmund. 1950. *Totem and Taboo.* London: Routledge and Kegan.

Fustel de Coulanges, N.D. 1956. *The Ancient City: An Anthropological View of Greece and Rome.* 1864. Reprint. New York: Anchor, Doubleday.

Geertz, Clifford. 1965. "Religion as a Cultural System." In *Reader in Comparative Religion: An Anthropological Approach.* 2d ed., edited by William Z. Vogt. 205–215. New York: Harper and Row.

————.1973. *The Interpretation of Cultures.* New York: Basic Books, Inc.

Girardot, Norman J. 1983. *Myth and Meaning in Early Taoism: The Theme of Chaos.* Berkeley: University of California Press.

Gluckman, Max. 1962. "Les Rites de Passage." In *Essays on the Ritual of Social Relations.* 1–52. Manchester, England: Manchester University Press.

Goody, Jack. 1961. "Religion and Ritual: The Definitional Problem." *British Journal of Sociology* 12:142–164.

Holloman, Regina E., and Serghei A. Arutiunov, eds. 1978. *Perspectives on Ethnicity.* The Hague, Netherlands: Mouton Publishers.

Hucker, Charles O. 1975. *China's Imperial Past: An Introduction to Chinese History and Culture.* Stanford: Stanford University Press.

Kaltenmark, Max. 1969. *Lao Tze and Taoism.* Palo Alto, California: Stanford University Press.

Kluckhohn, Clyde. 1942. "Myths and Rituals: A General Theory." In *Harvard Theological Review* 35:45–79. Cambridge, Mass.: Harvard University Press.

Kuper, Adam, ed. 1977. *The Social Anthropology of Radcliffe-Brown.* London: Routledge and Kegan Paul.

Langer, Susanne K. 1960. *Philosophy in a New Key: A Study of the Symbolism of Reason, Rite and Art.* Cambridge, Mass.: Harvard University Press.

Leach, Edmund. 1966. "On the Founding Fathers." *Current Anthropology* 7:560–567.

———.1968. "Ritual." In *International Encyclopedia of the Social Sciences*, edited by David Sills. Vol. 13. 520–526. New York: Macmillan.

———.1972. "The Structure of Symbolism." In *The Interpretation of Ritual*, edited by J. La Fontaine. London: Tavistock.

Legge, James. 1893. *Confucian Analects. The Chinese Classics.* Vol. 1 Oxford: Claringdon Press.

———.1959. "Introduction." In *Texts of Taoism*. Translated by James Legge. New York: Julian Press.

Lessa, William A., and Evon Z. Vogt, eds. 1965. *Reader in Comparative Religion: An Anthropological Approach.* 2d ed. New York: Harper and Row.

Levi-Strauss, Claude. 1966. *The Savage Mind.* Chicago: University of Chicago Press.

———.1963. "The Effectiveness of Symbols." In *Structural Anthropology*. Translated by Claire Jacobsen and Brooke Schoepf. 186–205. New York: Basic Books.

Lewis, Ioan. 1977. "Introduction." In *Symbols and Sentiments*, edited by Ioan Lewis. 1–24. New York: Academic Press.

Li Shih Chen. 1973. *Chinese Medicinal Herbs.* Translated and Researched by F. Porter Smith, and G. A. Stuart. 1578. Reprint. San Francisco: Georgetown Press.

Lubbock, J. 1870. *The Origin of Civilization and the Primitive Condition of Man; Mental and Social Condition of Savages.* London: Longmans, Green.

Maquet, Jacques, ed. 1982. *On Symbols in Anthropology: Essays in Honor of Harry Hoijer.* Malibu, California: Undena Publications.

Mauss, Marcel. 1954. *The Gift.* 1925. Reprint. London: Cohen and West.

Munn, Nancy. 1973. "Symbolism in a Ritual Context: Aspects of Symbolic Action." In *Handbook of Social and Cultural Anthropology*, edited by John J. Honigman. 579–612. Chicago: Rand McNally.

Needham, Rodney. 1975. "Polythetic Classification." *Man* 10:349–369.

Parsons, Talcott. 1963a. "On the Concept of Influence." *Public Opinion Quarterly* 27:37–62.

———.1963b. "On the Concept of Political Power." *Proceedings of the American Philosophical Society* 107:232–262.

Peacock, James L. 1975. *Consciousness and Change: Symbolic Anthropology in Evolutionary Perspective.* New York: John Wiley and Sons.

Rapoport, Rhona, and Robert N. Rapoport. 1974. "Four Themes in the Sociology of Leisure." *British Journal of Sociology* 25:215–229.

Rosaldo, Renato. 1968. "Metaphors of Hierarchy in a Mayan Ritual." *American Anthropologist* 70:524–536.

Royce, Anya Peterson. 1982. *Ethnic Identity: Strategies of Diversity.* Bloomington: Indiana University Press.

Smith, William Robertson. 1956. *The Religion of the Semites.* 1889. Reprint. New York: Meridian Books, World Publishing.

Southwold, Martin. 1978. "Buddhism and the Definition of Religion." *Man* 13:361–379.

Suzuki Daisetz. 1959. "Introduction." *The Texts of Taoism.* Translated by James Legge. New York: Julian Press.

Tu Wei Ming. 1985. "Ch'an in China: A Reflective Interpretation." In *Zen in China, Japan, East Asian Art,* edited by H. Brinker, R. P. Kramers, and C. Ouwehand. 9–26. New York: Peter Lang.

Turner, Victor. 1967. *The Forest of Symbols.* Ithaca, New York: Cornell University Press.

———.1969. *The Ritual Process.* Chicago: Aldine Publishing Company.

———.1975 *Revelation and Divination in Ndembu Ritual.* Ithaca, New York: Cornell University Press.

Tylor, Edward B. 1871. *Primitive Culture: Researches into the Development of Mythology, Philosophy, Religion, Language, Art and Custom.* London: J. Murray.

———.1965. "Animism." In *Reader in Comparative Religion: An Anthropological Approach.* 2d ed., edited by William A. Lessa, and Evon Z. Vogt. 10–12. New York: Harper and Row.

Gennep, Arnold L. Van. 1960. *The Rites of Passage.* Chicago: University of Chicago Press. [French edition. *Les Rites de Passage.* 1909. Paris: E. Nourry.]

Weber, Max. 1958. *The Protestant Ethic and the Spirit of Capitalism.* Translated by Talcott Parsons. New York: Charles Scribner's Sons.

Williams, C. A. S. 1974. *Outlines of Chinese Symbolism and Art Motives.* (Third Revised Edition) 1941. Reprint. Tokyo: Tuttle.

Wilson, Monica. 1957. *Rituals of Kinship Among the Nyakyusa.* London: Oxford University Press.

Zuesse, Evan M. 1987. "Ritual." In *The Encyclopedia of Religion,* edited by Mircea Eliade. Vol. 12. 405–422. New York: MacMillan.

Index

purity *(continued)*
109, 150, 154–155, 157, 168,
170, 176, 183, 213, 215–216,
221, 223, 230, 250, 260, 291, 299

R
raku, 68, 183, 187–188, 240–243,
245–246, 251, 283, 289
Raku Chōjirō (1452?–1589), 58,
187, 242, 289
Raku Kichizaemon, 251
rank, 35–36, 44, 63, 99, 133, 141,
143, 197, 222, 230, 233, 256, 279
Reisenji, 24
religion(s), 1, 4–6, 10, 13, 19, 21,
24, 213, 223, 262
renga, 31, 276, 280, 289
representative branch offices (*see*
shutchōjo)
respect (*see also* kei), 2–3, 9, 16,
29–30, 38, 42, 54, 58, 67, 70, 80,
82, 96, 98, 101, 165, 167, 172,
181, 192, 194, 216, 213,
ritual emblems of identity, 130
215, 229–231, 233–236, 250,
281, 292, 300–301
reverence, 30, 54, 215
rice, 34, 44, 108, 145, 167–172,
176, 180, 201–202, 212, 232,
239, 240, 257–258, 270, 277,
280, 285, 289, 302
rice wine (*see* saké)
rikka, 181–182, 289
Rikū (*see* Pai-chang)
Rikyū (*see* Sen Rikyū)
Rikyūdō, 48, 85, 242
Rikyūki, 103, 184, 242, 243, 289
rinji chaji, 103, 106, 271, 289
rinkan chanoyu, 290
Rinzai Zen, 24, 32, 47, 53, 89, 192,
197
ritual divider (*see* kekkai)
ritual message system, 9

ritual pollution, 215
River Hsi, 52
ro (*see also* hearth, fire pit), 57,
101, 103–104, 158, 173 229, 231,
233–234, 243, 254, 258, 265,
273–277, 287, 290, 293, 295,
297, 299, 301
roji, 41, 55, 104, 148–151, 153–157,
179–181, 216, 244, 255–256,
269, 284, 290, 292, 295, 297–299
roji gasa, 149, 156, 290
Rokujō, 255
Roman Empire, 14
Royce, Anya Peterson, 220
ryaku bon, 100, 227, 228, 290
ryūreidemae, 70, 291
Ryūseiken, 300

S
sabi, 245, 282
Sadler, 30, 37, 46, 54, 56–58, 67,
98, 134, 150, 155, 166, 215, 222,
250
sadōguchi, 158, 291
Saga (*see* Emperor Saga)
saishō, 39
Sakai School, 33, 34
Sakai, 33–38, 43–45, 47–48, 50, 64,
77, 91, 252, 287
saké, 24, 105–106, 149, 168–169,
171, 180, 241, 268–269, 274,
280, 287, 291
saké pourer (*see* kannabe)
Sakurai family, 86
salvation, 5–6, 10, 15, 19–20, 22,
25–32, 53, 59, 61, 130, 134 192,
210–211, 263
San Mon, 46, 241
Sangen'in, 241
Sanguisorba officinalis (burnet,
karaito sō), 184
Sanjōnishi Sanetaka, (1455–1537)
33